Worship

with

One

Accord

Worship

with

One

Accord

WHERE LITURGY AND
ECUMENISM EMBRACE

GEOFFREY WAINWRIGHT

New York   Oxford   •   Oxford University Press   1997

Oxford University Press

Oxford   New York
Athens   Auckland   Bangkok   Bogota   Bombay   Buenos Aires
Calcutta   Cape Town   Dar es Salaam   Delhi   Florence   Hong Kong
Istanbul   Karachi   Kuala Lumpur   Madras   Madrid   Melbourne
Mexico City   Nairobi   Paris   Singapore   Taipei   Tokyo   Toronto   Warsaw

and associated companies in
Berlin   Ibadan

Copyright © 1997 by Oxford University Press, Inc.

Published by Oxford University Press, Inc.
198 Madison Avenue, New York, New York 10016

Oxford is a registered trademark of Oxford University Press

Library of Congress Cataloging-in-Publication Data

Wainwright, Geoffrey, 1939–

Worship with one accord : where liturgy and ecumenism embrace /

Geoffrey Wainwright.

p.   cm.

Includes bibliographical references.

ISBN 0-19-511610-0

1. Liturgics and Christian union.   II. Title.

BX9.5.L55W35   1997

262'.001'1—dc21   96-53170

1 3 5 7 9 8 6 4 2

Printed in the United States of America
on acid-free paper

To
Wiebe Vos,
founder of *Studia Liturgica* and *Societas Liturgica,*
who believes that liturgy and ecumenism
should not simply embrace
but marry.

ation is to be gratefully received and effectively witnessed to. Worship practices should—in the delicate relationship between *signifying* what is already the case and *effecting* what is still to be—both reflect the existing degree of unity and further it.

The variety in this book arises from the several occasions that originally called forth its chapters (a list of these "sources" is given after the copyright page). Its coherence resides in its being the work of a thinker who claims to stand within evangelical, orthodox, catholic Christianity and seeks the manifestation of the church's unity for the glory of God and the salvation of the world. Most of the various papers have arisen out of my activities as an academic theologian. Concurrently, I have been engaged in more directly ecclesial forms of ecumenism, both in the Faith and Order Commission of the World Council of Churches (*Baptism, Eucharist and Ministry* and *Confessing the One Faith*) and in international bilateral dialogues (I chair on the Methodist side the Joint Commission between the Roman Catholic Church and the World Methodist Council); and a collection of my papers from those contexts—often with liturgical dimensions—has recently appeared with Abingdon Press/Kingswood Books under the title *Methodists in Dialogue.*

Conversations with my colleague Karen Westerfield Tucker helped me to find an appropriate sequence for presenting within a single set of covers the material in this book. The first chapter offers an interpretative history of the relations between the Liturgical and the Ecumenical Movements in the twentieth century. Chapter two then expounds the encompassing ecclesiology that takes worship as a primary duty of the church (with witness and service), and as its most enduring delight. Chapters three and four make the liturgical assembly the home of both Scripture and Tradition; this move may help in the regulation of the relations between these two, which is an indispensable criteriological concern in the search for ecclesial unity. Chapters five, six, and seven focus on the sacraments in an ecumenical perspective, treating the Faith and Order work on *Baptism, Eucharist and Ministry*, the "world church" discovered at Vatican II, and the inheritance which at least one world Christian communion (my own Methodist) needs to reclaim for itself and then offer to others. The following two chapters review liturgical revision, especially in the English-speaking world, stressing the ecumenical importance of the recovery of classical patterns. Chapters ten and eleven look at liturgical embodiments of the reconciliation that is integral to the Gospel and to its witness before the world (the Irish chapter springs from my longstanding and deep affection for St. Patrick's people). Chapters twelve and thirteen link worship with the ethical and the political, in the hope that the connections thus established will provide a framework for treating some issues that have proved theoretically and practically divisive among the churches. Chapter fourteen returns to the dogmatic heartland by displaying the profoundly trinitarian structure of Christian worship at a time when the doctrine of God is once more controversial. The concluding chapter arises from an attempt to speak of liturgy and ecumenism to an academic society many of whose members no longer manifest much enthusiasm for either; it ends with an autobiographical confession of commitment to the worship, mission, and unity of the church, called together to praise God and bear witness to the world.

In the revision of these chapters for present publication, some modest updating has been made in points of fact and information. In some smaller matters of judgment I have declined the advantages of retrospection that Monday morning provides not only to quarterbacks but also to liturgists and preachers. In any case, the decade from which these chapters come has seen me consistent in fundamental principles and in the larger arguments. Occasionally brief overlaps in material have been retained among the chapters for the sake of the integrity of the argument in each context. The scripture quotations have usually been taken from the Revised Standard Version.

My thanks are due to Virgil Funk for initiating this project, to Larry Johnson for carrying it along, and to Cynthia Read for seeing it through. The book is dedicated to a dear friend over the past three decades, whose cheerful commitment to the worship and unity of Christians has "endured through many afflictions and hardships" (2 Cor 6:4): Wiebe Vos, servant of the Word of God in the Netherlands Reformed Church.

Geoffrey Wainwright
Duke University
Michaelmas 1996

Sources

Chapter 1, "Where Liturgy and Ecumenism Embrace," was written for the *Festschrift* to celebrate Bishop Wacław Swierzawski and the twenty-fifth anniversary of the Liturgical Institute in the Pontifical Theological Academy of Cracow, *Euntes Docete* (Kraków: Papieska Akademia Teologiczna, 1993) 190-203. Chapter 2, "The Church as a Worshiping Community," appeared in *Pro Ecclesia* 3 (1994) 56-67; it had been delivered as a lecture to Baptist and Lutheran audiences. Chapter 3, "Bible and Liturgy: Daniélou's Work Revisited," is based on an address to the 1991 Toronto congress of *Societas Liturgica* that appeared as "'Bible et liturgie': Daniélou's Work Revisited," *Studia Liturgica* 22 (1992) 154-162 and "'Bible et liturgie' quarante ans après Daniélou," *La Maison-Dieu* no. 189 (1992) 41-53. Chapter 4, "Tradition as a Liturgical Act," was written for the *Festschrift* in honor of George H. Tavard, *The Quadrilog: Tradition and the Future of Ecumenism*, ed. Kenneth Hagen (Collegeville: The Liturgical Press, 1994) 129-146. Chapter 5, "The Lima Text in the History of Faith and Order," is an updated version of my presidential address to the 1985 Boston congress of *Societas Liturgica*; it originally appeared in *Studia Liturgica* 16 (1986) 6-21. Chapter 6, "Sacramental Theology and the World Church," was a plenary address to the Catholic Theological Society of America and appeared in its *Proceedings* 39 (1984) 69-83. Chapter 7, "The Sacraments in Wesleyan Perspective," was given to a convocation called by the United Methodist bishop of Western North Carolina and figured without bibliographical apparatus in *Doxology* 5 (1988) 5-20. Chapter 8, "Renewing Worship: The Recovery of Classical Patterns," was written, in connection with the then imminent publication of the Presbyterian *Book of Common Worship* (1993), at the invitation of *Theology Today* 48 (1991-1992) 45-55. Chapter 9, "Divided by a Common Language," is updated from the Centenary Address given to the Scottish Church Service Society (1983) and the Austin James Memorial Lecture (1985) given to the Australian Academy of Liturgy, the fullest version of which appeared hitherto in *Studia Liturgica* 17 (1987) 241-255. Chapter 10, "The Reconciliation of Divided Churches: A Witness to the Gospel," is updated from a plenary address delivered to the 1987 Brixen congress of *Societas Liturgica*; it first appeared in *Studia Liturgica* 18 (1988) 75-95. Chapter 11, "Reconciliation: Irish and Ecumenical," was given as a lecture at a conference in Belfast in May 1993 and published first in *Reconciliation in Religion and Society*, ed. Michael Hurley (Belfast: Institute of Irish Studies, 1994) 72-88. Chapter 12, "Eucharist and/as Ethics," was first delivered before a largely Lutheran audience at Valparaiso University; it appeared in *Worship* 62 (1988) 123-138. Chapter 13, "Praying for Kings: The Place of Human Rulers in the Divine Plan of Salvation," was presented at the 1986 Frederick Neumann Symposium on Theological Interpretation of Scripture, where the general theme was Church and State; the text appeared in *Ex Auditu* 2 (1986) 117-127. Chapter 14, "Trinitarian Worship," was first given as a lecture to the Mercersburg Society and appeared in The New Mercersburg Review no. 2 (1986) 3-11; in a slightly revised form, expanded by notes, it was printed in *Speaking the Christian God: The Holy Trinity and the Challenge of Feminism*, ed. Alvin F. Kimel (Grand Rapids: Eerdmans, 1992) 209-221. Chapter 15, "Canons, Cultures, and the Ecumenically Correct," was a paper presented to the American Theological Society in 1992 and appears here for the first time.

Contents

1

Where Liturgy and Ecumenism Embrace

FROM ITS INTERNATIONAL BEGINNINGS IN PROTESTANTISM AT THE TURN OF THE nineteenth century into the twentieth, the motto of the modern ecumenical movement has been "that they may be one." That invocation of John 17:21 immediately evoked the next clause, namely, "so that the world may believe that thou hast sent me." Thus ecumenism was placed in the service of evangelization. The restoration of Christian unity was necessary not only for the practical purposes of cooperation in missionary work but, more profoundly, for the sake of a more credible witness to the Gospel of reconciliation. If the churches could not demonstrate unity among themselves, how could they testify to the reconciliation of the world to God?

There is, however, another scriptural theme that runs as a golden thread through ecumenical endeavors in the twentieth century. Beginning perhaps with the increased participation of the Orthodox after the Patriarch of Constantinople's Ecumenical Appeal of 1920, there has grown an awareness that "right worship" can occur only when Christians are united in faith and life. Here the underlying biblical text is the apostolic exhortation to "have the same mind among you according to Christ Jesus, that you may with one heart and one mouth glorify God the Father of our Lord Jesus Christ" (Rom 15:5-6). Thus ecumenism's goal becomes not only evangelization but an acceptable doxology.

The Roman Catholic Church officially entered the ecumenical movement with the Second Vatican Council. That council also

1

endorsed the liturgical movement that was seeking to improve worship in the Catholic Church and elsewhere. At the time of Vatican II, the missionary movement was still being confidently pursued by Roman Catholics as well as by other Christians. While the respective conciliar documents on worship (*Sacrosanctum Concilium*), evangelization (*Ad Gentes*) and Christian unity (*Unitatis Redintegratio*) did not make extensive cross-references among the three concerns, there can be no doubt—the dogmatic constitution on the church, *Lumen Gentium*, is the best testimony—that liturgical reform, missionary endeavor, and the desire for the restoration of ecclesial relations all coalesced in the spirit of Vatican II.

By the end of this chapter I want to establish the theological connection between the church's mission to the world and the vocation of humankind to "glorify God and enjoy Him forever,"[1] with Christian unity being seen as not only the condition but also the result of both evangelization and worship. But meanwhile, neglecting for a moment an express concern with the church's missionary vocation, I want in particular to show, by historical narrative and examples, how the modern liturgical movement, which has run concurrently with the modern ecumenical movement, has itself worked ecumenically and contributed to greater unity among the churches; and how the ecumenical movement has looked for resources in liturgy and has affected the worship of the churches in the direction of a more common euchology.

In some cases it has been the same people who have led both ecumenical and liturgical movements in their own churches; but it is nevertheless possible to look on some twentieth-century leaders primarily as liturgists and others primarily as ecumenists. In the first half of this chapter I will notice some ways in which liturgists and the discipline of liturgiology have proceeded ecumenically and have had ecumenical effect. In the second half I will notice some ways in which ecumenists have turned their attention to liturgy, and how ecumenical endeavors have contributed responsibly towards an increasing, though not yet fully attained, *communio in sacris*.[2]

LITURGISTS AND ECUMENISM

Whereas the nineteenth-century precursors of the modern liturgical movement in the various ecclesial communities may have started their work in comparative independence of each other, they shared certain assumptions and goals. Thus mere archeology was never the motivation of the Benedictines at Solesmes with their Gregorian Chant, the German Lutherans around Wilhelm Löhe and his notion of the liturgy as "sacred drama," or the Oxford Movement and the Anglo-Catholics in the Church of England. Their "restorationism" sought for the present the purity of a *retour aux sources.* As we shall soon see, one of the principal achievements of the liturgical movement in our own time has consisted precisely in convergence and renewal by way of a *common* return to a *shared* Tradition that antedated the sixteenth and the eleventh centuries. Or again: the early twentieth-century pioneers of the modern liturgical movement characteristically considered the Sunday worship assembly as the place for sound biblical and dogmatic instruction and the equipment of the faithful for Christian witness in society and culture, whether one thinks of the Benedictines Lambert Beauduin in Belgium and Virgil Michel in the United States and the Augustinian canon Pius Parsch in Austria, or Gabriel Hebert and the "Parish and People" movement in the Anglican Church, or the Methodist Sacramental Fellowship in Britain. And, as we shall again see, these concerns for the contemporary church came to find an increasingly ecumenical expression.

However, before we enumerate some ecumenical achievements of the modern liturgical movement, we must first register the way in which liturgical scholarship has developed along transconfessional lines. The communication of information and practices across confessional boundaries has been indispensably facilitated by the growth of a body of scholars employing common methodologies in research and devoted to a recognizably similar vision of Christian worship. Protestant historians of the liturgy have cited, since their first publication, the works of the Tyrolese Catholic Josef Jungmann as a classic authority on the patristic period and the western rites.[3] The Anglican Benedictine Gregory Dix helped not only his fellow Anglicans but also Roman Catholics and Lutherans to recover "the shape of the liturgy."[4] The Russian-American Orthodox Alexander Schmemann provided for many also outside his own communion an "introduction to liturgical theology."[5] More recently, the Jesuit Robert Taft, who is an eastern rite Catholic, has embodied liturgical scholarship that is "beyond east and west."[6] The widest ecumenical range of liturgical research and renewal has been represented by the international review *Studia Liturgica* and the worldwide association *Societas Liturgica,* the twin offspring of the Netherlands Reformed pastor, Wiebe Vos.[7] The oldest and best doctoral program in liturgics in the United States, namely that of the University of Notre Dame, a Catholic institution, counts Orthodox and Protestants among its graduates as well as Catholics, and its professors include the Methodist James White and the Anglican Paul Bradshaw. J.G. Davies' *Dictionary of Liturgy and Worship* numbered a fully ecumenical range of contributors,[8] and the standard English-language manual *The Study of Liturgy* claims Roman Catholic, Anglican, Protestant, and Orthodox writers.[9]

Since the 1960s liturgical revisions in the Roman Catholic Church and those in most Protestant Churches have resulted in rites that converge with regard to both structure and even wording.[10] This has been achieved by means of mutual borrowings and critiques as the rites were being produced, and, above all, by means of a common return to the freshly investigated and interpreted texts of the early centuries. Following Vatican II, the work of the Roman consilium for the revision of the liturgy was accompanied by observers on behalf of the World Council of Churches (the British Methodist, Raymond George), the Anglican Communion (Ronald Jasper from England and Massey Shepherd from the United States), and the Lutheran World Federation (Eugene Brand from the United States), themselves leading figures in the liturgical commissions of their churches.[11] The outstanding achievements of the Missal of Paul VI (1969-1970) and the *Ordo Initiationis Christianae Adultorum* (1972) in some ways paralleled work that was already being accomplished in other churches, and in other ways inspired other churches in their own process of liturgical revision. Many churches now possess rites that in various ways view Christian initiation as a single coherent, though complex, ritual which, after evangelization and cate-chumenate, includes baptism, confirmation, and first communion after the pattern that *OICA* relearned from the patristic period.[12] Several churches now own eucharistic prayers closely based, like the Roman Eucharistic Prayer II, on the anaphora of the so-called *Apostolic Tradition* of Hippolytus[13] and other prayers, like the Roman Eucharistic Prayer IV, in the eastern mode of St. Basil.[14] The return to the patristic pattern of word and table has meant that the homily has once more become for Roman Catholics "a part of the liturgy itself,"[15] whereas Protestants have been developing a more frequent celebration of the Lord's Supper. Overall, there has grown a recovered awareness of Christian liturgy as the celebration of the paschal mystery, an anamnesis of Christ's death and resurrection,[16] including the adoption of an annual Easter Vigil by several Anglican and Protestant Churches under the inspiration of the Roman Catholic rite that underwent restoration and renewal already in the 1950s.[17]

Great Britain provides, in its "Joint Liturgical Group," a powerful example of a semi-official ecumenical body of liturgical scholars who were all active in the practical work of their own churches and whose collaborative publications exercised great influence throughout the British Isles. In particular, their two-year Sunday lectionary—prepared before the new Roman three-year *Ordo Lectionum Missae* (1969)—found its way into the revised service-books of the Methodist Church (*The Methodist Service Book*, 1975), the Church of Scotland (*The Book of Common Order*, 1979), the Church of England (*Alternative Service Book*, 1980), the United Reformed Church (*A Book of Services*, 1980), and the Church of Ireland (*Alternative Prayer Book*, 1984). The British Group also contributed significantly to the International Consultation on English Texts (later reborn as English Language Liturgical Consultation) which composed standard translations of ancient and classical liturgical texts, including the Lord's Prayer, the Apostles' and Nicene Creeds, the *Kyrie*, the *Gloria in Excelsis, Sursum Corda, Sanctus* and *Benedictus qui venit, Agnus Dei, Gloria Patri, Te Deum, Benedictus, Magnificat*, and *Nunc Dimittis*.[18]

Another semi-official ecumenical group of liturgical scholars has been the North American Consultation on Common Texts, whose influential *Common Lectionary* has been finding wide acceptance among Protestant and Anglican Churches not only in North America but also in Australia, New Zealand, and South Africa. Based on the Roman *Ordo Lectionum Missae*, the *Common Lectionary* differs from its source chiefly by allowing, in the "ordinary" Sundays after Pentecost, for a semi-continuous of the Old Testament: in the year of Matthew the Old Testament readings come from the Pentateuch, in the year of Mark from the Davidic narrative, and in the year of Luke from the prophets. An aim of all these lectionaries is obviously to immerse the hearers of the word into the entire history of salvation to which they belong and thereby equip them to become "doers of the word" in order to prolong that history by their witness.[19]

In the realm of music and hymnody, too, liturgy has taken on an increasingly ecumenical aspect. Already in the nineteenth century the translations of early Greek and medieval Latin hymns by John

Mason Neale (1818-1866) were finding their way into Anglican hymnals and thus reflecting the proto-ecumenical "branch theory" of some Anglicans that saw the "Church Catholic" as "Eastern, Western, British."[20] Catherine Winkworth (1827-1878), another skillful Anglican translator, for her part looked rather to German Protestant hymnody for deliberate ecumenical enrichment, and her texts were subsequently favored particularly by British Methodist as well as by American and Australian Lutheran hymnals.[21] In the second half of the twentieth century, Charles Wesley's hymns were borrowed from Methodist into English-language Catholic hymnals, whereas the German-language Catholic *Gotteslob* draws heavily on such Protestant hymn writers as Martin Luther, Paul Gerhardt, Joachim Neander, Philipp Nicolai, and Martin Rinckart. In the English-speaking world, it is now a matter of course that contemporary hymnals should be entirely ecumenical in range, and this applies *a fortiori* in cases where English is no more than a *lingua franca* (as in the *East Asia Christian Conference Hymnal*, 1963, and *Sound the Bamboo: Christian Conference of Asia Hymnal*, 1990). Musically, the settings of the French Jesuit Joseph Gelineau have stimulated a worldwide and ecumenical renewal of psalmody, mediated in part by the Reformed-ecumenical monastic community of Taizé. Chants of Russian Orthodox origin are now sung in churches of many denominations throughout the world, having been brought back home by participants in assemblies of the World Council of Churches.

In one other area liturgy has taken an ecumenical turn in our times, namely, the commemoration of the saints. On account of what they perceived as abuses in the medieval cult of the saints, the sixteenth-century Reformers either greatly reduced the *sanctorale* (as with Anglicans and Lutherans) or practically abandoned all liturgical mention of conspicuous Christians from the past (as with the Reformed). Allowing once more, however, for a modest commemoration of the saints (though rarely the invocation of their prayers), even churches having no formal process of canonization have begun to introduce or expand calendars in their official service-books. These calendars include figures from before the schisms of the eleventh and the sixteenth centuries (especially the martyrs of the early centuries, the missionaries to the nations, and the great patristic doctors of both the Greek and the Latin Churches—as far indeed as Thomas Aquinas in the case of the Anglican Churches of

Southern Africa and New Zealand and the Uniting Church in Australia); and from the times after the schisms the new calendars include figures not only from their own side but also from "the other party." To give a few examples: the (Protestant) Uniting Church in Australia names Ignatius Loyola, the North American *Lutheran Book of Worship* of 1978 mentions Calvin (though not Zwingli!), and the Anglican Church of New Zealand in its *Prayer Book* of 1988-1989 commemorates Maximilian Kolbe. Most remarkable of all, perhaps, is that the Church of King Henry VIII should now, in its *Alternative Service Book*, list for July 6th "Thomas More, martyr, 1535." The Uniting Church in Australia mentions the modern ecumenical pioneers Paul Couturier, W.A. Visser 't Hooft, and Pope John XXIII as "reformers of the church." As a Methodist, I am pleased to find John and Charles Wesley commemorated in the North American *Lutheran Book of Worship* and in all recent Anglican prayer books. If the Roman Catholic and the Orthodox Churches could ever follow that example, it would probably be taken by Methodists to constitute the biggest single step towards mutual recognition between those churches and Methodism.[22]

Having looked in representative ways at the ecumenical operation and fruits of the modern liturgical movement, we may now in turn examine how ecumenists have drawn on liturgical resources and moved the churches towards mutual recognizability in their worship and a more complete sacred communion among them.

ECUMENISTS AND LITURGY

From its beginnings the Faith and Order side of the modern ecumenical movement has known that the eventual restoration of Christian unity must take the route of mutual recognition by the churches in baptism, eucharist, and ministry. That was already clear at the first and second world conferences on Faith and Order, at Lausanne 1927 and Edinburgh 1937 respectively. Hence the "continuation committee," after Edinburgh 1937, set up three international theological commissions: one was to study ecclesiology in the broadest sense of the doctrines of "the church" held by the divided Christian communities; a second was to study the attitudes, laws, and customs of the various churches towards "intercommunion"; the third was to study, most concretely of all, the different "ways of worship" characteristically celebrated in the several ecclesial or confessional families. These studies could be resumed only after World War II, and the three reports were presented to the third world conference on Faith and Order at Lund in 1952.[23]

The most directly liturgical report was, of course, that on *Ways of Worship*. The longest part consisted in largely descriptive accounts of "the elements of liturgy" in their authors' respective ecclesial traditions: F.G. Van der Meer, Roman Catholic; G. Florovsky, Orthodox; A.G. Hebert, Anglican; H. Goltzen, German Lutheran; P. Edwall, Swedish Lutheran; W.D. Maxwell, (Reformed) Church of Scotland; J. Schweizer, Reformed Churches in German Switzerland; R.C. Johnson, Baptist, U.S.A.; J. Marsh, Congregationalist; H.F. Rall, Methodist, U.S.A.; and the Committee on Christian Relationships of the Religious Society of Friends in Great Britain, Quaker. These were followed by briefer, more systematic accounts of "The Inner Meanings of Word and Sacraments" according to the Orthodox (L. Gillet), Anglican (A.H. Couratin, G.W.H. Lampe, F.C.N. Hicks), Lutheran (W. Stählin, R. Will), Reformed (G. Van der Leeuw, A. Graf, R. Paquier), and Old Catholic (A.E. Rüthy) traditions. Finally came some individual reflections on "liturgy and devotion," treating particularly "Mariology" and, more broadly, "an approach to the work of reunion through common devotional understanding."

The work of mutual information in liturgical as well as in other matters was necessary, but progress towards unity would now require bolder steps. In the general history of Faith and Order, Lund 1952 is considered to mark a *shift* in method *away* from "comparative ecclesiology," in which the various churches offer predominantly descriptive statements of their respective positions and practices, and *towards* rather a "common concentration" on the Christological and trinitarian history of salvation, by which it is hoped that all may arrive at an agreed reading of the Gospel, a unified confession of the Christian faith, and a shared participation in the benefits of redemption. Whereas the studies in "ways of worship" preparatory to the Lund conference had taken place according to a comparative methodology, the Lund conference did indeed set Faith and Order on the track whereby a "theological commission" of confessionally very varied membership could now work at formulating an ecumenical statement on worship based on joint study of the Bible and of the Tradition broadly understood.

In preparing its "Report on Worship" for the third world conference on Faith and Order at Montreal 1963, this commission worked in three geographical sections: European, East Asian, and North American.[24] In the absence of a global meeting of the commission before Montreal itself, each geographical section furnished a separate part of the report.

The Europeans first offered some "general considerations" on "The Christian Tradition in Europe" (between "Christendom" and "secularization"), "The Interpretation of the Language of Worship" (the tensions between "biblical-traditional" and "modern" discourse), "Variety and Unity of Christian Worship" (both in "types" and in "forms"), "The Presence of History in Worship" (in terms of "anamnesis"), "The Importance of Sunday in Christian Worship" (as "the Lord's Day"), and "Meanings of the Word 'Liturgy'"; and then set forth some theological theses on "Creation and Worship," "Redemption and Worship," and "New Creation and Worship."

The East Asian section studied the relations between worship and the "mission," "unity," and "renewal" of the church, with a particular emphasis on questions of "indigenization."

The North American section began descriptively and analytically with "Worship in the North American Churches"; it turned to the Bible for the "Meaning and Practice of Worship in the Scriptures," examining "the matrix of worship in the Old Testament," "the New Testament vocabulary for worship," and the "interaction of kerygma and cultus," being concerned here with "the manner of God's presence in Christ" and the relation between "worship in cultus and in ethical obedience"; finally came a synthetic reflection on the problematic of "worship, intelligibility, and contemporary culture."

By the time of the Uppsala assembly in 1968, the World Council of Churches had become obsessed with the theologically fashionable question of secularization, and the assembly's discussion was dominated by this theme.[25] It was debated how far any "crisis in worship" reflected a "crisis of faith," and deep divergences became apparent between those who affirmed traditional practices and forms of liturgy and those who radically questioned not only inherited forms but even the very practice of worship and prayer. The controversy led to an inconclusive consultation on "Worship in a Secular Age" at Geneva in September 1969.[26] Even today the serious question of secularization, and the related questions of inculturation and acculturation, are far from resolved (all of which, incidentally, have implications for the church's mission of evangelization). But the more immediately significant study set in motion by Montreal

1963 was the resumption of work on the specific themes of baptism, eucharist, and ministry. And to these we shall soon return, after noting one practical result and one theoretical proposal of ecumenical origin that affected the liturgical life of the churches and recognized its importance.

The practical result of ecumenism to be particularly noticed was the creation of the Church of South India in 1947 and the provision of a liturgy for this church. The Church of South India brought together in an organic ecclesial union the fruit of missionary labors on the part of Anglicans, (British) Methodists, (Scottish and Swiss) Presbyterians, and (U.S.A.) Congregationalists. The new "liturgy committee" was described by one of its own members as "for the most part liturgically illiterate";[27] and yet they set about educating themselves while continuing, as another member put it, "to regard liturgiology as the handmaid rather than the mistress of liturgiography."[28]

The Church of South India attracted international attention by its *Order for the Lord's Supper* (1950, revised 1954, 1962, 1971-72), included since 1963 in *The Book of Common Worship*. The eucharist unfolds in a sequence that may be considered historically and theologically "classical" by the canons of modern liturgical scholarship. During an entrance hymn or psalm the ministers carry in the Scriptures. An opening prayer for purity is followed by an ancient hymn ("Glory to God in the Highest," or "Holy God, Holy and Mighty, Holy and Immortal") or a biblical litany of praise ("Worthy Is the Lamb"). Next may come a confession of sin and declaration of pardon, unless these have occurred before the service. The "Ministry of the Word of God" begins with the oration of the day, after which the Old Testament, the Epistle, and the Gospel are read, the sermon is preached, and the Creed is recited. Intercessions are made in litany form. The "Breaking of the Bread" opens with the exchange of the Peace, the entrance of the Gifts, a "prayer of the veil" ("Holy Father, you have opened a new and living way . . ."), and an invocation of "Jesus, our good High Priest" ("Be present, be present . . ."). The salutation ("The Lord be with you") and dialogue ("Lift up your hearts") lead into the eucharistic prayer (with preface, *Sanctus* and *Benedictus*, thanksgiving, institution narrative, anamnesis-oblation, epiclesis for consecration and fruits of communion, and doxology). The Lord's Prayer is followed by the fraction and communion, during which the "Lamb of God" may be sung. A post-communion prayer, including a brief commemoration of the saints, precedes the blessing and dismissal.

Much of the language of the C.S.I. rite, especially in the earliest versions, remains familiar to Anglicans and Methodists in the Cranmerian tradition, although a few touches derive also from the *Book of Common Order* of the Church of Scotland. The invocation of Jesus derives from the Mozarabic "*Adesto, adesto*," but the "main source for the recapturing of the classical heritage" was "the Syrian liturgies," which had known "centuries of use on South Indian soil by the Christians of St. Thomas."[29] According to Bishop T.S. Garrett, for a time chairman of the C.S.I. liturgy committee, the entire work had the "aim of reappropriating the great classical tradition of Christian worship, as found in the ancient liturgies, while subjecting it to the critical insights of the Reformation."[30] While culturally Indian features were to be found in the accompanying music and lyrics, the gestures of greeting, the vestments, and the vessels, it was the example of a successfully repristinated patristic structure of the rite which accounted for its considerable influence on liturgical revisions in several other parts of the English-speaking world. For our purposes, the *ecumenical* origins, procedures, and purposes of the Church of South India's *Lord's Supper or Holy Eucharist* are particularly noteworthy.

The theoretical proposal, from the side of ecumenism, that recognized the importance of liturgy came from the leading German Lutheran theologian active in Faith and Order, Edmund Schlink.[31] Schlink had observed that "members of divided Churches find it much easier to pray and witness together than to formulate common dogmatic statements." He sought to account for this by the "category shift" which takes place when the content stated in prayer and preaching is translated into the structures of dogma. In worship and witness we face God and our fellow human beings more directly. In dogmatic statements, however, we are (merely) *talking about* (the proper way) to worship and witness. The risk is that the teaching office or theologian withdraws to "a neutral position from which the encounter between God and man may be observed, described and be cast into didactic formulas." Schlink holds the "structural change" from doxology to doctrine responsible for some of the most persistent dogmatic problems in Christendom: the "interval" between doxology and doctrine allows differences of theory and formulation to appear. He believes that differing doctrinal statements should be "led back" to their *common* origin in liturgy, where their original unity can be recognized.

Schlink's stimulating essay exercised a great influence on doctrinal work in wide ecumenical circles. More particularly, the German Catholic liturgical historian and sacramental theologian H.J. Schulz was prepared to argue on the basis of their eucharistic liturgies that there already exists among Roman Catholics, the Orthodox, and some Protestants sufficient "unity of faith" for sacramental communion to be restored.[32] This went further than most were yet willing to accept. But the further reflection that, for instance, Faith and Order saw to be necessary certainly took place under the aegis of the Schlink proposal.

We return, therefore, to the ecumenical work on baptism, eucharist and ministry, where agreement in understanding and practice has been recognized from the start of Faith and Order to be indispensable to the restoration of ecclesial unity. Within the more general study of worship, Montreal 1963 stimulated the resumption of attention to these essential particularities. Two decades of drafting and redrafting by teams within Faith and Order, of consultation with specialist scholars and critique from the churches, finally produced the text on *Baptism, Eucharist and Ministry* (BEM) approved by the full Faith and Order Commission meeting at Lima, Peru, in January 1982 as sufficiently "mature" for transmission to the churches with a request for their response "at the highest appropriate level of authority."[33] This document received from the churches a quantity and a quality of attention unprecedented in the ecumenical movement.[34] The thorough, and generally positive, response of the Roman Catholic Church is what captures our attention here on account of its appreciation of the methods followed in BEM and of the potential significance of the results for church unity.

The official Roman Catholic response to BEM, issued by the Secretariat for Promoting Christian Unity in collaboration with the Sacred Congregation for the Doctrine of the Faith, expresses in the following terms its approval of the section on the eucharist, both with regard to content and with regard to the *lex orandi, lex credendi* methodology of the text:

> Catholics can recognize in the statement on the eucharist much that corresponds to the understanding and practice of the apostolic faith, or, as it is said in the document, the faith of the church through the ages.

We especially appreciate the following:
(a) The sources employed for the interpretation of the meaning of the eucharist and the form of celebration are Scripture and Tradition. The classical liturgies of the first millennium and patristic theology are important points of reference in this text.
(b) The eucharist is described as pertaining to the content of faith. It presents a strong Christological dimension, identifying the mystery of the eucharist in various ways with the real presence of the risen Lord and his sacrifice on the cross.
(c) The structure and ordering of the basic aspects of the document, as well as their relation to one another, conforms with Catholic teaching, specifically:
  —The presentation of the mystery of the eucharist follows the flow of classical eucharistic liturgies, with the eucharistic theology drawing heavily on the content of the traditional prayer and symbolic actions of these liturgies. The text draws on patristic sources for additional explication of the mystery of the eucharist.
  —There is strong emphasis on the Trinitarian dimension. The source and goal of the eucharist is identified as the Trinity.
  —The explanation of the content of the act of the church in the eucharistic prayer includes basic elements required by Catholic teaching as well: thanksgiving to the Father; memorial of the institution of the eucharist and the sacrifice of the cross; intercession made in union with Christ for the world; petition for the Spirit's coming on the bread and wine and on the community, in order that the bread and wine become the body and blood of Christ, and that the community be sanctified; the meal of the New Covenant.
(d) There is a strong eschatological dimension. The eucharist is viewed as a foretaste of Christ's parousia and of the final kingdom, given through the Spirit. It opens up the vision of the kingdom and the renewal of the world.
(e) The eucharist is presented as the central act of the church's worship. Because of this, the text recommends frequent celebration.
(f) The text has important ecclesiological dimensions and implications for mission.[35]

The Roman Catholic response in fact recognizes in this way the potential scope of the BEM statement on the eucharist: "If all the churches and ecclesial communities are able to accept at least the theological understanding and description of the celebration of the eucharist as described in BEM and implement it as part of their normal life, we believe that this would be an important development, and that these divided Christians now stood on a new level in regard to achieving common faith on the eucharist."[36] And with regard to the whole of BEM, even though "the text falls short at certain points," the Roman Catholic response declares that "if it were accepted by the various churches and ecclesial communities, it would bring the churches to an important step forward in the ecumenical movement, although still only one stage along the way in the ecumenical process of working towards visible unity of divided Christians."[37]

One byproduct of *Baptism, Eucharist and Ministry* has been the so-called Lima Liturgy. First prepared for celebration at the conclusion of the Faith and Order Commission meeting in Lima itself in January 1982, this text represents one way of bringing to liturgical expression the doctrinal agreements and convergences proposed in BEM.[38] A classically constructed rite in the western style (it places the Creed as a response to the proclamation of the word and even locates the peace in the Roman position before communion), the text of the liturgy is too heavily thematized around the three topics of baptism, eucharist, and ministry to be really suitable for regular use; but it has been used, with various adaptations, on important ecumenical occasions and even at local and parish level.[39] Such use testifies to a widespread longing among Christians for the possibility of a common celebration of a common faith and the goal of full unity in liturgy, doctrine, and life.

LITURGY, ECUMENISM, AND EVANGELIZATION

We liturgists and ecumenists are, in the unforgettable idiom of Wactaw Swierzawski and my own mother, "not so green as we are cabbage-looking." We are not so naïve as to think that the hard work of study, writing, and negotiation, necessary as these are, will of themselves achieve the desired unity of Christians in a single fellowship of worship and mission. They will amount to nothing without the blessing of God on what we take to be obedience to a divinely given task. Ecumenists and liturgists therefore regard as indispensable, and indeed as a foretaste of the deepened *communio in sacris* which the churches seek, prayer for Christian unity and for the world to which the Gospel is to be preached. This is why they collaborate, in preparation and in practice, in the composition and celebration of the annual Week of Prayer for Christian Unity and the week-in, week-out ecumenical prayer-cycle, *For All God's People*.[40]

According to the Fourth Gospel, Jesus promised that when he was "lifted up from the earth," on the cross and at the Father's right hand, he would "draw all people to himself" (Jn 12:32). According to a scriptural hymn, it is the sure purpose of God that "at the name of Jesus, every knee shall bow . . . and every tongue confess that Jesus Christ is Lord, to the glory of God the Father" (Phil 2:10-11). Given what St. Paul says elsewhere about the single Gospel, the one faith, and the unity of the body of Christ, then 2 Corinthians 4:13-15 indicates the part to be played by the church's evangelizing testimony in bringing the widest range of people to swell the eucharistic chorus whereby the triune God is universally praised:

> Having the same Spirit of faith as he had who wrote, "I believed, and so I spoke," we too believe, and so we speak, knowing that he who raised the Lord Jesus will raise us also with Jesus and bring us with you into his presence. For it is all for your sake, so that as grace extends to more and more people it may increase thanksgiving, to the glory of God.

Notes

1. The phrase is taken from the opening exchange of the Presbyterian Westminster Shorter Catechism of 1647-1648: "What is the chief end of man? Man's chief end is to glorify God, and to enjoy Him for ever."

2. I am here echoing the phrase, used in a slightly different context, of Vatican II concerning "*quaedam cum Ecclesia catholica communio, etsi non perfecta*" (*Unitatis redintegratio* 3).

3. Especially Jungmann's *Missarum Sollemnia* (Vienna: Herder, 1948-1949), and his book, first given as lectures at the University of Notre Dame in the summer of 1949, *The Early Liturgy* (Notre Dame: University of Notre Dame Press, 1959).

4. Gregory Dix, *The Shape of the Liturgy* (Westminster [London]: Dacre, 1945); cf. Hans-Christoph Schmidt-Lauber, *Die Eucharistie als Entfaltung der verba testamenti* (Kassel: Stauda, 1957).

5. Alexander Schmemann, *Introduction to Liturgical Theology* (Portland, ME: American Orthodox Press, 1966).

6. Robert F. Taft, *Beyond East and West: Problems in Liturgical Understanding* (Washington, D.C.: The Pastoral Press, 1984).

7. The first issue of *Studia Liturgica* appeared in 1962. The foundation

meeting of *Societas Liturgica* took place in 1967; the society now numbers over four hundred members, from all continents and confessions.

8. J.G. Davies, ed., *A Dictionary of Liturgy and Worship* (London: SCM Press, 1972), and thoroughly revised in 1986 as *A New Dictionary of Liturgy and Worship*. Similarly P.E. Fink, ed., *The New Dictionary of Sacramental Worship* (Collegeville: The Liturgical Press, 1990).

9. C. Jones, G. Wainwright, and E. Yarnold, eds., *The Study of Liturgy* (London: SPCK; New York: Oxford University Press, 1978), and a thoroughly revised edition in 1992.

10. For the notion of liturgical "convergence," see Max Thurian and Geoffrey Wainwright, *Baptism and Eucharist: Ecumenical Convergence in Celebration* (Geneva: World Council of Churches, 1983).

11. See Annibale Bugnini, *The Reform of the Liturgy 1948-1975*, trans. Matthew J. O'Connell (Collegeville: The Liturgical Press, 1990) 200.

12. See, for example, the Presbyterian Church in the U.S.A., *Holy Baptism and Services for the Renewal of Baptism* (1985) and then *The Book of Common Worship* (1993).

13. Thus the North American *Lutheran Book of Worship* (1979) (The Great Thanksgiving IV); The Church of England, *Alternative Service Book 1980* (Holy Communion A, Third Eucharistic Prayer); Presbyterian Church in the U.S.A., *The Service for the Lord's Day*, 1984 (Great Prayer of Thanksgiving D; redesignated G in *The Book of Common Worship*, 1993); United Church of Canada (Methodist-Presbyterian-Congregationalist), *A Sunday Liturgy*, 1984 (Eucharistic Prayer II); Anglican Church of Canada, *The Book of Alternative Services*, 1985 (Eucharistic Prayer 2); the Anglican Church of the Province of Southern Africa, *An Anglican Prayer Book*, 1989 (Fourth Eucharistic Prayer); the German Lutheran *Erneuerte Agende*, 1990 (text number 484).

14. Thus the Episcopal Church in the U.S.A., *The Book of Common Prayer*, 1979 (Holy Eucharist II, Eucharistic Prayer D); Presbyterian Church in the U.S.A., *The Service for the Lord's Day*, 1984 (Great Prayer of Thanksgiving E; redesignated F in *The Book of Common Worship*, 1993); United Church of Canada, *A Sunday Liturgy*, 1984 (Eucharistic Prayer V); Anglican Church of Canada, *The Book of Alternative Services*, 1985 (Eucharistic Prayer 6); Uniting Church in Australia (Methodist-Presbyterian-Congregationalist), *Uniting in Worship*, 1988 (Alternative Great Prayer of Thanksgiving H).

15. Vatican Council II, *Sacrosanctum Concilium* 52 (see also 35.2).

16. See Max Thurian, *L'Eucharistie: Mémorial du Seigneur, sacrifice d'action de grâce et d'intercession* (Neuchâtel: Delachaux & Niestlé, 1959; Wacław Swierzawski, *Dynamiczna "Pamiątka" Pana: Eucharystyczna anamneza Misterium Paschalnego i jego egzystencialna dynamika* (Cracow: Polish Theological Society, 1980).

17. Thus the Episcopal Church in the U.S.A. (*The Book of Common Prayer*, 1979), the Anglican Church of Canada (*The Book of Alternative Services*,

1985), the Anglican Church of the Province of Southern Africa (*An Anglican Prayer Book*, 1989), the North American *Lutheran Book of Worship*, 1978, the Presbyterian Church in the U.S.A. (*Liturgical Year*, 1992; *The Book of Common Worship*, 1993), and *The United Methodist Book of Worship*, 1992.

18. International Consultation on English Texts, *Prayers We Have in Common* (Philadelphia: Fortress Press, 1970, 2d edition, 1975); English Language Liturgical Consultation, *Praying Together* (Nashville: Abingdon Press, 1988).

19. It may also be noted that in English as in other languages the Scriptures are often read from translations of the Bible that have been prepared by ecumenical teams of scholars: the American "(New) Revised Standard Version" has its counterpart in the French "Traduction oecuménique de la Bible" and the German "Einheitsübersetzung."

20. See A.G. Lough, *The Influence of John Mason Neale* (London: SPCK, 1962).

21. See G. Wainwright, "Catherine Winkworth - 'Königin der Uebersetzerinnen' deutscher Kirchenlieder," in *Liturgie und Frauenfrage— Ein Beitrag zur Frauenforschung aus liturgiewissenschaftlicher Sicht*, ed. T. Berger and A. Gerhards (St. Ottilen: EOS-Verlag, 1990) 289-305.

22. See G. Wainwright, "John Wesley and the Communion of Saints," *One in Christ* 27 (1991) 332-345.

23. *The Nature of the Church*, ed. R. Newton Flew (London: SCM Press, 1952); *Intercommunion*, ed. Donald Baillie and John Marsh (London: SCM Press, 1952); *Ways of Worship*, ed. Pehr Edwall, Eric Hayman, and William D. Maxwell (London: SCM Press, 1951).

24. See *Report on Worship*, Faith and Order Paper no. 39 (Geneva: World Council of Churches, 1963); and for the Montreal conference itself, *The Fourth World Conference on Faith and Order*: Montreal 1963, ed. P.C. Rodger and L. Vischer (London: SCM Press, 1964) 69-80 ("Worship and the Oneness of Christ's Church").

25. See *The Uppsala Report 1968*, ed. Norman Goodall (Geneva: World Council of Churches, 1968) 74-85; see also the commentaries in *Studia Liturgica* 6:2 (1969).

26. See the report *Worship Today* and the papers assembled in *Studia Liturgica* 7:2-3 (1970), also published as *Worship and Secularization*, ed. W. Vos (Bussum [Holland]: Paul Brand, 1970).

27. Arthur Marcus Ward, *The Pilgrim Church* (London: Epworth Press, 1953) 130.

28. T.S. Garrett, *Worship in the Church of South India* (London: Lutterworth Press, 1958), extensively revised edition 1965, p. 16.

29. Ibid. 11.

30. Ibid. 10.

31. E. Schlink, "Die Struktur der dogmatischen Aussage als ökumenisches Problem," *Kerygma und Dogma* 3 (1957) 251-306.

32. H.J. Schultz, *Oekumenische Glaubenseinheit aus eucharistischer Ueberlieferung* (Paderborn: Bonifacius, 1976).

33. For the story of the text's preparation, see the account given by me as the chairman of the final redaction: G. Wainwright, "The Lima Text in the History of Faith and Order," *Studia Liturgica* 16 (1986) 6-21; updated as chapter 5 in the present volume.

34. See *Baptism, Eucharist and Ministry 1982-1990: Report on the Process and Responses*, Faith and Order Paper no. 149 (Geneva: World Council of Churches, 1990).

35. *Churches Respond to BEM*, ed. Max Thurian, vol. 6 (Geneva: World Council of Churches, 1988) 1-40, in particular 16-17.

36. Ibid. 38.

37. Ibid. 4.

38. The text of the Lima liturgy is found with commentary in *Baptism and Eucharist: Ecumenical Convergence in Celebration*, ed. M. Thurian and G. Wainwright (Geneva: World Council of Churches, 1983) 241-255.

39. The United Methodist Church (U.S.A.) made the Lima liturgy available in its collection of supplemental eucharistic prayers, *Holy Communion*, 1987; and the same is true of the German Lutheran *Erneuerte Agende*, 1990.

40. *For All God's People* (Geneva: World Council of Churches, 1978), revised as *With All God's People* (1989).

2

The Church as a
Worshiping Community

An Eschatological Game

CHRISTIAN WORSHIP, ACCORDING TO THE SWISS REFORMED THEOLOGIAN JEAN-Jacques von Allmen, is "an eschatological game."[1] There are indeed several features of worship that make the comparison to a *game* appropriate. First, Christian worship is governed by the rules inherent in our being the redeemed creatures of God. Second, there is room within the rules for improvisation, since the "service" of God is in fact "our perfect freedom."[2] Third, there exist many well-tried moves, since the game has already been played by many generations of our predecessors in the faith. Lastly, worship, like any good game, contains its own purpose, which in this case is none other than "man's chief end," namely "to glorify God and enjoy Him for ever."[3]

The seriousness of this game of worship was already recognized by the Roman Catholic theologian Romano Guardini when, in his chapter on "the playfulness of the liturgy," he brought the earnestness with which children amuse themselves into connection with the entrance prayer of the presiding minister in the Roman rite as it then was: "I will go to the altar of God, to the God who rejoices my youth."[4] Worship is in fact so serious that it merits von Allmen's designation of it as an *eschatological* game. And that is the perspective in which I want to explore our theme. It will require us to begin at the end, with the book of Revelation and the worship that is there envisioned in the divine city, in the final kingdom of God. But we shall be aware also that the church on earth and in history remains a community of pilgrims on its way to the definitive destination. The historic church is stretched between what is *already possible* in virtue of God's decisive achievements for our salvation and the certainty of God's promises and ultimate triumph—and what is *still necessary* because the kingdoms of this world have not yet become the kingdom of God and of his Christ. Through theological reflection in this eschatological perspective, and drawing on the experience of Christian worship down the centuries, we shall try to detect a normative shape and content for the church's gathering as a liturgical community.[5]

WORSHIP IN THE CITY OF GOD

At the beginning of the book of Revelation St. John tells us that he "was in the Spirit on the Lord's day" (Rv 1:10). Exegetes commonly hold that the visionary's ensuing accounts of life and events in the heavenly Jerusalem reflect in some ways the worship practices in the churches of his time, either in the regular Sunday gathering or at Easter (depending on the sense of "Lord's Day").[6] By divine inspiration St. John's experience of contemporary Christian liturgy was "heightened" into the vision of worship in the city of God. In turn, the inspired writer's heavenly vision has helped to shape the understanding and performance of worship in the earthly church down the centuries.

It is perhaps the Eastern Orthodox Churches which have been most deliberate in modelling their worship on the vision of St. John. Curiously, they do not read from the book of Revelation in their lectionary cycles. This is presumably in accord with a principle formulated in another context by a Catholic exegete, Pierre Benoit: "One does not read a rubric out, one does what it says."[7] The Orthodox understand their liturgy as "heaven upon earth." Many visitors have caught a sense of this. An exemplary and significant story concerns the conversion of Russia a millennium ago. The emissaries of Prince Vladimir of Kiev found Muslim worship frenzied and foul-smelling, and "beheld no glory" in the ceremonies of Western Christians. But in Constantinople "the Greeks led us to the buildings where they worship their God, and we knew not whether we were in heaven or on earth. For on earth there is no such splendor or beauty, and we are at a loss to describe it. We know only that God dwells there among men, and their service is fairer than the ceremonies of other nations."[8]

The *"theologia crucis"* in Protestant traditions will perhaps hold us back from such a degree of "realized" eschatology, but there are features in the heavenly worship described in the book of Revelation that affect, or should affect, our worship also. Here I will highlight the character of worship as (1) praise, (2) festive banquet, and (3) communion of the saints. The emphasis will fall on the *anticipatory* character of what is "already possible" in the worship of the earthly church.

Praise

Before the throne of God "the living creatures . . . never cease to sing, 'Holy, holy, holy, is the Lord God Almighty, who was and is and is to come!' And whenever the living creatures give glory and honor and thanks to him who is seated on the throne, who lives for ever and ever, the twenty-four elders fall down before him who is seated on the throne and worship him who lives for ever and ever; they cast their crowns before the throne, singing, 'Worthy art thou, our Lord and God, to receive glory and honor and power, for thou didst create all things, and by thy will they existed and were created'" (Rv 4:8-11). Then "the Lamb" is included by "a new song": "Worthy is the Lamb who was slain, to receive power and wealth and wisdom and might and honor and glory and blessing" (Rv 5:8-14). A multitude of martyrs joins in the praise: "Salvation belongs to our God who sits upon the throne, and to the Lamb" (Rv 7:9-12). Further on, we hear praise of the "King of the ages" (Rv 15:3-4), who has "taken [his] great power and begun to reign" (Rv 11:16-18).

Thus God is praised in heaven for creation, redemption, and rule. The earthly church already joins in that praise in faith and hope.

One manifestation is to speak in "the tongues of angels" (1 Cor 13:1).[9] That is fine, the apostle Paul implies, as long as it is accompanied by charity. If tongues-speaking is to occur in corporate worship, it should be with interpretation for the edification of the community (1 Cor 14:26-28). With or without glossolalia, services among Pentecostals and charismatics usually include a high proportion of praise.

It is the *singing* of praise which most readily allows for communal expression. Fragmentary hymns are found in the New Testament and in early patristic texts, and by the time of the great Fathers such as Ambrose, Augustine, and Chrysostom we have explicit evidence that the whole congregation joined in the singing.[10] Moreover, God is "doubly praised" in the hymn—by the words and by the music. Hymn-singing has been a prominent feature of corporate worship in most Protestant traditions, which would endorse the rationale offered by Isaac Watts:

> Praise ye the Lord! 'Tis good to raise
> Your hearts and voices in his praise:
> His nature and his works invite
> To make this duty our delight.

Duty and delight combine in this anticipatory attainment of "man's chief end," "to glorify God and enjoy him for ever," and it is God's being, character, and acts—"his nature and his works"—which evoke our praise.[11]

Another high expression of praise occurs in classical orders of the Lord's Supper with the anaphora or great prayer of thanksgiving. One traditional designation for the eucharist is the "sacrifice of praise" (*sacrificium laudis*). The eucharistic prayer begins with the summons "Lift up your hearts," a phrase of much significance in Calvin's interpretation of the Lord's Supper. The opening phase of the prayer praises God's transcendent glory and leads into the song where the earthly church joins with the whole company of heaven: "Holy, holy, holy, Lord God of hosts: Heaven and earth are full of thy glory: Glory be to thee, O Lord most High!" Then the prayer gives thanks for the redeeming work of the Son and invokes the Spirit, so that through communion with Christ we may, in communion with all his people, enjoy his present and future benefits. A trinitarian doxology concludes the prayer.[12] In the Amen said by all, the words of the presider are endorsed by the whole community as their own.[13]

Festive Banquet

In Revelation 19 the "hallelujah chorus" gives way to the wedding feast of the Lamb with his bride, the church: "Hallelujah! For the Lord our God the Almighty reigns. Let us rejoice and exult and give him the glory, for the marriage of the Lamb has come" (Rv 19:6-7). And "Blessed are those who are invited to the marriage supper of the Lamb" (Rv 19:9). Already in Revelation 3:20, even in the letter to the "lukewarm" church of Laodicea, the exalted Christ says, "Behold, I stand at the door and knock; if any one hears my voice and opens the door, I will come in to him and eat with him, and he with me."

The liturgies of the church have consistently looked on the Lord's Supper as a foretaste of the marriage feast of the Lamb. This comes to expression, for example, in various formulations in the prayers after communion in the rites dating from the patristic west: the earthly and temporal communion is a "pledge" (*pignus*), "promise" (*promissio*), or "prefiguration" (*praefiguratio*) of the heavenly and eternal; what is now performed in an image will then be enjoyed manifestly ("*ut quod in imagine gerimus sacramenti, manifesta perceptione sumamus*"), what is now done in appearance will then be received in truth ("*ut quae nunc specie gerimus, rerum veritate capiamus*").[14] Such an unimpeachably Protestant source as the rite composed by John à Lasco in 1550 for Dutch refugees in England moves along the same lines:

> I hope that you all, in sitting down at this Supper, have per-
> ceived by the eye of your faith that blessed time in the kingdom
> of God when you will sit at table with Abraham, Isaac and
> Jacob; and that you are already, through trust in the righteous-
> ness, merit, and victory of Christ the Lord (in the communion
> of which you have now been sealed), just as sure of sitting
> down there as we have now surely all sat down together at this
> table of the Lord.

In my own Methodist tradition, a section of the Wesleys' *Hymns on the Lord's Supper* (1745) is entitled "The Sacrament a Pledge of Heaven," where the words "type," "earnest," and "taste" recur and much is made of the "joy" and "hope" as we "here begin by faith to eat / The supper of the Lamb" (hymn 97).

In his letter of 10 September 1784 to "our brethren in America" John Wesley advised all "the elders to administer the Supper of the Lord on every Lord's Day." That exact formulation shows Wesley to have appreciated the connection established by the Lord's resurrection between his meal and his day. As the day of resurrection, Sunday is the appropriate day for the Lord's people to gather in his name, week by week, to find him in their midst in the meal he instituted for the proclamation of his death until his coming again (cf. Mt 18:20; 1 Cor 11:26). In sad historical fact, Wesley was no more able than Luther, Calvin, and the English reformers had been to reestablish the weekly communion of the Christian people that had marked the early centuries of the church's life[15] before being lost in the Constantinian Middle Ages.

Communion of the Saints

In Revelation 7:9-17 we have already seen the multitude of the martyrs gather around the throne to worship God and the Lamb. They come "from every nation, from all tribes and peoples and tongues," and they utter their praise with a single voice. The martyrs are also eager for the final triumph of God: "How long, O Lord?" (Rv 6:9-11).

When Christians on earth gather for worship, they too form an assembly, a congregation. What joins them together most profoundly is not a merely human sense of fellowship but rather the divine reality in which they have a common share, namely the *"koinonia"* of participation in Christ (1 Cor 1:9; Heb 3:14) and in the Holy Spirit (2 Cor 13:14; Heb 6:4). They have been baptized into the body of Christ and made to drink of the one Spirit (1 Cor 12:12-13). They remain one body through partaking of the one bread, which gives participation in the body of Christ (1 Cor 10:16-17), and through drinking the new wine by which the Spirit gives them the joy of the kingdom (cf. Mt 26:29; Rom 14:17; 1 Cor 10:16; Eph 5:18-20).[16]

Every local congregation has in varying measures the possibility to anticipate that community across time and space which characterizes the inhabitants of the city of God in the final kingdom. The church is both a cultural and a transcultural community. Each local gathering takes place in a particular historical and geographical context; it has the chance of including in its worship elements and features from past times and from different places. It can pray for "the whole state of Christ's church militant here in earth" and also bless God's name for "all thy servants departed this life in thy faith and fear" (to speak with the Book of Common Prayer). Opportunity may also arise for a congregation to diversify itself historically and geographically through the welcome afforded to Christians coming from different ecclesial traditions as well as from different parts of the world.

Theological controversy has surrounded the present relation between God's people on earth and those who may already be enjoying closer fellowship with God. What is the proper understanding and form of that more comprehensive "communion of the saints" which embraces all who—on this or the other side of death— live in Christ? The Orthodox give visual expression to that communion in the icons that surround the gathered congregation and are believed in some way to convey the heavenly company of those by whom God has graced the church in every generation. In reaction to medieval western abuses that depended on claims to too detailed a knowledge of the afterlife, Protestants have usually been reticent about any practice that went beyond a simple confidence that departed believers remain "safe in the arms of Jesus." Nevertheless, some have been willing to envisage and execute at least a fellowship of praise between the church militant and the church triumphant. Thus, for example, Charles Wesley makes the invitation, "Come, let us join our friends above," and in another hymn offers this vision:

> Happy the souls to Jesus joined,
> And saved by grace alone;
> Walking in all Thy ways we find
> Our heaven on earth begun.

> The church triumphant in Thy love,
> Their mighty joys we know;
> They sing the Lamb in hymns above,
> And we in hymns below.

> Thee in Thy glorious realm they praise,
> And bow before Thy throne;
> We in the kingdom of Thy grace,
> The kingdoms are but one.

> The holy to the holiest leads,
> From hence our spirits rise,
> And he that in Thy statutes treads
> Shall meet Thee in the skies.[17]

Again, for fear of impugning Christ's unique mediation, Protestants have usually been unwilling to ask for the prayers of the saints in heaven. But it should be remembered that "the prayer of a righteous person avails much" (Jas 5:16). And while nomination to the company of the righteous remains God's prerogative, "the prayers of the saints" rise acceptably with the incense before the heavenly throne (Rv 5:8; 8:3-4).

WORSHIP IN THE MIDST OF THE WORLD

So far, we have emphasized those features of worship by which the church on earth, in doing what is "already possible," *anticipates* worship in the city of God: praising God, feasting with Christ, sharing with all the saints. But certain familiar liturgical practices are conspicuous by their absence from the vision given in the book of Revelation. In the heavenly city there is no preaching, no baptizing, and no continuing need for forgiveness and intercession. But it is "still necessary" for the earthly church, by virtue of its location in the midst of the world, to be a community that announces the Gospel, admits new members to the Body of Christ, and seeks the removal of all that blocks or interrupts the fullness of God's rule. In considering (1) proclamation, (2) baptism, and (3) reconciliation, we shall not be forfeiting our eschatological orientation, for these features of worship in the midst of the world are to be seen as *preparing* for worship in the city of God.

Proclamation

The biblical rationale for preaching is classically set out in Romans 10:13-17: "For 'every one who calls upon the name of the Lord will be saved.' But how are men to call upon him in whom they have not believed? And how are they to believe in him of whom they have never heard? And how are they to hear without a preacher? And how can men preach unless they are sent? . . . So faith comes from what is heard, and what is heard comes by the preaching of Christ."

As the church follows the Lord's apostolic commission to "make disciples of all nations" (Mt 28:19), primary evangelism typically takes place beyond the Christian worship assembly. It is more like what I experienced as a missionary in West Africa a generation ago, where the whole village would gather in the shade of a tree to hear the Gospel for the first time. In our own culture, however, the regular Sunday service will likely include some who have been for some time on the fringes of the congregation and still have not responded fully to the Gospel. All members of the congregation can in fact profit from hearing the Gospel again and again, as they seek to grow in the faith and to work that faith out in their own existence. Here, therefore, the evangelism is suitably recapitulatory. Preaching is a matter of rehearsing the saving revelation of God to which the Bible testifies, so that attentive hearers may be ever more intimately included in the continuing story of God's presence and action for the salvation of the world. The Scriptures will be read and expounded and applied to the lives of the congregation and the individuals within it and on its edges. In this way the pilgrim people is encouraged on its journey towards the kingdom.

Baptism

The offer and acceptance of the Gospel are decisively sealed in baptism, where the candidate confesses Christ and receives the gift of the triune God in whose name the baptism is administered: adoption as the Father's child (Rom 8:15-17; Gal 4:4-7), incorporation into the Son and his saving work (Rom 6:1-23; 1 Cor 12:12-13; Gal 3:27), and renewal by the Holy Spirit (Jn 3:3-5; Ti 3:3-7), and all this with a view to the "day of redemption" (2 Cor 1:22; Eph 4:30).

In the earliest church baptism appears to have taken place away from the worship assembly. At least in its narrative accounts, the New Testament suggests that baptism took place upon the immediate response to primary evangelization (Acts 2:41; 8:38; 16:33; 19:5). When a preparatory catechumenate developed, those who had thereby gained more detailed instruction in the faith were finally baptized in a place dictated by decency and then brought clothed into the congregation to join for the first time fully in its prayers and receive holy communion for the first time: so it appears from the so-called *Apostolic Tradition* of Hippolytus at the beginning of the third century; and in its public architecture from the fourth century onwards, the church built separate baptisteries next to the bishop's cathedral so that the people baptized there could then join at once in the worship of the whole congregation.

Over the centuries the location and timing of baptism in relation to the regular assembly of the congregation have varied. As part of its effort to strengthen the sense of the church as the baptismal community, both baptized and baptizing, the twentieth-century liturgical movement has sought to bring the administration of baptism into the presence of the entire congregation. A fine example is the renewed Easter Vigil of the Roman rite. Many Protestant denominations now on occasion include baptisms in their Sunday morning services.

Where baptisms are administered within the regular assembly, the most appropriate ordering of the service is probably that which lets baptism follow directly on the sermon. This expresses the fact that baptism signifies the Gospel as appropriated by faith: the word has been preached and has elicited response, and now that same sequence of offered and accepted grace comes to expression in the dominical ordinance of baptism. On Sundays where there are no baptisms, it is also suitable at this point in the service for worshipers to bear witness to the grace they have received and the faith they profess. This may be done either by open testimonies or by a creedal confession, especially in churches that freely adopt the classical symbols as an expression of the faith once delivered to the saints. In both cases believers can understand themselves as recapitulating their baptism and, it may be hoped, going forward under the baptismal sign of death to sin and living unto God (Rom 6).

Reconciliation

The reconciling love and action of God toward the world is already a reality in Christ, but the world for its part still needs to let itself be reconciled to God (2 Cor 5:19-20). Even among Christians, sin unaccountably persists toward God and neighbor, so that renewed repentance and reconciliation remain necessary. Until humans are fully reconciled to God and to one another, the kingdom will not have finally come, and so intercession will continue to be required for the overcoming of all that opposes God's will.

The world enters Christian worship most obviously as an object of intercession. This follows the apostolic injunction of 1 Timothy 2:1, which is grounded in the belief that God "desires all men to be saved and to come to the knowledge of the truth" (1 Tim 2:4). Free passage for the preaching of the Gospel is also a reason for praying for peace in the world (1 Tim 2:2).

Compassion for people in their immediate circumstances of distress is itself sufficient motivation for intercession on the part of followers of a Christ who healed and helped. When Jesus "went about doing good" (Acts 10:38), his deeds were signs of the messianic kingdom (Mt 11:2-6; Lk 7:18-23). Until death has been finally abolished and God has wiped away the tears from every eye (Rv 21:4), it remains necessary to pray for the removal of all that contradicts and frustrates the fullness of the kingdom.

As Christians, we ourselves give evidence of the present incompleteness of God's rule when we fall back into sin. Then we need penitently to ask God for renewed forgiveness and to seek reconciliation with the neighbor whom we have offended. In classical liturgies the exchange of a greeting or a kiss is the sign that Christian brothers and sisters are at peace with one another. (In the Byzantine rite the place for this, in accordance with Matthew 5:23-24, is before the gifts are brought to the altar. In the Roman rite the *"pax"* takes place immediately before communion itself.)

THE SHAPE OF THE LITURGY

Having detected, through a theological reading of the Scriptures and of the liturgical traditions of the church, the features in Christian worship that, in the midst of the world, either anticipate or prepare for worship in the city of God, we may now briefly look in a more practical way for the "shape" of a service that includes those features in suitable sequence and proportion.[18] Here the Scriptures offer us little direct guidance, although the Emmaus story (Lk 24:13-35) and the account of Paul at Troas (Acts 20:7-11) may already suggest a regular Sunday service of word and table.

The earliest extant account of a full Sunday service dates from Justin Martyr's *Apology* I in the middle of the second century. In Justin's description of the church at Rome one can detect a basic structure of Christian worship that has lasted despite the accretions by which intervening generations have overlaid it and the excisions by which they have sometimes truncated it. Here is Justin's text (from *Apology* I. 67):

> And on the day called Sunday an assembly is held in one place of all who live in town or country, and the records of the apostles or the writings of the prophets are read as time allows. Then, when the reader has finished, the president in a discourse admonishes and exhorts us to imitate these good things. Then we all stand up together and send up prayers; and as we said before, when we have finished praying, bread and wine and water are brought up, and the president likewise sends up prayers and thanksgivings to the best of his ability, and the people assent, saying the Amen; and the elements over which thanks have been given are distributed, and everyone partakes; and they are sent through the deacons to those who are not

present . . . And we all assemble together on Sunday, because it is the first day, on which God transformed darkness and matter, and made the world; and Jesus Christ our Savior rose from the dead on that day . . .

A little earlier Justin had given more information about the prayer of the presiding minister over the bread and the cup: "he sends up praise and glory to the Father of all in the name of the Son and of the Holy Spirit, and gives thanks at some length that we have been deemed worthy of these things from him"; and "We bless the Maker of all things through his Son Jesus Christ and through the Holy Spirit over all that we offer."

It is quite possible to see in Justin's order of service the firm lines of a rite that liturgical revisers in the twentieth century have sought to restore, either by the docking of excrescences or by the rebuilding of missing parts:

1. the reading of the Scriptures, Old Testament ("prophets") and New ("apostles");
2. the sermon;
3. the (intercessory) prayers of the people;
4. the bringing of the bread and wine;
5. the great prayer of thanksgiving ("praise and glory to God") for creation, redemption, and the prospect of the kingdom;
6. communion in bread and wine.

That outline now appears, by a remarkable consensus among the historians and theologians of Christian worship, as the preferred basic order for the Sunday assembly in the service books of churches across a very broad confessional spectrum.

Into this order, and without obscuring it, it is quite possible to fit the other features I have mentioned. Confession of sin and prayer for forgiveness can appropriately come at the very beginning, so that, as the first- or second-century *Didache* suggests in accord with a very widespread religious intuition, "your offering may be pure." As indicated earlier, the sermon may be followed by baptism or by renewed confessions of faith. A greeting of peace may intervene between the prayers of intercession (Justin's place for it, according to *Apology* I. 65) and the presentation of the bread and wine. The communion of the saints is suitably remembered towards the end of the great prayer of thanksgiving or after the communion.

In the first part of such an order, the principal sense is that of preparing for God's kingdom by doing what is still necessary in the midst of the world: the proclamation of the Gospel, the invited response of faith, the prayers of intercession, the needed reconciliation to God and neighbor. In the second part, the emphasis moves to the anticipation that is already possible of worship in the city of God: the praise of God, the meal at the Lord's table, the fellowship of all the saints in Christ from every time and place. Only hymns are lacking: these are not structurally determinative; they may accompany any other element of the service; and since they often, in their own right, convey praise, they may help to keep that note present throughout, since the glory of God should dominate every act of worship on the part of those invited to enjoy God for ever.

****

Conclusion: A Vital Rhythm

The worship of God is the most eschatological activity of the church, since it will endure into the final kingdom and indeed become so all-pervasive that there will be no need for a temple in the city of God, for "its temple is the Lord God the Almighty and the Lamb," and "the glory of God is its light, and its lamp is the Lamb" (Rv 21:22-23). This emphasis on *leitourgia* is not to deny the importance of *martyria* and *diakonia*—the church as a "witnessing community" and a "caring community." Indeed we have seen a number of intrinsic connections between the church as a "worshiping community" and its responsibility for the spread of the Gospel in the world and the building up of a reconciled fellowship of mutual love. When it is not directly worshiping God in the assembly as its most immediate anticipation of the heavenly city, the Christian community should be about its business of preparing for the kingdom in the midst of the world; and the most direct forms of that (which find echoes and impulses in the sermon and the intercessions of the liturgical assembly) are the evangelism and the diaconal ministry which take place on the world's terrain.

To return at the end to Jean-Jacques von Allmen, we may find the Swiss Reformed theologian speaking also of the earthly church as engaged in a vital rhythm of breathing in and breathing out, *sustolé* and *diastolé*.[19] The church alternately gathers and disperses. When it assembles "in the Spirit on the Lord's day," it anticipates in worship the joys of heaven but also bears the burden of a world that has not yet let itself be redeemed. When the church scatters for mission and service, it is sustained by the divine life on which it has drawn in the Bread come down from heaven and which it now offers again to the world.

Notes

1. Jean-Jacques von Allmen, "Worship and the Holy Spirit," *Studia Liturgica* 2 (1963) 124-135.

2. From morning prayer in the Anglican Book of Common Prayer.

3. *Westminster Shorter Catechism.*

4. Romano Guardini, *The Spirit of the Liturgy* (London: Sheed and Ward, 1930). The text is from the Vulgate of Psalm 42 (43):4.

5. In my usage "liturgical" has very little to do with "read" as opposed to "extemporary" prayers or with dressing up in garments from times past. There is no such thing as a "non-liturgical" church since liturgy is by etymology simply "public service" and therefore the "corporate worship" of any Christian community.

6. See, for example, Massey H. Shepherd Jr., *The Paschal Liturgy and the Apocalypse* (Richmond, VA: John Knox Press, 1960); Pierre Prigent, *Apocalypse et liturgie* (Neuchâtel: Delachaux et Niestlé, 1964); Edouard Cothenet, *Exégèse et liturgie* (Paris: Editions du Cerf, 1988), particularly 235-323; Leonard L. Thompson, *The Book of Revelation: Apocalypse and Empire* (New York: Oxford University Press, 1990), particularly 53-73.

7. "On ne récite pas une rubrique, on l'exécute"; see Pierre Benoit, "Le récit de la cène dans Lc. xxii, 15-20," *Revue biblique* 48 (1939) 357-393.

8. The "Primary Chronicle," quoted from James H. Billington, *The Icon and the Axe* (New York: Random House, 1966) 6.

9. See William J. Samarin, *Tongues of Men and Angels: The Religious Language of Pentecostalism* (New York: MacMillan, 1972).

10. James McKinnon, *Music in Early Christian Literature* (New York: Cambridge University Press, 1987).

11. For further theological use of this hymn, see Geoffrey Wainwright, "The Praise of God in the Theological Reflection of the Church," *Interpretation* 39 (1985) 34-45.

12. For a developed treatment of the classical anaphora in a perspective similar to the present chapter, see Geoffrey Wainwright, "La prière eucharistique, lieu eschatologique," in A.M. Triacca and A. Pistoia, eds., *Eschatologie et liturgie* (Rome: CLV, 1985) 312-329.

13. "To this you say Amen. To say Amen is to append your signature" (St. Augustine; Migne: *Patrologia Latina* 46:836). According to St. Jerome the people's Amen resounded like heavenly thunder in the Roman basilica (Migne: *Patrologia Latina* 26:381).

14. For details, see Geoffrey Wainwright, *Eucharist and Eschatology*, rev. ed. (New York: Oxford University Press, 1981) 51-55.

15. See below on Justin Martyr.

16. For this last association of ideas, see Pierre Lebeau, *Le Vin nouveau du royaume* (Paris: Desclée de Brouwer, 1966).

17. John and Charles Wesley, *Hymns on the Lord's Supper* (1745) 96.

18. I am here borrowing the notion of shape from the influential work of Gregory Dix, *The Shape of the Liturgy* (Westminster, London: Dacre Press, 1945).

19. Jean-Jacques von Allmen, *Essai sur le repas du Seigneur* (Neuchâtel: Delachaux et Niestlé, 1966) 111-116, 120.

3

"Bible and Liturgy":
Daniélou's Work Revisited

IF ONE WERE TO NAME JEAN DANIÉLOU'S ACADEMIC DISCIPLINE, IT WOULD probably be patristics. As a patrologist, he recalled attention, by his monographic studies, to those fertile if eccentric giants, Origen[1] and Gregory of Nyssa.[2] As a historian of dogma, he recounted the development of Christian doctrine and thought in a way that did greater justice to semitic strands in the early church (Jewish and Syrian), without neglecting the more familiar currents in the Greek and Latin areas.[3] Yet Daniélou was no narrow student of the Fathers and the councils of the first centuries. In his many writings he brought together a number of academic disciplines and ecclesiastical movements that coalesced in the 1940s, 50s and early 60s to provide, as it turned out, the intellectual foundations for the Second Vatican Council. Besides his patristic interests, Daniélou drew on and contributed to biblical theology, liturgics, ecclesiology, and ecumenism. How "deliberately" ecumenical Daniélou himself was, I (as a Protestant) do not know; but certainly his work benefited from, and helped to shape, the convergence that developed among Catholics, Orthodox, and classical Protestants in matters of Scripture and Tradition in those years, and which has made possible the continuing serious doctrinal efforts in the various interconfessional bilateral dialogues since Vatican II and in the multilateral context of Faith and Order (for example, *Baptism, Eucharist and Ministry* and *Towards the Common Expression of the Apostolic Faith Today*). Daniélou was a bright figure in a generation that counted many stars: Yves

Congar, Henri de Lubac, Lucien Cerfaux, Karl and Hugo Rahner, Josef Andreas Jungmann, and (unless he is too young) Louis Bouyer.

The announcement of a congress of Societas Liturgica on the theme of "Bible and Liturgy" inevitably recalled that generation, and particularly Jean Daniélou. For, after all, he published a book under that title, *Bible et liturgie*, in the "Lex Orandi" series.[4] So I re-read that book, together with what is in some ways the preparatory book, *Sacramentum Futuri*.[5] This last-named book consists of *"études sur les origines de la typologie biblique."* These "origins" are both intra-scriptural and (as the Fathers develop hints within the Scriptures) patristic. On that basis, Daniélou then expounds, in *Bible et liturgie*, *"la théologie biblique des sacrements et des fêtes d'après les pères de l'Église."*

It seems to me that, a generation later, these studies of Daniélou may still have a contribution to make in the discussion of several questions that are of concern today. These are questions that I hear or raise as a systematic theologian in the presence of liturgical scholars who are discussing "Bible and liturgy." Some may be tempted to think Daniélou's approach outdated, given the changes that have intervened in church and culture since he wrote the studies mentioned. Certainly the intellectual climate is different. But not all changes have been for the good. And outmoded as Daniélou may appear in the light of intellectual fashion, the dogmatician in me wants to assert that he proposed, and still encourages, valid answers to a number of questions that arise perennially for the church in relation to the world and manifest themselves focally in the understanding and use of the Bible and in the practice of the liturgy.

My remarks fall into two groups, with three questions in each group. The first set has to do with history, more particularly with the history of salvation, and more particularly yet with the history of salvation as it is focused in Jesus the Christ. The second set has to do with the modalities—linguistic, symbolic, institutional—by which that history is "told," "prolonged," "entered into." Obviously, these two groups of interests are linked. From a Christian and churchly viewpoint, they comprise Tradition, first considered as content, then as process.

HISTORY AND SALVATION

Daniélou broadly shared a view of redemptive history that was familiar to Protestants through the work of their biblical theologians, above all Oscar Cullmann. Both in the formal presentation of his material and in the substance of his understanding, Daniélou accepts as given the scriptural order of creation, paradise, Adam and Eve, the flood; Israel in Egypt and exodus; the vicissitudes of the chosen people in the promised land, in exile and restoration; messianic prophesy; the coming of Christ in incarnation, earthly ministry, death and resurrection; the foundation of the church and its continuing life in the Spirit; the expectation of a final and universal kingdom of God. Using the key category of *typology*, Daniélou emphasizes the continuities in the narrative, the constancies of God's operation in human history, the movement forward (which is not necessarily a naïve "progress") to a divinely appointed goal. Jesus as the Christ is the fulfillment of the Old Testament promises, and this fulfillment will one day reach its consummation in the final kingdom of God, of which the church enjoys already an anticipation. The patristic use of typology arose, at least in part, in controversy with Jews and with Gnostics: *"La typologie . . . marque à la fois contre les gnostiques l'unité des deux Testaments et contre les Juifs la supériorité du Nouveau."*[6]

This vision immediately brings us into contact with a number of issues that are currently in hot debate. To name only three: (1) the relationship between Christianity and Judaism; (2) the relationship of the Christian faith to "other religions"; (3) ecumenical relations among Christians.

Christianity and Judaism

More precisely (at least according to the apostle Paul), the question would be that of Jews who (for the most part) do not (yet) accept Jesus as the Christ. The apostle does not spell out the means by which finally "all Israel will be saved" (Rom 11:26), but meanwhile his practice certainly includes preaching the Gospel to Jews as well as to Gentiles. Today, however, some Christians consider such evangelization as inappropriate towards Jews and attribute a positive role to "Judaism"—as a somehow autonomous religion—in the continuing history of salvation. Among scholars, a sign of this is the preference given to the term "Hebrew Bible" or the designation of the two Testaments as simply "the first" and "the second."

Undoubtedly, we Christians—especially of European stock—have much cause for repentance in our historical relations with Jews. Thus we should beware of any unguarded use of the term "superiority" such as may perhaps be found in the sentence quoted from Daniélou. But it is difficult to see how Christians could, without undermining their own faith, give up the category of "the Christ" as their first identification of Jesus (Mt 16:16; Jn 1:41; Acts 2:36; Rom 1:1-7, etc.). The Scriptures of Israel—and the history to which those Scriptures bore witness—provided the earliest Christians with the framework, both real and literary, in which to confess and interpret Jesus. In return, the Scriptures and history of Israel were given a Christological interpretation. Like it or not, the early church engaged in a "battle for the Scriptures," and the Scriptures of Israel became, in Christian eyes, the "Old Testament"—viewed positively insofar as it witnessed to God's purpose and promises, and yet as insufficient in the light of the events around Jesus that constituted the New Testament and to which the apostolic writings bore witness.

In the context of liturgy, the current uncertainties among Christians are refracted in the debate concerning the proper use of Old Testament readings. Can there be a reading of "the Hebrew Scriptures" in "their own right"? Or is not a Christian interpretation also—and always—required? This controversy may even, in a mild form, underlie the dissatisfaction many express over the selection and brevity of Old Testament texts in the Roman Order of Readings for Mass of 1969. Criticism is made of the use of these texts in the service of a narrow and artificial "typology." In my view, typology—precisely because it respects the concrete history of salvation to which the Scriptures bear literary witness—provides an appropriate, and even indispensable, though perhaps not the only, way of relating the Old Testament and the New. And renewed attention to Daniélou's work can help us recover a generous, though by no means wild or uncontrolled, use of it.

The Christian Faith and "Other Religions"

According to the Christian Scriptures, the history of salvation found its focus—in both a real and a literary way—first in Israel, then more particularly in Jesus as the Christ, and then again in the church as the company of those, both Jew and Gentile, who are joined to Christ through acceptance of the Gospel. If "election" appears to lead to a narrowing of the focus, the narrowing is temporary and remains in the service of God's universal purpose.

From their beginnings, Christian reflection and practice have had to face the question of the present state and future destiny of human beings outside the institutional history of the church. Generally, the church has considered itself to bear the responsibility of proclaiming Christ to every creature, while entertaining a measure of hope—sometimes more generous, sometimes less generous—for the salvation of those who should die without hearing the Gospel. Today, however, there is quite a widespread crisis, in the more liberal theological circles, concerning the necessity or desirability of evangelization. These doubts are often coupled with feelings of guilt concerning the way in which "western civilization," whether in its form as Christendom or in its more modern forms of rationalism and technology, is said to have overrun and suppressed other cultures. Multiculturalism would include a respect for other religions, all the more so since a pluralist epistemology would relativize all claims—and perhaps especially the Christian—to be in touch with ultimate truth.

Daniélou's work could remind contemporary theologians of the biblical and patristic resources for expressing a characteristically Christian view on the relations between the universal and the particular in matters of salvation. For the Scriptures, the Fathers and the liturgies know about "Adam and Christ"; and they display ways in which anthropological and religious constants (say, the "sacrifice" of which Klaus-Peter Jörns spoke in his address to the Congress of Societas Liturgica,[7] or "judgment") get transformed when included in the history of creation, fall, and redemption.[8]

Liturgists would do well to reflect on why the Roman authorities rejected the Bangalore New Orders of the Mass for India (which included, for instance, readings and citations from Hindu scriptures) and approved the Missal for the Dioceses of Zaïre (with its hopeful attitude towards the African ancestors).

Ecumenism within Christianity

Many feel that the ecumenical movement has completed its course. Christians of different communities have now become much more friendly towards each other. Remaining differences, whether of a doctrinal or an institutional kind, can, it is thought, easily be maintained without any harm. Whenever it seems good to them, individual Christians can now cross confessional lines to worship and work together as occasion allows.

Such resignation is to betray the original ecumenical vision. One valuable service which Daniélou's works can perform is to recall weary ecumenists to the task of seeking an ecclesial unity grounded upon substantial agreement in the scriptural and patristic faith as this comes to expression in the classic liturgies of the early church. The official Roman response to the Lima document on *Baptism, Eucharist and Ministry* recognized that herein lay the considerable degree of success attaching especially to the Faith and Order text on the eucharist: "The sources employed for the interpretation of the eucharist and the form of celebration are Scripture and tradition. The classical liturgies of the first millennium and patristic theology are important points of reference in this text ... The presentation of the mystery of the eucharist follows the flow of classical eucharistic liturgies, with the eucharistic theology drawing heavily on the content of the traditional prayer and symbolic actions of these liturgies. The text draws on patristic sources for additional explication of the mystery of the eucharist."[9]

A contribution which liturgical theologians might offer is close examination of the relations between the anamnetic, epicletic, and proleptic dimensions that mark Christian worship as part of salvation history. This could help pastoral and doctrinal authorities in the churches as they seek to discern the various stages along the way towards deeper ecclesial unity at which a greater sharing in liturgy and sacraments becomes appropriate.

Underlying the problems—represented above—that some theologians now find with salvation history may be the current questioning, in intellectual circles, of "linear history." In addition to "deconstructionist" attacks on coherence in general (and deconstructionism is still fashionable among North American academics despite its demise in France), left-wing political motives cause some to oppose any philosophy of history or any historiography that may appear to favor a triumphalism of "the victors" over "the victims." In fact, however, the Christian view of salvation history has never been naïvely "linear": the purpose, presence, and action of a triune God who is Lord of creation and time calls forth the notions of anamnesis, epiclesis, and prolepsis; and this very same God seeks to liberate—for history and eternity—all who are entrapped in sin and its consequences.[10]

MODALITIES OF PARTICIPATION

In *Bible et liturgie* Jean Daniélou presents—chiefly in terms of sacraments and calendar—the liturgical application of typology.

The realities of salvation history, to which the Old and New Testaments bear literary witness, are made available in the church's worship, in order that successive generations of believers may appropriate them and thereby become part of the company of those who will enjoy the glorious consummation of God's purpose for humankind. Daniélou demonstrates this understanding and function of the Christian liturgy from the practice of the rites themselves and from patristic expositions of them. In baptism, for example, the prayer over the water may evoke creation and the flood, the crossing of the Red Sea and the Jordan, Jesus' baptism in the river and on the cross; and the candidates' passage through the element of water, thus consecrated, becomes the sacramental sign of their inclusion into the realities of redemption prefigured in the Old Covenant, actualized in Christ, and now granted to believers by their incorporation into Christ in anticipation of their resurrection into the definitive kingdom of God. "*Ainsi, mémorial efficace de la mort et de la résurrection du Christ, considérés comme baptême par le Christ lui-même (Luc 12.50), le baptême est aussi prophétie efficace de la mort et de la résurrection eschatologique.*"[11]

Here again, Daniélou's work brings us into touch with three sets of issues that are controversial at the present time: (1) the viability of the inherited Christian vocabulary; (2) the relation between word and sacrament; (3) the status and function of the (scriptural) canon.

The Christian Vocabulary

Cultural changes intervening between biblical times and the modern period have—increasingly in the second half of the twentieth century—caused theologians to worry about the continuing intelligibility of the traditional language of the Christian faith. But it would be simplistic to say that we must choose between "the language of Canaan" and "the language of CNN" [Cable Network News, the international television service originating in the United States]. Christians may rightly use one "language" for their internal discourse within the church, and another for their external work in apologetics, evangelism, or dialogue; such differentiation of language in different contexts is a normal part of the linguistic phenomenon. Even within the liturgy, different ways of speech may be appropriate in (say) the eucharistic prayer (with its fixity and its solemnity) and the sermon (a flexible and unrepeatable address to an assembly).

Yet it remains of vital importance that the linguistic and symbolic treasury of the Bible and the Fathers be maintained, for it is the vehicle for recounting the story of salvation and for participating in that story as it continues towards consummation. The Christian liturgy is the privileged place for the enactment and continuation, in words and gestures, of the realities of redemption.

Intelligent, active, and effective participation in the liturgy requires, on the human side, a mental and practical catechesis concerning the traditional rites of the church. In the North American context, the Protestant theologian George Lindbeck has argued in a much noticed book, *The Nature of Doctrine: Religion and Theology in a Postliberal Age*, precisely for the renewed necessity of just such an instruction and apprenticeship for membership in a distinctive ecclesial community that can no longer count on the surrounding culture to transmit the Christian story.[12] Daniélou's *Bible et liturgie* could prove to be an excellent manual for teachers.

Word and Sacrament

One might have hoped, in a century of ecumenism, that the old polemical distinction between Protestantism and Catholicism as respectively the "church of the word" and the "church of the sacrament" had by now been overcome. Unfortunately, the responses of the churches to the Lima document on *Baptism, Eucharist and Ministry* show that this is not yet fully the case.

Liturgists, of all people, should be able to help the dogmaticians escape from this false dilemma. For a typological understanding and practice of the liturgy, such as Daniélou represents, brings together into a complex semiotic totality the originating events of salvation history, the Scriptures which bear witness to them and interpret them, the icons that depict them, the readings, sermons, prayers, and formularies that proclaim the history in verbal form, the material elements and bodily gestures that concretize the assembly's participation in the continuing story. By means of all the senses—hearing, seeing, taste, touch, smell—a story is incarnated that gets told and pondered in an intelligible way through speech.

The Scriptural Canon

The whole notion of a norm and standard internal to western or universal civilization—of "classic" works of art, literature, philosophy—is under attack among the liberal intelligentsia in North America, perhaps also in Europe. For some, the very word "canon"— a straight rod, a measuring stick—would be a symbol of phallocracy. This crisis of the canonical or the classical has found its way into theology. The permanent identity of Christianity is thereby placed at stake.

Daniélou's liturgico-typological approach supplies a means whereby the scriptural story can reach into the present. The lines of the biblical story's dynamic were perceived and prolonged by the patristic interpreters who developed an understanding and practice of the rites and preaching of the church that allowed for successive generations to be included in the story by word and sacrament. In the time of the church, the liturgy has functioned as a hermeneutical continuum and a vehicle of appropriation for the formative story. As long as the liturgical tradition remains unbroken and continues to be governed by the Scriptures whose reading it includes, successive generations will have the opportunity of coming to the Christian faith by means of an intelligible story that summons its hearers to let themselves become part of it. It is, moreover, the continued presence of the Scriptures in the liturgy that—humanly speaking— allows the originating realities of salvation history to perpetuate themselves as permanent archetypes, rather than as mere prototypes on which later generations might be tempted to "improve."

****

My tribute to Jean Daniélou has been to suggest that the present generation has much to (re-)learn from him concerning "Bible and liturgy."

Notes

1. *Origène* (Paris: La Table Ronde, 1948); English translation: *Origen* (New York: Sheed & Ward, 1955).

2. *Platonisme et théologie mystique: Essai sur la doctrine spirituelle de saint Grégoire de Nysse* (Paris: Aubier-Montaigne, 1944); *L'être et le temps chez Grégoire de Nysse* (Leiden: Brill, 1970).

3. See the three volumes on the development of Christian doctrine before the Council of Nicea: 1. *Théologie du judéo-christianisme*; 2. *Message évangélique et culture hellénistique*; 3. *Les Origines du christianisme latin* (Paris: Desclée, 1958, 1961; and Editions du Cerf, 1978); English translation: 1.

Theology of Jewish Christianity; 2. *Gospel Message and Hellenistic Culture*; 3. *The Origins of Latin Christianity* (London: Darton, Longmann and Todd, 1964, 1973, 1977); see also J. Daniélou and H. Marrou, *Des origines à saint Grégoire le Grand*, vol. 1 of *Nouvelle histoire de l'église* (Paris: Seuil, 1963); English translation: *The First Six Hundred Years* (New York: McGraw-Hill, 1964).

4. *Bible et liturgie* (Paris: Editions du Cerf, 1951); English translation: *The Bible and the Liturgy* (Notre Dame: University of Notre Dame Press, 1956).

5. *Sacramentum Futuri* (Paris: Beauchesne, 1950); English translation: *From Shadows to Reality* (London: Burns and Oates, 1960).

6. Ibid. x.

7. See Klaus-Peter Jörns, "Liturgy: Cradle of Scripture," *Studia Liturgica* 22 (1992) 28-29.

8. See further by Daniélou, *Le Mystère du salut des nations: la sphère et la croix* (Paris: Seuil, 1946); English translation: *The Salvation of the Nations* (Notre Dame: University of Notre Dame Press, 1962); *Le Mystère de l'avent* (Paris: Seuil, 1948); English translation: *The Advent of Salvation: A Comparative Study of Non-Christian Religions and Christianity* (New York: Paulist Press, 1962); and *Mythes païens, mystère chrétien* (Paris: Arthème Fayard, 1966); English translation: *Myth and Mystery* (New York: Hawthorn, 1968).

9. M. Thurian, ed., *Churches Respond to BEM, vol. 6* (Geneva: World Council of Churches, 1988) 16.

10. See J. Daniélou, *Essai sur le mystère de l'histoire* (Paris: Seuil, 1953); English translation: *The Lord of History: Reflections on the Inner Meaning of History* (London: Longmans, 1958).

11. *Bible et liturgie* 109f. Extracts from *Bible et liturgie* concerning baptism and confirmation were published in the Foi Vivante paperback series under the significant title of *L'Entrée dans l'histoire du salut* (Paris: Seuil, 1967).

12. George Lindbeck, *The Nature of Doctrine: Religion and Theology in a Postliberal Age* (Philadelphia: Westminster Press, 1984), esp. 128-138.

understanding and practice of liturgy and tradition in the ecumenical present.[2]

THE LORD'S SUPPER

We may begin with 1 Corinthians 11:23-26, where the Apostle Paul employs the technical rabbinical terms for traditioning, *mâsar* and *qibbêl*, or *paradounai* and *paralambanein*: "For I *received* (*parelabon*) of the Lord *what* (*ho*) I also *delivered* (*paredôka*) to you, *that* (*hoti*) the Lord Jesus on the night when he was betrayed took bread, and when he had given thanks, he broke it, and said, 'This is my body, which is for you. Do this in remembrance of me.' In the same way also the cup, after supper, saying, 'This cup is the new covenant in my blood. Do this, as often as you drink it, in remembrance of me.' For as often as you eat this bread and drink this cup, you proclaim the Lord's death until he comes."

That is usually called, even by liturgists, "the institution narrative." It is in fact much less a narrative than a "rubric," culminating in the twofold "command to repeat": "Do this in remembrance of me." Now the proper thing to do with a rubric is not to read it but to perform it, as Pierre Benoit said in accounting for the absence of "the command to repeat" from Matthew and Mark and (we might extend the argument) of the entire "institution narrative" from some early eucharistic prayers: "*On ne récite pas une rubrique, on l'exécute.*"[3] Without endorsing Hans Lietzmann's exegesis that Paul is in 1 Corinthians 11:23-26 claiming to be the *first* to receive from the Lord (a new form of) the Lord's Supper (a hellenistic memorial meal rather than the Jerusalemite festive meal),[4] we may therefore suggest that *what* St. Paul received "from the Lord," doubtless by a traditionary process, was in fact the beginning of Christian worship, "the first Mass" (as they used to say). At the Last Supper Jesus provided his church with the means of perpetuating the redemptive event of his own impending death and resurrection, the offering which inaugurated the new covenant. The ecclesial celebration of the sacrament carries forward the history of salvation and of the church. It will be celebrated "until he comes" or—taking up Joachim Jeremias' observation that *achri ou* with aorist subjunctive often carries a final sense—"with a view to His coming" (*bis* [*es so weit ist, dass*] *er kommt*).[5] At the last, the sacrament will give way to what it anticipates, namely, the Marriage Feast of the Lamb (Rv 19:7-9).

PREACHING

Moving on to 1 Corinthians 15:1-7, we find the same terminology for the traditionary process and the same substantive content, only the form is now that of preaching rather than the eucharistic meal: "Now I would remind you in what terms I preached to you the Gospel (*to euangelion ho euêngelisamên humin*), which you received (*ho kai paralabete*), in which you stand, by which you are saved, if you hold it fast (*katechein*)—unless you believed in vain. For I *delivered* (*paredôka*) to you as of first importance *what* I also *received* (*ho kai parelabon*), *that* (*hoti*) Christ died for our sins in accordance with the Scriptures, that he was buried, that he was raised on the third day in accordance with the Scriptures, and that he appeared to Cephas, then to the twelve . . ." What Paul hands on is "the Gospel" or the Paschal Mystery itself: "Christ, our paschal lamb, has been sacrificed" (1 Cor 5:7). The core of the kerygma is "Christ crucified" (1 Cor 1:23) whom God has raised from the dead (1 Cor 15:12-20).

During his earthly ministry Jesus had said to those whom he sent out in his name, "Whoever hears you hears me" (Lk 10:16). After his death and resurrection, his promised accompaniment of his apostles to the close of the age, as in Matthew 28:16-20, grounds a perhaps even stronger identification between his messengers and the One who has become the Proclaimed: Lutheran exegetes in particular are fond of arguing that, according to Paul's use of the noun *euangelion* and the verb *euangelizesthai*, "Gospel" is both content and action, with Christ both its author and its object.[6] Or in the words, on the Reformed side, of the marginal addition to the Second Helvetic Confession: "The preaching of the Word of God is itself the word of God (*praedicatio verbi divini est verbum divinum*)."

According to Romans 10, the purpose and result of preaching is that people may "confess with [their] lips that 'Jesus is Lord' and believe in [their] hearts that God raised him from the dead," so that they may "call on the name of the Lord" and "be saved." Thus they join in the anticipation of that final worship when "at the name of Jesus every knee shall bow . . . and every tongue confess that 'Jesus Christ is Lord', to the glory of God the Father" (Phil 2:10-11). Or to put the apostolic testimony in another way: as believers speak out, so the grace of God abounds to more and more, and the eucharistic chorus is swelled: "We too believe, and so we speak, knowing that he who raised the Lord Jesus will raise us also with Jesus and bring us with you into his presence. For it is all for your sake, so that as grace extends to more and more people it may increase thanksgiving, to the glory of God" (2 Cor 4:13-15).

Having begun with the eucharist and with preaching, which are the preeminent instances of "word and sacrament," we turn now to other forms of worship which in their very substance and action constitute the Tradition. First we examine a trio that employs above all the spoken word: the recitation of creeds, the saying of prayers, and the singing of hymns. The point is neatly made in a verse by the nineteenth-century Anglican hymn writer Samuel John Stone:

> Ancient Prayer and Song liturgic,
> Creeds that change not to the end,
> As His gift we have received them,
> As His charge we will defend.[7]

We note at the outset that each appears as "gift" and "charge," "*Gabe*" and "*Aufgabe*," as is characteristic of the traditionary process.

CREEDS

From the fourth century we know of a ceremony that took place some weeks or days before baptism, the *traditio symboli*, whereby the creed was "passed on" to the candidates who then, after learning it, "returned" it—the *redditio*—to the bishop.[8]

The *traditio et redditio symboli* is best viewed as a rehearsal for the act of confessing the faith that was integral to baptism itself.[9] The first form that we know of the words spoken at baptism consists in the threefold creedal questions put by the minister to the candidate and the latter's responses of "I believe," upon which the candidate was each time immersed. Thus, in the so-called *Apostolic Tradition* of Hippolytus, which dates from the early third century:

> The minister of baptism shall lay hand on the candidate, saying: "Do you believe in God the Father almighty?"
> And the one who is being baptized shall say: "I believe."
> And forthwith the giver, having his hand placed upon the baptizand's head, shall baptize him once.
> And then he shall say: "Do you believe in Christ Jesus, the Son of God, who was born of the Holy Spirit from the Virgin Mary, and was crucified under Pontius Pilate, and died, and rose again on the third day alive from the dead, and ascended into

heaven, and sits at the right hand of the Father, and will come to judge the living and the dead?"
And when he has said, "I believe," he shall be baptized again. And the minister shall say again: "Do you believe in the Holy Spirit and the Holy Church and the resurrection of the flesh?" Then the one being baptized shall say: "I believe," and thus he shall be baptized a third time.[10]

The trinitarian creedal structure clearly matches the "command to baptize" recorded of the risen Lord in Matthew 28:19: "Go therefore and make disciples of all nations, baptizing them in the name of the Father and of the Son and of the Holy Spirit, teaching them to observe all that I have commanded you; and lo, I am with you always, to the close of the age." This justifies the fact that, even after he had ceased to hold that the Apostles' Creed was dictated by Christ himself, the great nineteenth-century Danish preacher and theologian N.F.S. Grundtvig could still consider the western baptismal creed as "a word from the Lord's own mouth."

The significance of that baptism "in the name of the Father, the Son, and the Holy Spirit" has been well brought out by Markus Barth in terms of Matthean exegesis: it is baptism into the crucified and risen Christ, the Father's chosen and anointed Son, who himself baptizes with the Holy Spirit that is now being poured out on all flesh.[11] According to the church's canonical reading of the broader apostolic witness contained in the entire New Testament, baptism in the water of God's creation signifies and effects: inclusion, by grace and faith, into the redeeming death and resurrection of Christ; the gift of the Holy Spirit whereby the children of God *in Filio* cry "Abba, Father"; incorporation into the church; and inheritance in the promised final kingdom. Thus each later confession of the baptismal creed, as the anamnesis of baptism, summarizes and takes up the history of salvation and locates the believer within it. And thus does the *traditio symboli* contribute to the formation and renewal of the worshiping community.

THE LORD'S PRAYER

Emerging perhaps at a slightly later date in the patristic period than the *traditio et redditio symboli* was another double ceremony of "handing over" and "rendition," the *traditio et redditio orationis dominicae*. The Lord's Prayer was taught to the baptismal candidates after they had "returned" the creed, and, still before baptism, they had to "repeat" the prayer in preparation for their first "sacramental" use of it, which would occur at the eucharistic communion that followed immediately on their baptism.[12]

Jesus had promised his disciples that whenever they gathered in his name for prayer, he would be in the midst of them. This would ensure the Father's hearing them (Mt 18:19-20). The presupposition was that their prayer would follow the model and spirit of Jesus' instruction:

> Pray then like this:
> Our Father who art in heaven,
> Hallowed be thy name.
> Thy kingdom come,
> Thy will be done,
>   On earth as it is in heaven.
> Give us this day our bread for the morrow;
> And forgive us our debts,
>   As we also have forgiven our debtors;
> And do not put us to the test,
>   But deliver us from evil.
>   (Mt 6:9-13)

When the Church Fathers discuss prayer, this is *the* prayer they write about. Tertullian calls it a "summary of the entire Gospel (*brevarium totius evangelii*)," and Cyprian a "compend of our heavenly teaching (*nostris coelestis doctrinae compendium*)."[13] In our own time, the exegete Heinz Schürmann says the Lord's Prayer is "the key to the preaching of Jesus";[14] and the theological historian Yves Congar writes that "When I say the 'Our Father,' I have already included everything which will be given me to know only in the Revelation of glory."[15]

Three instances may be given of the ways in which the church continued to pray after the fashion of the Lord's Prayer and thereby allowed the prayer to constitute its Tradition in the interval between Christ's announcement of the kingdom and the kingdom's final arrival. First we know from Justin Martyr, in the middle of the second century, that petitionary and intercessionary prayers formed part of the regular Sunday gathering for worship: common prayers were made "for ourselves . . . and for all others everywhere, that, having learned the truth, we may be deemed worthy to be found good citizens also in our actions and guardians of the commandments, so that we may be saved with eternal salvation."[16] The classical "prayers of the people" continued to seek the spread of the Gospel, the conversion of the world, and the perseverance of the faithful, all with a view to the coming of God's kingdom.[17]

Second, we may notice a prayer from the ancient *Didache* which has found favor as an offertory prayer in modern liturgical revival:

> As this broken bread was scattered over the mountains, and when brought together became one, so let your Church be brought together from the ends of the earth into your kingdom; for yours are the glory and the power through Jesus Christ for evermore.[18]

Finally may be mentioned the *Sanctus*, which is found already in Revelation 4:8 and came to be a fixture in the eucharistic anaphora or great prayer of thanksgiving. With the "Holy, holy, holy" the church on earth joins in the hallowing of God's name which is the accomplishment of "angels and archangels and all the company of heaven."[19]

SONG LITURGIC

Twentieth-century biblical scholarship has recalled attention to the primitive Christian hymns embedded in the texts of the New Testament. Christocentrically, but always with reference to God the Father, they celebrate the divine origin of Christ, his role in creation, redemption, and consummation, and his sovereign status. Characteristic are Colossians 1:15-20 and, most famously, Philippians 2:5-11.

An early post-apostolic example is the *Phôs hilaron*:

> Hail, gladdening light, of His pure glory poured,
> Who is the immortal Father, heavenly, blest,
> Holiest of Holies, Jesus Christ, our Lord!
> Now we come to the sun's hour of rest.
> The lights of evening round us shine.
> We hymn the Father, Son, and Holy Spirit divine.
> Worthiest art Thou at all times to be sung
> With undefilèd tongue,
> Son of God, giver of life, alone;
> Therefore in all the world Thy glories, Lord, they own.[20]

In the fourth century this was joined by the western *Te Deum*. Both have remained in constant use in the churches. Addressed in the present to the divine Persons, they enact the praise that is due God's being, nature, and works and thereby locate the worshipers in the salvation which God graciously bestows and will bestow in the final kingdom. The same is achieved by the church's constant use of the psalms of David, often interpreted Christologically (whether as *vox Christi* or as *vox ad Christum*) and concluding with a trinitarian doxology.

Later hymn writers frequently take up the practice of patristic preachers in focusing the past and future of salvation history upon a liturgical "today," whereby that history is resumed, advanced, and anticipated. I select two examples from my own Methodist tradition. First, some verses from Charles Wesley's "Hymn for Ascension Day":

> Hail the day that sees Him rise,
> Ravished from our wistful eyes!
> Christ, awhile to mortals given,
> Reascends His native heaven.
>
> Him though highest heaven receives,
> Still He loves the earth He leaves;
> Though returning to His throne,
> Still He calls mankind His own.
>
> See! He lifts His hands above;
> See! He shows the prints of love;
> Hark! His gracious lips bestow
> Blessings on His Church below.
>
> Master, parted from our sight,
> High above yon azure height,
> Grant our hearts may thither rise,
> Following Thee beyond the skies.[21]

And then from another Wesley hymn, in anticipation of the final Advent:

> Lo! He comes with clouds descending,
> Once for favoured sinners slain;
> Thousand thousand saints attending,
> Swell the triumph of His train:
> Hallelujah!
> God appears on earth to reign.[22]

After the oral forms of "ancient prayer and song liturgic, creeds that change not to the end," we turn to two sacraments that in our context are also to be considered in their constitutive function for Tradition. Medieval western theology appropriately viewed baptism and ordination as *deputationes ad cultum*. Baptism and ordination are themselves liturgical acts that induct persons into membership of, and particular roles in, the worshiping community. Thereby the baptized and the ordained become, "incidentally," carriers of the Tradition.

BAPTISM

According to the so-called *Apostolic Tradition* of Hippolytus, it is baptism which first allows a person to "pray with the faithful," to exchange the kiss of peace, to offer gifts at the eucharist, and to receive the communion. Henceforth one becomes, no longer merely a receiver of the Gospel through listening to teaching, the reading of the Scriptures, and the oral word of the sermon, but now one who, as a member of the celebrating community, actively embodies the faith. A secondary sign of this is the putting on of the white "garment of righteousness," having been "washed in the blood of the Lamb" (cf. Rv 7:14).[23]

Here the existential and ethical implications of baptism come into play. The *results* of participation in Christ's death and resurrection and incorporation into his Body are presented by the New Testament in liturgical or cultic terms. In 1 Corinthians 6:19-20 St. Paul asks the rhetorical question: "Do you not know that your body is a temple of the Holy Spirit within you, which you have from God? You are not your own; you were bought with a price. So glorify God in your body." And similarly in 2 Corinthians 6:16-7:1: "What agreement has the temple of God with idols? For we are the temple of the living God; as God has said, 'I will live in them, and I will be their God, and they shall be my people' . . . Since we have these promises, beloved, let us cleanse ourselves from every defilement of body and spirit, and make holiness perfect in the fear of God." Or again in Romans 12:1-2: "I appeal to you therefore, brothers and sisters, by the mercies of God, to present your bodies as a living sacrifice, holy and acceptable to God, which is your spiritual worship. Do not be conformed to this world but be transformed by the renewal of your mind, that you may prove what is the will of God, what is good, and acceptable, and perfect."

The existential and ethical comportment of Christians may, by the witness it makes, have the incidental effect of bringing others to glorify God. So, according to Matthew 5:16: "Let your light so shine before others, that they may see your good works and give glory to your Father who is in heaven." Or, as echoed by 1 Peter 2:12: "Maintain good conduct among the Gentiles, so that in case they speak against you as wrongdoers, they may see your good works and glorify God on the day of visitation."

ORDINATION

The prayer for the ordination of a bishop in the *Apostolic Tradition* exercised great influence, directly or indirectly, in many parts of the east, and in our time it has reemerged as a source for the revision of the rite in several western churches. While "princely" and "pastoral" themes echo the Old Testament notion of a "royal shepherd," they are integrated into a priestly framework which makes the principal ministry of a bishop liturgical. The prayer of Hippolytus reads in large part:

> God and Father of our Lord Jesus Christ, you foreordained from the beginning a race of righteous men from Abraham; you appointed princes and priests, and did not leave your sanctuary without a ministry. From the beginning of the age it was your good pleasure to be glorified in those whom you have chosen: now pour forth that power which is from you, of the princely Spirit which you granted through your beloved Son Jesus Christ to your holy apostles who established the Church in every place as your sanctuary, to the unceasing glory and praise of your name.

> You who know the hearts of all, bestow upon this your servant, whom you have chosen for the episcopate, to feed your holy flock and to exercise the high-priesthood before you blamelessly, serving night and day; to propitiate your countenance unceasingly, and to offer you the gifts of your holy Church; and by the Spirit of high-priesthood to have the power to forgive sins according to your command, to confer orders according to your bidding, to loose every bond according to the power which you gave to the apostles, to please you in gentleness and a pure heart, offering to you a sweet-smelling savor, through your child Jesus Christ our Lord, with whom be glory and power and honor to you, with the holy Spirit, both now and to the ages of ages. Amen.[24]

Correspondingly, Vatican II's Constitution on the Sacred Liturgy calls the worship assembly "the preeminent manifestation of the Church," marked by the "full, active participation of all God's holy people, especially in the same eucharist, in a single prayer, at one altar at which the bishop presides, surrounded by his college of priests and by his ministers."[25]

The building up of this worshiping community is the purpose of the traditionary process. In the patristic and medieval periods the bishop's duties were recognized to include evangelizing, preaching, and teaching.[26] At the ordination of a bishop the eighth-century Byzantine rite prays for "him who has been elected to undertake the gospel."[27] The ninth- or tenth-century Armenian rite of ordination to the priesthood contains the petition for the ordinand "that he may stand firm and without blemish in the priesthood before you in the catholic Church, built and established on the rock of faith; without shame, to epitomize rightly the word of the preaching, to sow abroad the quickening and orthodox faith of the apostolic Church in all places to them that listen."[28]

Ancient prayers of ordination do not forget that the Gospel is to be spread outward. In closely similar phraseology, a Georgian prayer for the ordination of a bishop refers to "teachers, by whom has been spread over the whole earth the knowledge of your truth, vouchsafed to those born of men by the Prince your only-begotten Son, whom from generation to generation you manifested to your chosen ones"; the East Syrian rite to "apostles and prophets, teachers and priests, by whose work might be multiplied the knowledge of the truth which your only-begotten Son gave to the human race"; and a West Syrian prayer to the gift of "leaders, so that we might please you by making the knowledge of the name of your Christ multiplied and glorified throughout the world."[29] In the medieval west a Gallican prayer in the Roman rite for bishops asks that "their feet, by your aid, may be beautiful for bringing good tidings of peace, for bringing your good tidings of good [Is 52:7; Rom 10:15]. Give them, Lord, a ministry of reconciliation [2 Cor 5:18] in word and deeds and in power of signs and of wonders [Rom 15:18-19]. May their speech and preaching be not with enticing words of human wisdom, but in demonstration of the Spirit and of power [1 Cor 2:4; 1 Thes 1:5]."[30]

The strongly Pauline character of those prayers recalls the ministry of the apostle, who saw his evangelizing work in liturgical terms. Paul uses the verb *latreuô* in Romans 1:9, the sense of which C.K.

Barrett neatly captures as "I render God spiritual service in proclaiming the Gospel of his Son."[31] In Romans 15:15-16 the apostle writes: "On some points I have written to you very boldly, by way of reminder, because of the grace given me by God to be a minister (*leitourgos*) of Christ Jesus to the Gentiles in the priestly service (*hierourgôn*) of the Gospel of God, so that the offering (*prosphora*) of the Gentiles may be acceptable, sanctified by the Holy Spirit." His expected apostolic martyrdom, which was but the culmination of a ministry of mortal hardship (2 Cor 4:7-12; 6:4-5; Gal 6:17), St. Paul interpreted in terms of sacrifice (2 Tim 4:6), "poured out as a libation upon the sacrificial offering of your faith" (Phil 2:17). The successors in the apostolic tradition may expect no less: it is their service to the worshiping community's service of God.

After the spoken word and the sacramental act we may now turn to two objects whose liturgical use also constitutes the Tradition. I refer to the book of the Scriptures and to icons.

THE SCRIPTURES

Some weeks before the *traditio symboli* and the *traditio orationis dominicae*, candidates for baptism in the patristic church in parts of the west also received the *traditio evangelii*, to which was transferred the name of *apertio aurium*. The candidates had their "ears opened" by the "tradition of the Gospel," as the beginnings of the four Gospels were read and expounded to them, and they could thenceforth "hear the Gospel" in the eucharistic assembly.[32] They thus became part of a community that was so deeply constituted by the Gospel that it was considered an act of apostasy to "surrender" its Scriptures into the wrong hands in times of persecution: in a kind of negative example of tradition, the *traditores* were betrayers or traitors.

When the churches confess the divine inspiration of the Scriptures, room is left for various modalities of the Spirit's action in the composing, sorting, and understanding of the texts, and among these must certainly be included the creative, selective, and interpretative force of the liturgy. As to the origin of the Scriptures, much of their material—and by no means only the hymns we mentioned earlier—has been judged by contemporary scholarship to have had its *Sitz im Leben* in the worship of the believing community.[33] As to the choice of the writings that would eventually be recognized as canonical, George Tavard has rightly stressed the part played in the "reception" of a book by the "experience of the Word" as he "imposed himself with power" in the reading of the book "in the continued Pentecost of liturgical worship."[34] Finally, therefore, as to the hermeneutic of Scripture, the liturgical assembly and rite provide a connatural context and purpose.

The canonical Scriptures serve as the internal norm of the Tradition and thereby also as an instrument of its transmission. The fact that, at the sheer level of producing manuscripts, the Scriptures were copied principally for liturgical use is an indication of the purpose of the Tradition in worship. The normativity for the Tradition of the liturgically preserved Scriptures is illustrated by the way their reading has, ordinarily, provided guidance for the ongoing life of the church and of the individual faithful—and, extraordinarily, sparked reformation or renewal where need or opportunity arose.

ICONS

Liturgical icons are characteristic of the eastern churches rather than the western, but help towards understanding and appreciating their action upon the Tradition can be found in some observations of George Tavard concerning the communion of saints. When the international dialogue between the Roman Catholic Church and the World Methodist Council began to tackle the theme of the apostolic Tradition, Tavard proposed to the Joint Commission the serendipitous and fruitful motto of "koinonia in time."[35] Viewing the proclamation of the Gospel in the administration of the sacraments, he noted that "receiving and transmitting the Gospel manifests and promotes the communion of saints, both holy things and holy persons": "Tradition is the tradition of holy things; their reception makes the faithful holy (*Ta agia tois agiois*, 'holy things for the holy,' in the liturgy of St. John Chrysostom)." At each moment "this Tradition lives from the riches of the Gospel as received from the previous generation[s]," and while "Tradition looks forward, beyond history, to the full epiphany of the divine glory in the kingdom of God," there are "anticipations and previews of the kingdom, when the Church is truly experienced as the communion of saints."

Tavard's stimulation allowed the Singapore 1991 report of the Catholics and the Methodists at several places to view the communion of the saints as both an agent in and a purpose of the Apostolic Tradition:[36]

To be sure that we are hearing the Word, we maintain communion with those who have heard and obeyed the Word before us (18).

The Holy Spirit has enabled the faithful to confess Christ in every generation, and the Church continues in this communion of saints (33).

When Christians recite the Creed within a liturgical setting, they do more than list a set of beliefs; they identify themselves with that great company "whose lives are hid with Christ in God" (37).

In places that are hostile to Christianity, missionary endeavour has been difficult, and fidelity to the Gospel has proved very costly. The picture in Hebrews of the saints who watch from heaven and encourage us is pertinent here (47).

While all the baptized make up the communion of saints, they also recognize the conspicuous presence of divine grace in specific persons—the Saints—whose lives and example testify, even to the shedding of their blood for Jesus, to the transforming action of the Spirit of God in every generation. The "cloud of witnesses" transcends denominational barriers (66).

The saints in heaven are held as instances of Christ's "closest love" and as present tokens of the ultimate fulfillment of all God's purposes (75).

Against that background, Western Christians also should be able to recognize that liturgical icons—on the ceilings, walls, screens of the churches—are signs of the cumulative transgenerational presence of the saints amid the earthly worshiping community; or we may say that the contemporary generation of worshipers is lifted to join the heavenly company from all times and places. Once more, the Tradition is displayed as a liturgical event which gathers up past, present, and future.

Everything that has so far been said about varieties of word and sacrament, of persons, functions, and liturgical objects, presupposes the presence and action of the Holy Spirit to constitute Christian worship and *ipso facto* the Tradition. As a final, but fundamental, feature of the liturgy we must therefore treat the explicit invocation of the Holy Spirit.

THE INVOCATION OF THE SPIRIT

In the eastern churches again, the Tradition is customarily understood in strongly pneumatological terms. Vladimir Lossky called

Tradition "the life of the Holy Spirit in the Church, communicating to each member of the Body of Christ the faculty of hearing, of receiving, of knowing the truth in the Light that belongs to it, and not according to the natural light of human reason."[37] Paul Evdokimov called the Holy Spirit *"l'Esprit de la Transmission"*: "The time of the Spirit is the time of Tradition, essentially marked by its apostolic origins and its openness to the Parousia ... The *Acts of the Apostles*, Acts of the Church until the end of the world, constitute the *Gospel of the Holy Spirit* ... Even outside the gathering of councils, the epiclesis of conciliarity is permanently operative; it is the epiclesis of Tradition, of the uninterrupted life of the Church."[38]

The term "epiclesis" gives the clue to the constitutively liturgical character of the Tradition. In its technical sense among liturgiologists, the epiclesis is the specific prayer to God, appropriately for the Holy Spirit, to consecrate the materials, the assembly, and the action for the realization of the sacramental event. Typical is the epiclesis in the Byzantine Liturgy of St. John Chrysostom: "We pray and beseech and entreat you, send down your Holy Spirit on us and on these gifts set forth; and make this bread the precious body of your Christ, changing it by your Holy Spirit, Amen; and that which is in this cup the precious blood of your Christ, changing it by your Holy Spirit, Amen; so that they may become to those who partake for vigilance of soul, for fellowship with the Holy Spirit, for the fullness of the kingdom of heaven, for boldness toward you, not for judgement or condemnation."[39] Suitable variations are made in the case of the elements, actions, and purposes of baptism and chrismation,[40] whereas ordination prayers often have the appearance of a single expanded epiclesis.

Despite lingering controversies between east and west over a "moment of consecration" at the eucharist (reflecting different views on the respective roles of the trinitarian persons and even perhaps the *filioque* debate), and despite continuing Protestant hesitations over the propriety of invoking the Spirit on "inanimate" elements, the twentieth-century liturgical movement has rediscovered for the west the pneumatological, and even the specifically epicletic, dimension of Christian worship.[41] An ecumenical indication of this is provided by the quite widespread welcome given, even from unexpected quarters, by the responding churches to the theme of "invocation of the Spirit" in Faith and Order's Lima text, *Baptism, Eucharist and Ministry*.[42] The Anglican Church of Canada, for example, notes that "the emphasis on epiklesis not only restores the importance of the role of the Holy Spirit in the operation of the sacraments, but also it makes clear that the sacraments are prayer actions and not mechanical means of grace," and the Evangelical Lutheran Church of Bavaria "sees expressed [in the efficacy of the Holy Ghost] that the church does not control the gift of the sacrament, but entreats the presence of God. This wards off at the same time a magical understanding of the *verba testamenti.*"[43]

What applies focally to specific moments in sacramental rites applies generally to Christian worship in its entirety and thereby to the Tradition: the Holy Spirit is integral to its substantive content and to the traditionary process. Without the Spirit who is invoked in worship, there is no Tradition or tradition.

****

In conclusion, two points remain to be briefly made. Defensively, it may be necessary to ward off any charge of "liturgical fundamentalism" that may be raised against the foregoing argument. Positively, I need to redeem my obliquely made promise at the start that my thesis has hopeful implications for ecumenism.

Against any charge of mindless, passive invariability it should be sufficient to affirm that the active and intelligent receptivity called forth by divine Revelation in its originating moments continues to mark Christian worship and the ongoing traditionary process it constitutes. What is received has in fact to be actively and intelligently appropriated, assimilated and applied in the ever-new here and now. The present and local horizon is integral to the hermeneutical procedure and to the ritual performance. George Tavard has put the matter well in terms of culture: "At first sight there would seem to be no diversities in regard to the reception of the gospel: all must listen to it (*fides ex auditu*, Rom 10:17), accept it, and live a life of obedience to it (the 'new obedience' of the Reformers). But in fact there is diversity in reception that is due to the inculturation of the gospel in the many cultures of the world . . . What one receives is the gospel as previously received in a certain culture, expressed in a given language, embodied in certain customs and institutions. This gospel is always in tension with its social context. For the context has been shaped by human traditions that preceded the preaching of the gospel, or that have grown outside of it, or that are more or less in conflict with it, or even that have been inspired by it."[44]

As Tavard recognizes, complex and subtle discernment is therefore required: "The present in which we live affects our reception of the gospel. It colours the way we assimilate it and pass it on. In other words, Tradition, both as reception and as handing on, requires discernment. One should assess the meaning and value of past documents, and one can do this only in the light of contemporary culture and of present needs. Yet there must also be a critical discernment of one's discernment. In the cumulative effect of the Tradition, many things—customs, practices of piety, pious opinions, methods of meditation and self-discipline, ethical conclusions, practical applications—have accrued to the core of Tradition. The community and its members must be capable of sorting out the essential from the permissible, the permanent from the provisional."[45]

This is where the liturgical nature of Tradition comes in, and the ecumenical promise of such an understanding and practice. For communities that gather faithfully and expectantly in the name of "Jesus Christ, the same yesterday, today, and forever" open themselves to reformation and renewal by the triune God who is the origin, sustenance, and goal of the Tradition. It is no accident that the twentieth-century liturgical and ecumenical movements have gone hand in hand, allowing the churches to converge in their understanding and practice of the Gospel as, with the help of the biblical and patristic movements, they have sought to penetrate again to the core of the Tradition and allow it to reconfigure them.[46]

There is still a way to go. But the recovery of unity *coram Deo* is vital, for only as they live together in harmony with one another and in accord with Christ Jesus can Christians fulfill the purpose and reach the goal of Tradition: "with one heart and one voice to glorify the God and Father of our Lord Jesus Christ" (Rom 15:5-6).

Notes

1. J.B. Bossuet, *Instruction sur les états d'oraison* (1697) Book VI.

2. It is useful, though sometimes difficult, to make a distinction between Tradition (initial capital) and tradition (lower case). I have tried to follow the usage of the World Conference on Faith and Order at Montreal in 1963 by using a capital T where the stress is on the substantive *"paradosis of the kerygma"* and a small t for the transmission process or for particular traditions.

3. Pierre Benoit, "Le récit de la cène dans Lc. xxii, 15-20)," *Revue biblique* 48 (1939) 386.

4. Hans Lietzmann, *Messe und Herrenmahl*, 3d ed. (Berlin: de Gruyter, 1955).

5. Joachim Jeremias, *Die Abendmahlsworte Jesu*, 3d ed. (Göttingen: Vandenhoeck & Ruprecht, 1960) 244.

6. See, for instance, G. Friedrich, *euangelizomai, euangelion* in G. Kittel, *Theologisches Wörterbuch zum Neuen Testament*, vol. 2, pp. 715-733.

7. Samuel John Stone, *Poems and Hymns* (London: Methuen, 1903) 245.

8. We know of the practice in Jerusalem from Etheria's *Pilgrimage*, in Rome from Rufinus' *Commentary on the Apostles' Creed*, and in North Africa from Augustine's *Sermons* (56-59 or 212-215). The two-part rite was spread throughout the west. There was geographical variety in the days appointed for its performance. The history may be traced in Alois Stenzel, *Die Taufe: Eine genetische Erklärung der Taufliturgie* (Innsbruck: Rauch, 1958) or in J.D.C. Fisher, *Christian Initiation: Baptism in the Medieval West* (London: SPCK, 1965).

9. Stenzel distinguishes between a stress at the *redditio symboli* on the accuracy of the candidate's learning of the *content* of the faith (the *fides quae creditur*) on the one hand, and on the other hand, the profession of faith at the baptism itself as the commitment of belief (the *fides qua creditur*). But such a distinction seems a trifle artificial in this context.

10. Translation largely borrowed from G.J. Cuming, *Hippolytus: A Text for Students* (Bramcote, Notts.: Grove Books, 1976) 19. In a recovery of the Tradition, modern liturgical revision has reclaimed the interrogative form of the profession of faith immediately *before* the baptism, while retaining also the pronouncement by the minister, "I baptize you . . .," which appears to have been unnecessary as long as the baptismal questions and responses occurred in the water.

11. Markus Barth, *Die Taufe—ein Sakrament?* (Zollikon-Zurich: Evangelischer Verlag, 1951) 525-554.

12. For the history, see again Stenzel or Fisher.

13. Tertullian, *De Oratione* 1; Cyprian, *De Oratione Dominica* 9.

14. H. Schürmann, *Das Gebet des Herrn*, 4th ed. (Freiburg: Herder, 1981) 14.

15. Y.M.-J. Congar, *La Tradition et les traditions*, vol. 2 (Paris: Arthème Fayard, 1963) 185. In this section (181-191) Congar is treating the liturgy as the first among *"les principaux monuments de la Tradition."*

16. Justin, *Apology* I. 67 (for regular Sunday worship) and 65 (for the content of the prayers). Translation from R.C.D. Jasper and G.J. Cuming, *Prayers of the Eucharist: Early and Reformed*, 3d ed. (New York: Pueblo Publishing Co., 1987) 28-29.

17. See Paul de Clerck, *La "Prière universelle" dans les liturgies latines anciennes: Témoignages patristiques et textes liturgiques* (Münster: Aschendorff, 1977).

18. Translation is from Jasper and Cuming, *Prayers of the Eucharist* 23.

19. The dating of the *Sanctus* in the eucharistic prayer and its place in the structure of the various anaphoras is historically debated; see, most recently, B.D. Spinks, *The Sanctus in the Eucharistic Prayer* (Cambridge: Cambridge University Press, 1991).

20. Translation by John Keble.

21. First published in 1739, the hymn is found in *The Poetical Works of John and Charles Wesley*, ed. George Osborn, vol. 1 (London: Weslyan-Methodist Conference Office, 1868) 187-188, and in many Methodist and other hymnals.

22. First published in 1758 under the title "Thy Kingdom Come," the hymn is found in *The Poetical Works*, ed. Osborn, vol. 6 (1870) 143-144, and in many Methodist and other hymnals.

23. It is, of course, the martyrs who by their "baptism of blood" most powerfully embody the Tradition of the Gospel and the Faith.

24. Translation from Paul F. Bradshaw, *Ordination Rites of the Ancient Churches of East and West* (New York: Pueblo Publishing Co., 1990) 107.

25. *Sacrosanctum Concilium* 41; translation from the International Commission on English in the Liturgy, *Documents on the Liturgy 1963-1979* (Collegeville: The Liturgical Press, 1982) 12-13.

26. See Bernard Cooke, *Ministry to Word and Sacraments* (Philadelphia: Fortress Press, 1976) 78, 85, 255-256, 430.

27. Bradshaw, *Ordination Rites* 133.

28. Ibid. 130.

29. Ibid. 171-172, 164, 184 respectively.

30. Ibid. 229.

31. C.K. Barrett, *The Epistle to the Romans* (London: Black, 1957) 24.

32. See Stenzel, *Die Taufe*, esp. 64-67, 151-152 (n. 251), 189-193.

33. For a summary including both the Old Testament and the New Testament material, see G. Wainwright, *Doxology* (New York: Oxford University Press, 1980) 151-163.

34. George Tavard, *Holy Writ or Holy Church: The Crisis of the Protestant Reformation* (London: Burns & Oates, 1959) 6-8.

35. George Tavard, "Tradition as Koinonia in Historical Perspective," *One in Christ* 24 (1988) 97-111.

36. *The Apostolic Tradition: Report of the Joint Commission between the Roman Catholic Church and the World Methodist Council, Fifth Series, 1986-1991*, reprinted in several places, such as *Origins* 21 (19 September 1991) 237-247, *Catholic International* 3 (1-14 February 1992) 106-120, and *One in Christ* 28 (1992) 49-73.

37. Vladimir Lossky, *In the Image and Likeness of God* (Crestwood, NY: St. Vladimir's Seminary Press, 1974) 141-168 ("Tradition and traditions") here 152.

38. Paul Evdokimov, *L'Orthodoxie* (Neuchâtel: Delachaux et Niestlé, 1959) 196-197.

39. Translation from Jasper and Cuming, *Prayers of the Eucharist* 133.

40. See E.G.C.F. Atchley, *On the Epiclesis of the Eucharistic Liturgy and in the Consecration of the Font* (London: Oxford University Press, 1935).

41. See John H. McKenna, *Eucharist and Holy Spirit: The Eucharistic Epiclesis in Twentieth-Century Theology* (Great Wakering, Essex: Mayhew-McCrimmon, 1975).

42. See *Baptism, Eucharist and Ministry 1982-1990: Report on the Process and Responses*, Faith and Order Paper no. 149 (Geneva: World Council of Churches, 1990) 67-68, 114-116.

43. Ibid. 68.

44. Tavard, "Tradition as Koinonia" 101-102.

45. Ibid. 107.

46. See G. Wainwright, "Renewing Worship: The Recovery of Classical Patterns," *Theology Today* 48 (April 1992) 45-55; reprinted as Chapter 8 of this volume.

5

The Lima Text in the
History of Faith and Order

ON 12 JANUARY 1982 THE 120 MEMBERS OF THE WORLD COUNCIL OF Churches Commission on Faith and Order, meeting at Lima (Peru), voted with strict unanimity that the text on *Baptism, Eucharist and Ministry* (BEM) was sufficiently "mature" to be transmitted to the churches for their response and reception.[1] That decision marked the provisional climax of a journey that had begun at least fifty-five years earlier, at the First World Conference on Faith and Order in Lausanne (Switzerland) in 1927. My purpose now is to retrace that itinerary, speaking first of the long approach, next of the conditions of travel, then of a first arrival (Lima itself), and finally of the continuation of the journey; for BEM has turned into a document that many churches are willing to carry with them on the voyage toward fuller unity.

A LONG APPROACH

Getting Under Way

The beginnings go back to the pre-history of Faith and Order. The course of that movement has been largely charted according to the Chicago-Lambeth Quadrilateral of 1886-1888, with its fixed points in the Scriptures, the ancient creeds, the gospel sacraments of baptism and the Lord's Supper, and the episcopal ordering of the church. The final report of Lausanne 1927[2] included the first two points under "the Church's common confession of faith," while two further sections were devoted to "the sacraments" and to "the ministry of the Church." There was agreement "that sacraments are of divine appointment and that the Church ought thankfully to observe them as divine gifts," as "means of grace through which God works invisibly in us." More precisely:

> We believe that in baptism administered with water in the name of the Father, the Son, and the Holy Spirit, for the remission of sins, we are baptized into one body . . .

> We believe that in the holy communion our Lord is present, that we have fellowship with God our Father in Jesus Christ his Son, our living Lord, who is our one Bread, given for the life of the world, sustaining the life of all his people, and that we are in fellowship with all others who are united to him. We agree that the sacrament of the Lord's supper is the Church's most sacred act of worship, in which the Lord's atoning death is commemorated and proclaimed, and that it is a sacrifice of praise and thanksgiving and an act of solemn self-oblation.

Regarding baptism, existing differences in "conception, interpretation, and mode" are not further specified; regarding the eucharist, the report mentions "divergent views, especially as to (1) the mode and manner of the presence of our Lord; (2) the conception of the commemoration and the sacrifice; (3) the relation of the elements to the grace conveyed; and (4) the relation between the minister of this sacrament and the validity and efficacy of the rite." The report concludes: "We are aware that the reality of the divine presence and gift in this sacrament cannot be adequately apprehended by human thought or expressed in human language. We close this statement with the prayer that the differences which prevent full communion at the present time may be removed."

Concerning the ordained ministry, the members of the Lausanne conference recorded themselves as "in substantial accord" over the following five propositions:

> 1. The ministry is a gift of God through Christ to his Church and is essential to the being and well-being of the Church.

> 2. The ministry is perpetually authorised and made effective through Christ and his Spirit.

> 3. The purpose of the ministry is to impart to men the saving and sanctifying benefits of Christ through pastoral service, the preaching of the gospel, and the administration of the sacraments, to be made effective by faith.

4. The ministry is entrusted with the government and discipline of the Church, in whole or in part.

5. Men gifted for the work of the ministry, called by the Spirit and accepted by the Church, are commissioned through an act of ordination by prayer and the laying on of hands to exercise the function of this ministry.

It was recognized that "the provision of a ministry acknowledged in every part of the Church as possessing the sanction of the whole Church is an urgent need."

Concerning the more precise structures of ministry, the Lausanne report concluded:

> In view of (1) the place which the episcopate, the councils of presbyters, and the congregation of the faithful, respectively, has in the constitution of the early Church, and (2) the fact that episcopal, presbyteral, and congregational systems of government are each today, and have been for centuries, accepted by great communions in Christendom, and (3) the fact that episcopal, presbyteral and congregational systems are each believed by many to be essential to the good order of the Church, we therefore recognize that these several elements must all, under conditions which require further study, have an appropriate place in the order of life of a reunited Church, and that each separate communion, recalling the abundant blessing of God vouchsafed to its ministry in the past, should gladly bring to the common life of the united Church its own spiritual treasures.

Retrospectively, it is evident how much of BEM was already foreshadowed at Lausanne in 1927. Much of the intervening process consisted in providing a more detailed grounding for the agreements of principle and moderating as far as possible the continuing disagreements.

The Second World Conference on Faith and Order met at Edinburgh in 1937.[3] It devoted attention to the understanding of grace, to the word of God and testimony to it in Scripture and tradition, to the doctrine of the church and its relation to the kingdom, to models of ecclesial unity, and to ministry and sacraments. Not much progress is observable in the latter areas. Indeed much of that section of the final report is given over to the stating of differences, the rejection of some potential misunderstandings, the defensive formulation of certain other positions, and to footnotes in which particular churches and traditions make their own additions or disclaimers.

Throughout this early period the (Greek) Orthodox found it necessary to state and repeat their own ecclesial self-understanding and claims; while at Edinburgh the Baptist delegates declared that they could (only) "accept as applying to the baptism of believers, i.e. of those who are capable of making a personal profession of faith" the "statement which has been passed by their brethren who practice infant baptism."

The most positive development at Edinburgh came in connection with the eucharist:

> The important thing is that we should celebrate the eucharist with the unfailing use of bread and wine, and of prayer, and of the words of institution, and with agreements as to its essential and spiritual meaning.

> If sacrifice is understood as it was by our Lord and his followers and in the early Church, it includes, not his death only, but the obedience of his earthly ministry, and his risen and ascended life, in which he still does his Father's will and ever liveth to make intercession for us. Such a sacrifice can never be repeated, but is proclaimed and set forth in the eucharistic action of the whole Church when we come to God in Christ at the eucharist or Lord's supper. For us, the secret of joining in that sacrifice is both the worship and the service of God; corporate because we are joined to Christ, and in him to each other (1 Cor. 10:17); individual, because each one of us makes the corporate act of self-oblation his own; and not ceremonial only, but also profoundly ethical because the keynote of all sacrifice and offering is *Lo! I come to do thy will, O God.* We believe also that the eucharist is a supreme moment of prayer because the Lord is the celebrant or minister for us at every celebration, and it is in his prayers for God's gifts and for us all that we join. According to the New Testament accounts of the institution, his prayer is itself a giving of thanks; so that the Lord's supper is both a *verbum visibile* of the divine grace, and the supreme thanksgiving (*Eucharistia*) of the people of God. We are throughout in the realm of Spirit. It is through the Holy Spirit that the blessing and the gift are given. The presence, which we do not try to define, is a spiritual presence. We begin from the historical fact of the Incarnation in the power of the Holy Spirit, and we are already moving forward to the complete spiritual reality of the coming of the Lord and the life of the heavenly city.

From Lund to Accra

Faith and Order work was interrupted by the Second World War. Afterwards three theological commissions pursued the still necessary comparative studies that had been bequeathed to them by Edinburgh. Churches and traditions stated and compared their respective positions on "The Nature of the Church," "Ways of Worship," and "Intercommunion." The secretary of the second commission was Wiebe Vos, destined to become the founder of *Societas Liturgica*. The work of the commissions was transmuted by a great advance in methodology on the part of the Third World Conference on Faith and Order at Lund (Sweden) in 1952:[4]

> We have seen clearly that we can make no real advance toward unity if we only compare our several conceptions of the nature of the Church and the traditions in which they are embodied. But once again it has been proved true that as we seek to draw closer to Christ we come closer to one another. We need, therefore, to penetrate behind our divisions to a deeper and richer understanding of the mystery of the God-given union of Christ with his Church. We need increasingly to realise that the separate histories of our churches find their full meaning only if seen in the perspective of God's dealings with his whole people.

Instead of talking to one another around the circumference of a circle, the churches were henceforth to move in towards its center. It must be remembered that the 1950s were the heyday of "biblical theology," of the *Heilsgeschichte* perspective, of the Barthian "Christological concentration." These would make possible the report on "The Meaning of Baptism," which was published in 1960 as part of *One Lord, One Baptism*,[5] received commendation from the Fourth World Conference on Faith and Order at Montreal in 1963, and remained fundamental to the work on BEM.

Lund itself had adopted from the commission on intercommunion a paragraph which became basic to the sustained work on the eucharist when it was taken up after the plenary meeting of the Commission on Faith and Order at Aarhus (Denmark) in 1964:

> This dominical sacrament of Christ's Body and Blood, controlled by the words of institution, with the use of the appointed elements of bread and wine, is: (a) a memorial of

Christ's incarnation and earthly ministry, of his death and resurrection; (b) a sacrament in which he is truly present to give himself to us, uniting us to himself, to his eternal sacrifice, and to one another; and (c) eschatologically, an anticipation of our fellowship with Christ in his eternal kingdom.[6]

Nuances were added by Montreal in 1963:[7]

In the holy eucharist or Lord's supper, constantly repeated and always including both word and sacrament, we proclaim and celebrate a memorial of the saving acts of God (1 Cor. 11:23-26).

What God did in the incarnation, life, death, resurrection and ascension of Christ, he does not do again. The events are unique; they cannot be repeated or extended or continued. Yet in this memorial we do not only recall past events: God makes them present through the Holy Spirit who takes of the things of Christ and declares them to us, thus making us participants in Christ . . .

The Lord's supper, a gift of God to his Church, is a sacrament of the presence of the crucified and glorified Christ until he comes, and a means whereby the sacrifice of the cross, which we proclaim, is operative within the Church. In the Lord's supper the members of the body of Christ are sustained in their unity with their Head and Saviour who offered himself on the cross; by him, with him and in him who is our great High Priest and Intercessor we offer to the Father, in the power of the Holy Spirit, our praise, thanksgiving and intercession. With contrite hearts we offer ourselves as a living and holy sacrifice, a sacrifice which must be expressed in the whole of our daily lives. Thus united to our Lord, and to the Church triumphant, and in fellowship with the whole Church on earth, we are renewed in the covenant sealed by the blood of Christ. In the Supper we also anticipate the marriage-supper of the Lamb in the Kingdom of God.

At Aarhus, Jean-Jacques von Allmen was commissioned to write his study *Le Repas du Seigneur*, published also in English as *The Lord's Supper*.[8] My own association with the future BEM began with my attendance at Aarhus as a youth delegate, looking for the subject of a doctoral dissertation; the eventual result was my book *Eucharist and Eschatology*.[9]

It was Montreal that re-launched, since as long ago as Edinburgh 1937, the theme of the "special ministry" of the ordained. The Christological, pneumatological, ecclesiological, and missiological contexts were remarked on. A new emphasis was placed on the location of the special ministry "in today's world," suggesting the need for "more flexible forms of ministry." This latter concern marked further work up to and including Accra (Ghana) 1974; but thereafter it clearly emerged that the churches were suspicious of a path that might be taken as an attempt to bypass long-standing questions about the validity of orders and the proper sacramental structure of the ordained ministry.

There is neither time nor need to tell the details of the route through plenary meetings of Faith and Order at Bristol 1967 and Louvain 1971 to the full draft of Accra 1974, *One Baptism, One Eucharist, and a Mutually Recognized Ministry.*[10]

From Accra to Lima

The Accra document remains readily accessible. In an unprecedented step the Fifth Assembly of the World Council of Churches at Nairobi (Kenya) in 1975 sent the text to the churches for comment with a view to revision. More than 150 responses were received in Geneva. These were analyzed at a consultation in Crêt-Bérard (Switzerland) in June 1977 and at the plenary meeting of Faith and Order at Bangalore (India) in 1978.[11] Special themes emerged as needing particular attention. They received this at a significant encounter on infant baptism and believers' baptism that took place on Southern Baptist territory at Louisville, Kentucky, in 1978; at a consultation on *episcopé* (oversight) and episcopacy in Geneva 1979; and at an Orthodox consultation at Chambésy (Switzerland) in the same year. All the while, a small group of us worked at re-drafting, and we continued to meet a couple of times a year until the plenary at Lima 1982. That "first arrival" will be spoken of later in this chapter. Meanwhile, I want to offer some reflections on the voyage up to that point.

CONDITIONS OF TRAVEL

Of the several circumstances that characterize the journey, five will be mentioned.

Choice of Companions

Faith and Order is a multilateral endeavor, which differs from bilateral dialogues in a number of ways. Bilateral dialogues have usually begun between partners most immediately likely to prove sympathetic to each other; or else, more recently, they have been started by such unlikely partners that the danger of going too far seemed small. Naturally enough, bilaterals have limited themselves either to safe generalities or to the very particular issues that have divided the two sides. Faith and Order, however, has engaged the widest confessional range of participants ever to assemble and cooperate. The blurb of the English edition of BEM lists Eastern Orthodox, Oriental Orthodox, Roman Catholic, Old Catholic, Lutheran, Anglican, Reformed, Methodist, United, Disciples, Baptist, Adventist, and Pentecostal. This means, first, that it is impossible to dodge the awkward interlocutor; second, that each participant must have eyes right around the head in order to see how particular formulations will affect each and every partner and one's relations with them; third, that *all* controversial matters, even where only some of the participants are directly interested, demand treatment; and fourth, that expectations will differ as to what can and must be achieved. The complexity of the enterprise should be apparent.

A second point of interest in the matter of company kept concerns Roman Catholic participation. Following the official entry of the Roman Catholic Church into the ecumenical movement with Vatican II, Catholic theologians have served as full members of the Faith and Order Commission, even though their church does not belong to the WCC. They have usually numbered about a dozen. In the elaboration of BEM they have contributed with loyalty, sensitivity, and effectiveness.

Third, the decades have seen a notable increase of participants from Asia, Africa, Latin America, and Oceania. The single most recurrent issue that several of them have raised is that of the food and drink used at the Lord's Supper, a matter very circumspectly dealt with in the commentary to paragraph 28 on the eucharist. More generally, however, their presence has increasingly signaled the urgency for the older churches of the northern hemisphere to set their own house in order. These churches bear the responsibility of historic divisions and their spread and continuance. It is an awful legacy to hand on to churches in those parts of the world where it appears that the center of gravity of the universal church will soon lie.

Different Starting Points

Churches started out on the Faith and Order journey from very different points. Each was marked by a history of debates within its own bounds and of controversies with other communities. Matters of baptism, eucharist, and ministry had often been close to the heart of the separation or had become so. Obvious examples are the Lutheran revolt against "the sacrifice of the Mass," the divisions among Protestants over the mode of Christ's eucharistic presence, the rise of "anabaptism" over against both Catholic and Protestant pedobaptism and ecclesiologies, the disputed ordering of the church between Episcopalians, Presbyterians, and Independents, the mode and validity of ministerial succession as between the Anglicans, the Reformed, and the Roman Catholics. Words and concepts have acquired different connotations over separate and controversial histories. At Lima I ironically observed that our text was not the "perfect" document any one of us could have produced had we been working alone, either as individuals or as confessions. The point is, we all came to the task from our different backgrounds.

Search for a Common Language

In fact, however, the second third of the twentieth century had witnessed a marvelous confluence of various "movements" that had affected wide areas of Christendom over confessional boundaries: the biblical theology movement, the liturgical movement, the ecumenical movement in its more technical sense, the movement to discover our common patristic roots and even to recover the controversial figures of later history in their originality and authenticity. These movements provided us with a common language and with a greater possibility of substantive understanding and agreement. The process of producing BEM profited from that; indeed BEM is unthinkable without their contribution.

It took until the time of Lima for that "atmosphere" to percolate to the leaders and people of the churches. It then became vital that the opportunity be seized to act upon BEM while the movement for responsible decision was present and the chances for a favorable outcome were good. Such a conjuncture might not rise again for a long time.

Re-Reading the Guides

Doctrinal and practical decisions presuppose norms. Work on BEM was greatly assisted by developments concerning Scripture and Tradition. Whereas it cannot be claimed that all differences have been reconciled in the area of authentic testimony to the faith, it is certainly remarkable that as Vatican II was shifting from "the two sources of revelation" to the eventual constitution *Dei Verbum*, so Protestants and Orthodox at Montreal were converging in their views on "Scripture, Tradition and traditions." On all sides, Scripture is seen as the internal norm of the Tradition, while the Tradition constitutes the indispensable context for interpreting the Scriptures. Despite differing nuances among the collaborators, BEM operates within that broad perspective. This becomes explicit in the discussion of the New Testament and later developments and crises that have arisen in the course of history, as in paragraph 11 on *Baptism* and paragraphs 10, 17 (commentary), 19-22 and 33 on *Ministry*. Positively, BEM results from the attempt to re-read the Scriptures and the Tradition *in common*, with the help of responsible exegesis and historiography and with a hermeneutical interest in both truth and unity.

Ships That Pass in the Night?

During the last quarter of Faith and Order's voyage towards Lima, traffic on the ecumenical seas had become busier. In particular, Vatican II had occasioned the launching of several bilateral dialogues between the Roman Catholic Church and other partners among the world Christian communions. Their reports—often treating the same themes as BEM—appeared sooner and distracted attention from the slower progress of Faith and Order. Some ecumenists indeed feared—and others hoped—that the multilateral dialogue was being left behind altogether. But, as has already been hinted, multilateral and bilateral dialogues are rather different exercises; and they need not be rivals. In point of fact, there was some overlap among the personnel; and certainly ideas, and often phraseology, flowed easily among the participants. It would be a difficult matter to decide in which way many of the borrowings had occurred.

In March 1985 the world Christian communities and Faith and Order joined in a fourth "Forum" to compare the interim results of BEM and the various bilateral dialogues on those issues. The compatibility, and indeed the agreement, between the several documents proved noteworthy. More generally, a certain convergence had taken place between the "models of unity" set up as the final goals of ecumenism, whether the "reconciled diversity" which some participants in bilateral dialogues have preferred or the "organic union" which was the dominant vision in classical Faith and Order.

A FIRST ARRIVAL

Landfall took place in Peru in January 1982. The definitive establishment of BEM will be briefly described, and then several of its characteristics will be mentioned.

The Lima Text

To Lima was brought a near-definitive draft, which had been circulated to Commission members several months earlier. A first plenary session nevertheless resulted in 192 more written suggestions for amendment. These were sifted by our drafting group over several late sittings. An emended text was again submitted to the plenary Commission, and last-minute changes were to be incorporated only if unanimously and instantly accepted by a troika of J.M.R. Tillard (Roman Catholic), J.D. Zizioulas (Orthodox), and myself (Protestant). As indicated at the outset, the final text was unanimously sent to the churches as the best we could do.

Its Nature

The Lima text does not constitute a strict consensus. It is a document of *convergence*. To vary the metaphor from the dominant one of seafaring to another: the text suggests that the churches are in fact playing in the same ballpark in matters of baptism, eucharist, and ministry. Not everyone takes up the same position, but all stand within a defined terrain and are reasonably well agreed on the rules of the game. The churches themselves must decide what more is necessary before consensus can be declared. An explicit case of that is found in paragraph 13 of the *Eucharist* section, where the commentary asks the churches whether remaining differences on the *mode* of Christ's unanimously affirmed "real presence" can be "accommodated within the convergence formulated in the text itself."

Its Achievements

Let me, out of modesty, list only one principal achievement from each section.

The first section offers the lineaments of an understanding and practice of Christian initiation which can include both churches which baptize infants and churches which baptize only upon personal profession of faith. It was generally felt that the Louisville consultation, which brought together participants in roughly equal numbers from each side of that divide, had made solid progress on the issue; and the Lima text in fact takes up all five of the recommendations from Louisville. Commonalities between the positions are emphasized, as on grace and faith. "The necessity of faith for the reception of the salvation embodied and set forth in baptism is acknowledged by all churches" (8); as also on the communal dimension of baptism: "Both the baptism of believers and the baptism of infants take place in the Church as the community of faith" (12); as again on the human renewal of baptism: "Baptism needs to be constantly reaffirmed" (14, commentary).

Regarding the eucharist, anamnesis and epiclesis are made fundamental to the celebration, in line with the best insights of sacramental and liturgical theology in the twentieth century. Without being committed to the precise nuances of any particular version of the "memorial" theory, the Lima text employs the general principle as a means of confessing and conceiving the presence and sacrifice of Christ in the eucharist which undercuts later western controversies on the issues. The Lima text stands close to the "effective proclamation" of the Windsor statement on the eucharist from the Anglican/Roman Catholic International Commission (ARCIC). Or as I said in presenting the notion at Lima: A memorial is now widely understood as "a word, act or rite given to us by God, as a command and a promise, to put us in touch, by the Holy Spirit, with the saving activity of God which is being commemorated."

The chief gain on ministry was the idea that the ordained ministry focuses and represents the ministry of the whole body headed by Christ. It functions "not in an exclusive way" but so as to "assemble and build up the body of Christ," "providing the focus for the unity of the life and witness of the community" (13 and commentary). If some "may appropriately be called priests," it is "because they fulfill a particular priestly service by strengthening and building up the royal and prophetic priesthood of the faithful through word and sacraments, through their prayers of intercession, and through their pastoral guidance of the community" (17). The language of hierarchy is avoided. There is no talk of "steps" or "grades" in ministry. The ladder is replaced by the horizontal plane. The key notions are those of the "centering" of the community, particularly in its liturgy, and of the exercise of "wider" responsibilities. The ordained are "called to exercise wise and loving leadership on the basis of the Word of God" (16). "Deacons represent to the Church its calling as servant in the world" (31).

Its Tendencies

An Anglican archbishop complained to me that "the method of Lima, like that of ARCIC, is Catholic"; he meant the expansion from Scripture to later Tradition. Others have spotted regrettably "catholicizing" tendencies at particular points. Some object to the frequent use of "baptism" as the active subject of a sentence: "Baptism is incorporation into Christ . . ." (1); "The baptism which makes Christians partakers of the mystery of Christ's death and resurrection . . ." (4); "Baptism initiates the reality of the new life . . ." (7). There is, however, no thought of making baptism an independent instrument of salvation. Whatever baptism is and does, it is and does as "a gift of God" (1; 8). The offending sentences are shorthand for "God through baptism . . ." Some consider that the eucharistic section gives short shrift to preaching; but the principle is in fact clearly stated: "The eucharist, which always includes both word and sacrament, is a proclamation and celebration of the work of God" (3); "Since the *anamnesis* of Christ is the very content of the preached Word as it is of the eucharistic meal, each reinforces the other. The celebration of the eucharist properly includes the proclamation of the Word" (12; cf. 27). Some, again, scent a clericalism in the attention devoted to the ordained ministry; but this is to minimize the opening six paragraphs on "the calling of the whole people of God" and the insistence throughout the section on ministry that the ordained ministry must be understood in and for the whole community; it is also to ignore the fact that differences over the ordering of the life of the church reflect differences in fundamental perceptions of the operation of grace, of the church's standing before God, its mission in the world, its self-identity both in time and in space.

If such suspicions of "catholicizing" tendencies were aroused in some Protestant circles, it is perhaps comforting to note that some Catholics considered the Lima text as remaining a "fundamentally Protestant document."

Its Open Questions

The questions that were left open by the Lima text were of at least four varieties.

1. Some questions are deliberately left open, whether on a temporary or a permanent basis. The mode of Christ's eucharistic presence has already been mentioned (see 13 and commentary). Regarding the role of the Holy Spirit in Christian initiation, it is stated that "the Holy Spirit is at work in the lives of people before, in and after their baptism" (5); however, "Christians differ in their understanding as to where the sign of the gift of the Spirit is to be found" (14). The churches are asked to continue listening to one another on the issue of women's ordination (18; 54).

2. Some questions are diplomatically said to require "further study." This is the case with those "African churches which practise baptism of the Holy Spirit without water, through the laying on of hands, while recognizing other churches' baptism" (21, commentary c). It is also the case with the eucharistic bread and wine or other "local food and drink" (28, commentary).

3. Some challenges are issued to the churches: over the possibility of "equivalent alternatives" in patterns of initiation within a single community (12, commentary); over the interposition of "further and separate" rites "between baptism and admission to communion" (14, commentary b; cf. *Eucharist* 19, commentary); over "indiscriminate baptism" (21, commentary b); over "old controversies" about eucharistic sacrifice (8, commentary); over the "moment of consecration" (14, commentary); over the frequency of celebration and communion (30-31); over the use and disposal of eucharistic remains (32); over "the threefold ministry of bishop, presbyter and deacon" as "an expression of the unity we seek and also as a means for achieving it" (22); over "the need of reform" in the "threefold pattern" (24); over the need for episcopal churches to "regain their lost unity" among themselves as part of the wider process in which non-episcopal churches also enter the episcopal succession (38).

4. Some questions were either voluntarily or involuntarily not raised or faced:

(a) From out of left field (to revert to baseball), there came at Lima the question from an American Episcopalian: should not the statement on ministry say something about the papacy? It was immediately decided that such an undiscussed question would be premature. Nevertheless, the bilateral dialogues in which Rome has been involved have come round to treat the theme. It will eventually have to figure on the multilateral agenda.

(b) Paragraph 14 on baptism, for example, states that "baptism. . . signifies and effects" both "participation in Christ's death and resurrection" and "the receiving of the Spirit." But nowhere is an attempt made to give an account of the efficacy of the sacraments. The statement on the eucharist emphasizes "the mystery." Lund, on "Ways of Worship," recognized that there were "various opinions on the nature and efficacy of ritual acts." My suspicion is that some of the deepest differences in the sacramental area rest upon the anthropology and theology of *signs*: how far does the performance of signs *presuppose* already the existence of the reality signified? How far does the performance of signs *produce* the reality which they signify? My hope is that the general notions of "performative language" and "effective signification"—to which contemporary sacramental theology has been helped by linguistic philosophy and cultural anthropology—will provide an enabling conceptual framework in which the churches can accept the Lima formulations.

(c) Who has the right and responsibility, in a divided Christendom, to baptize, to eucharistize, and to ordain as, or as part of, the one Church of Jesus Christ? That fundamental question underlies the talk of "mutual recognition" found in Lima. To recognize the baptisms, eucharists, and ministries of "other" communities is, to that degree, to recognize those communities as "church." To recognize "other" communities as church is, to that degree, to recognize the sacraments celebrated in and by them. The Lima text is intended as a contribution to achieving the necessary and sufficient agreement in understanding and practice that will permit the identification of "church" over the widest possible range of communities claiming to be Christian.

(d) The question arises whether the Lima text carries an implicit ecclesiology. I think it would be compatible with the "eucharistic ecclesiology" advocated by N. Afanasiev and several other Orthodox writers. The eucharist is seen by Lima as "the central act of the Church's worship" (1), and there are many indications that the nature and functions of the church are "read off" the liturgical assembly, which Vatican II called the *"praecipua manifestatio ecclesiae."* Others have sought in Lima a "koinonia" ecclesiology of the kind adumbrated in the Final Report of ARCIC and which since has become prominent again in Faith and Order.[12] The ideas would overlap considerably. It is noteworthy that the notion of "community," "communion," and "participation" figured prominently already in the 1960 Faith and Order report on "The divine Trinity and the unity of the Church," published as part of *One Lord, One Baptism*. But the question remains as to how such "koinonia" is recognized and created.

(e) Lima never raises the question of whether "the sacraments are necessary for salvation." Edinburgh 1937 recognized "divergence of doctrine among us" on the matter. At Lund in 1952 all agreed that *"Deus non alligatur sacramentis."* My impression is that Lima would be compatible with the view I have proposed elsewhere of the church and the sacraments as "non-exclusive promises."[13]

THE CONTINUATION

BEM was placed before the churches in 1982. It has attracted a gratifying amount of attention in many circles of the church's life. Six volumes of official responses have been received,[14] and a first summing up appeared in 1990.[15] Three sets of remarks are in order.

Response and Reception

The vital question was that of the "extent to which your church can recognize in this text the faith of the Church through the ages." This was a subtle inquiry: the churches are not simply being asked whether the Lima text accords with what each of them has taught, even though that would be part of their answer; rather, the door was also left open for a church to recognize in the Lima text "the faith of the Church" and to admit its own need to come into conformity with that faith. In so far as a church recognizes in the Lima text "the faith of the Church," it will be willing for the text to work its way into its own life. In so far as a church affirms the Lima text, it becomes appropriate to ask what "guidance your church can take from this text for its worship, educational, ethical, and spiritual life and witness." That is the profounder process of reception.

The Dogmatic Context

Baptism, eucharist, and ministry are not simply three doctrinal areas among many. They bring into focus many other themes of dogmatic importance, such as the doctrines of God, of Christ, of the Spirit, of creation, redemption, and consummation. Yet Lima does not say everything that needs to be said to register agreement on these matters. BEM must therefore be placed in the larger context of a further study that itself resumes an issue already foreshadowed at Lausanne in 1927: "Towards the common expression of the apostolic faith today." A considerable document is now circulating among the churches under the title *Confessing the One Faith: An Ecumenical Explication of the Apostolic Faith as It Is Confessed in the Nicene-Constantinopolitan Creed (381).*[16]

The Destination

The constitutional aim of the WCC, which Faith and Order has the special responsibility of keeping before the Council, is to assist the churches towards "visible unity in one faith and in one eucharistic fellowship." It is only then that the church can truly be what Vatican II called it: "a sign and instrument of communion with God and of unity among all people." Obedience to the Lord's will for the unity of his disciples is a condition for bringing the world to believe (Jn 17:20-23). The church is already called to live "in such harmony with one another, in accord with Christ Jesus, that you may with one mind and voice glorify the God and Father of our Lord Jesus Christ" (Rom 15:5-6). In that way it can contribute toward the day when "at the name of Jesus every knee will bow, and every tongue confess that Jesus Christ is Lord, to the glory of God the Father" (Phil 2:10-11).[17]

Notes

1. The Lima text itself was published as *Baptism, Eucharist and Ministry*, Faith and Order Paper no. 111 (Geneva: World Council of Churches, 1982) and was eventually translated into some forty languages. The record of the meeting is found in *Towards Visible Unity: Commission on Faith and Order. Lima 1982.* Vol. 1. *Minutes and Addresses*, Faith and Order Paper no. 112 (Geneva: World Council of Churches, 1982); note especially pp. 80-84.

2. See *Faith and Order. Proceedings of the World Conference, Lausanne, August 3-21, 1927*, ed. H.N. Bate (London: SCM, 1927), in particular 466-473.

3. See *The Second World Conference on Faith and Order, Held at Edinburgh, August 3-18, 1937*, ed. L. Hodgson (London: SCM, 1938), in particular 219-269.

4. See *The Third World Confernece on Faith and Order, Held at Lund, August 15th to 28th, 1952*, ed. O.S. Tomkins (London: SCM, 1953), in particular 15-65 (here p. 15).

5. *One Lord, One Baptism*, Faith and Order Paper no. 32 (London: SCM, 1961).

6. Tomkins, *The Third World Conference* 53-54; cf. *Intercommunion: The Report of the Theological Commission Appointed by the Continuation Committee of the World Conference on Faith and Order, Together with a Selection from the Material Presented to the Commission*, ed. Donald Baillie and John Marsh (London: SCM, 1952), in particular 41-42.

7. *The Fourth World Conference on Faith and Order, Montreal 1963*, Faith and Order Paper no. 42, ed. P.C. Rodger and Lukas Vischer (London: SCM, and New York: Association Press, 1964) 73-74.

8. Jean-Jacques von Allmen, *Essai sur le repas du Seigneur* (Neuchâtel: Delachaux et Niestlé, 1966); *The Lord's Supper* (London: Lutterworth, and Richmond, VA: John Knox, 1969).

9. Geoffrey Wainwright, *Eucharist and Eschatology* (London: Epworth, 1971; updated New York: Oxford University Press, 1981).

10. *One Baptism, One Eucharist, and a Mutually Recognized Ministry*, Faith and Order Paper no. 73 (Geneva: World Council of Churches, 1975).

11. See *Sharing in One Hope. Commission on Faith and Order, Bangalore 1978*, Faith and Order Paper no. 92 (Geneva: World Council of Churches, 1978) 247-256. At Bangalore I chaired the section on the BEM theme and did so again at Lima in 1982.

12. See, from Santiago de Compostela 1993, *On the Way to Fuller Koinonia. Official Report of the Fifth World Conference on Faith and Order*, Faith and Order Paper no. 166, ed. T.F. Best and G. Gassmann (Geneva: World Council of Churches, 1994), especially 36-128, 223-295.

13. See G. Wainwright, *Doxology* (London: Epworth, and New York: Oxford University Press, 1980) 145-146.

14. *Churches Respond to BEM: Official Responses to the "Baptism, Eucharist and Ministry" Text*, ed. Max Thurian, 6 vols. (Geneva: World Council of Churches, 1986-1988). With very few exceptions (chiefly from among some of the smaller Protestant bodies), the official responses were strongly positive; even where problems remained, it was usually acknowledged that progress had been made and helpful perspectives set. The response of the Roman Catholic Church (vol. 6, pp. 1-40), although raising difficulties of an ecclesiological nature, was most appreciative of the ways in which BEM had employed Scripture and Tradition (particularly the liturgical tradition) in arriving at statements largely congruent with Catholic sacramental teaching, especially on baptism and eucharist; see G. Wainwright, "The Roman Catholic Response to 'Baptism, Eucharist and Ministry': The

Ecclesiological Dimension," in *A Promise of Presence: Studies in Honor of David N. Power, O.M.I.*, ed. M. Downey and R. Fragomeni (Washington, DC: The Pastoral Press, 1993) 187-206.

15. *Baptism, Eucharist and Ministry 1982-1990*, Faith and Order Paper no. 149 (Geneva: World Council of Churches, 1990).

16. Faith and Order Paper no. 153, revised edition (Geneva: World Council of Churches, 1991).

17. Efforts were made at the Seventh Assembly of the World Council of Churches (Canberra, 1991) and at the Fifth World Conference on Faith and Order (Santiago de Compostela) to call the World Council of Churches back to its primary task as an instrument of the churches in their search for Christian unity; see, respectively, *Signs of the Spirit. Official Report, Seventh Assembly, Canberra, Australia, 7-20 February 1991*, ed. Michael Kinnamon (Geneva: World Council of Churches, and Grand Rapids: Eerdmans, 1991), esp. 279-286 (reports by Orthodox and Evangelical participants), and *On the Way to Fuller Koinonia*, esp. 135-142 (address by Cardinal Edward Cassidy of the Pontifical Council for Promoting Christian Unity) and 167-194 (a very mixed bag). It is clear that "faith and order" work remains vital to restoration of church unity, whatever the context in which it is pursued; see G. Wainwright, "Faith and Order within or without the World Council of Churches," *Ecumenical Review* 45 (1993) 118-121.

6

Sacramental Theology and the World Church

IN THE LAST DECADE OR TWO OF HIS LIFE, KARL RAHNER DETECTED THE emergent reality of a new era in the history of the church and, whether consequently or antecedently, in the history of the world.[1] His idea of an incipient "world church" was prompted by the specifically Catholic experience of the Second Vatican Council, which brought together in Rome some two thousand bishops from all six continents. Rahner was a European, and more particularly a German-speaking European. His active ecumenism bloomed late; it was practically limited to contacts with Germanic Lutheranism, and it remained to the end rather bookish. For good or ill, my own cultural and ecclesial perspectives differ considerably from Rahner's. I am a minister of the British Methodist Church, with whose maternal milk I took in a commitment to ecumenism in its classical Faith and Order form, including the goal of organic unity such as has been achieved or attempted among local and regional churches of different denominations in many parts of the British Commonwealth. I worked for six years as a missionary in French-speaking Equatorial Africa, and since 1979 I have lived in the United States. These differences need to be kept in mind as I seek to interact with Rahner's concept of a world church, and more particularly from the angle of sacramental theology.

The world church appears first in Rahner's eyes as an historico-geographical phenomenon. But even then it is not merely a matter of extension in time and space. Diachronic and synchronic questions of *culture* arise concerning the church's relation to a developing universal civilization and to regional and provincial particularities. Rahner also knew that the worldwide spread of Christianity was not simply a matter of arithmetic. A presence in diaspora raises *soteriological* questions concerning the church's place and role in the prosecution of God's plan for the world, the attainment of God's kingdom.[2] We shall, then, concentrate on the cultural and soteriological aspects, themselves partly overlapping, of the notion and reality of a world church as they come to significant expression in the major sacraments of baptism and eucharist.[3]

In Rahner's later years, his conception of the sacraments underwent, according to his own avowal, "a copernican revolution."[4] In his little book on *Kirche und Sakramente* (1960), Rahner's thought substantially followed the sequence of God, Christ, the church, the sacraments, the life of Christians in the world.[5] In a couple of essays written after Vatican II, however, his argument moved rather from God's presence in secular human life to the sacraments and to the church itself.[6] My contention is that both procedures are valuable, indeed necessary; and I will suggest that the first movement is in fact a baptismal movement, and the second a eucharistic. The two principal sacraments and the two movements embody the dialectical relationship between church and world that obtains both soteriologically and culturally.

Since Vatican II marked a turning point for Rahner, it will be good to begin there. My concrete examples will, however, be taken largely from another process in which the world church has been anticipated and striven for. I refer to the twentieth-century movement of Faith and Order, in which Roman Catholic theologians have participated fully and officially since Vatican II, and which reached a provisional climax in the 1982 Lima text on *Baptism, Eucharist and Ministry.*[7]

THE CHURCH AS SACRAMENT

The dogmatic constitution *Lumen Gentium* began by saying that the church is "like a sacrament" (*veluti sacramentum*) of the world's salvation.[8] St. Augustine, in line with the New Testament's linguistic use of *mysterium Dei*, had declared that "the sacrament of God is none other than Christ" (Ep. 187.34; PL 33:846). In his book

Catholicisme (1938) Henri de Lubac concluded that "if Jesus Christ is the sacrament of God, the Church is for us the sacrament of Christ."[9] This basic insight was followed out Christologically and ecclesiologically by Edward Schillebeeckx and Otto Semmelroth in their respective books *Christus, sacrament van de Godsontmoeting* (1957) and *Die Kirche als Ursakrament* (1953).[10] Rahner's small book on *Church and Sacraments* adopted this perspective, though he would later safeguard the Christological priority by distinguishing between Christ as *Ursakrament* and the church as *Grundsakrament*, just as Leo Scheffczyk much later would distinguish between Christ as *Ursakrament* and, looking forward to the septenary of sacraments, the church as *Ganzsakrament*.[11] By Vatican II the Benelux and the German experts were able to introduce the sacramentality of the church as a main ecclesiological category, though only after a struggle, and the apparent novelty had to be explained on its first occurrence in *Lumen Gentium*.[12]

It was there stated that "the church in Christ is, as it were, the sacrament, that is, the *sign* and *instrument*, of intimate union with God and of the unity of all humankind." Sacramentally the church appears as both a present *anticipation* of salvation and also a *tool* for its realization on a universal scale. W. Beinert has suggested that the church's instrumental role was a characteristic emphasis of O. Semmelroth, whereas for Rahner the weight lay already on the less active sign-character of the church.[13] Despite such possible differences of accent, it will be remembered that a sacrament is traditionally an *efficacious* sign, and that, conversely, the *witness* of the church to the world operates at the level of signs which are not simply identical with the reality of God's kingdom which they proclaim.

It would not be too far from the thought of *Lumen Gentium* to say that the whole fallen world stands under the saving love of God, and that the believing church is given the cooperative task of evangelization: Repent and believe the Gospel! In broad terms, that had been also the missionary perspective in which that world church had come into being, whose first official epiphany had been for Karl Rahner the Second Vatican Council with its bishops from every corner of the earth. By world mission was understood the institutional "expansion of Christianity" which was more or less identified with the Roman Catholic Church. The church was a *Heilsanstalt* into which one entered by getting oneself baptized in response to the evangelical proclamation.

That vision was not strange, *mutatis mutandis*, to Protestantism either, as its reflection in the very titles of historical works by A. Harnack and K. Latourette shows.[14] True, the Lutheran Peter Brunner had criticized Rahner for "inserting" the church between Christ and the sacraments directly instituted by him; but even if classical Protestantism liked to think of the church as *creatura Verbi* and therefore also, albeit less explicitly, the "creature of the sacraments," yet Brunner had to admit that Protestants too know the church as the *bearer* of the word and the sacraments.[15] Moreover, the German Lutheran ritual of baptism still reads from the false ending of Mark:

> Go into all the world and preach the Gospel to the whole creation. Whoever believes and is baptized will be saved; but whoever does not believe will be condemned.

That is perhaps not altogether different in principle from Pope Boniface VIII's bull of 1302, *Unam Sanctam*:

> There is one holy catholic and apostolic church, and outside this church there is neither salvation nor remission of sins . . . It is altogether necessary to salvation for every human creature to be subject to the Roman pontiff.

Now I am not about to defend Boniface VIII, or even the false ending of Mark; but I do want to hold on to their positive thrust. They affirm that salvation is given in Christ, and that Christ has a visible people in the world, namely his church with the sacraments he has given it. The Lima document makes that claim:

> Baptism is the sign of new life through Jesus Christ. It unites the one baptized with Christ and with his people . . . (B # 2)

> Through baptism, Christians are brought into union with Christ, with each other and with the Church of every time and place . . . (B # 6)

> The eucharist is essentially the sacrament of the gift which God makes to us in Christ through the power of the Holy Spirit. Every Christian receives this gift of salvation through communion in the body and blood of Christ. In the eucharistic meal, in the eating and drinking of the bread and wine, Christ grants communion with himself. God himself acts, giving life to the body of Christ and renewing each member . . . (E # 2)

If these passages were taken on their own, they might seem to confirm the worst fears of Protestants concerning the *opus operatum*. But in fact the Lima text on baptism goes on to say:

> Baptism is both God's gift *and our human response to that gift*. It looks towards a growth into the measure of the stature of the fullness of Christ (Eph 4:13). The necessity of faith for the reception of the salvation embodied and set forth in baptism is acknowledged by all churches ... (B # 8)

And the text on the eucharist states:

> While Christ's real presence in the eucharist does not depend on the faith of the individual, all [churches] agree that to discern the body and blood of Christ, faith is required ... (E # 13)

That recognition of the human element in fundamental soteriology will eventually have consequences at the cultural level.

But first we need to face the ecumenical question in relation to the sacraments and the world church. The long years of work leading up to the Lima text revealed that simplistic appeals to baptismal unity were premature. Paragraph 6 of the text on baptism is much more nuanced:

> Our common baptism, which unites us to Christ in faith, is ... a basic bond of unity. We are one people and are called to confess and serve one Lord in each place and in all the world ... When baptismal unity is realized in one holy, catholic and apostolic Church, a genuine Christian witness can be made to the healing and reconciling love of God. Therefore, our one baptism into Christ constitutes a call to the churches to overcome their divisions and visibly manifest their fellowship.

The mordant commentary follows:

> The inability of the churches mutually to recognize their various practices of baptism as sharing in the one baptism, and their actual dividedness in spite of mutual baptismal recognition, have given dramatic visibility to the broken witness of the Church. The readiness of the churches in some places and times to allow differences of sex, race, or social status to divide the body of Christ has further called into question genuine baptismal unity of the Christian community (Gal 3:27-28) and has seriously compromised its witness.

The text on the eucharist makes a similar point with regard to compromised witness:

> Insofar as Christians cannot unite in full fellowship around the same table to eat the same loaf and drink from the same cup, their missionary witness is weakened at both the individual and the corporate levels. (E # 26)

Even more boldly, the text on the eucharist declares that *our own salvation* is called into question:

> Through the eucharist the all-renewing grace of God penetrates and restores human personality and dignity. The eucharist involves the believers in the central event of the world's history. As participants in the eucharist, therefore, we prove inconsistent if we are not actively participating in this ongoing restoration of the world's situation and the human condition. The eucharist shows that our behaviour is inconsistent in face of the reconciling presence of God in human history: we are placed under *continual judgment* by the persistence of unjust relationships of all kinds in our society, the manifold divisions on account of human pride, material interest and power politics and, above all, the obstinacy of unjustifiable confessional oppositions within the body of Christ. (E # 20)

With "unjustifiable confessional oppositions" is raised an issue which had occupied Karl Rahner for at least two decades and which he brought into a specifically ecumenical context in the 1983 manifesto co-authored with Heinrich Fries regarding the substantial possibility of church unity now.[16] Rahner distinguished—with a sharpness I am not sure is practicable—between dogmatic unity and theological pluralism. The former was necessary; the latter was inevitable and indeed welcome. That at least a relative distinction may be possible is suggested by the Lima text regarding the eucharistic presence. The commentary to paragraph 13 reads:

> Many churches believe that by the words of Jesus and by the power of the Holy Spirit, the bread and wine of the eucharist become, in a real through mysterious manner, the body and blood of the risen Christ, i.e., of the living Christ present in all his fullness . . . Some other churches, while affirming a real presence of Christ at the eucharist, do not link that presence so definitely with the signs of bread and wine. The decision remains for the churches whether this difference can be accommodated within the convergence formulated in the text itself.

The commentary to paragraph 15 returns to the question of different "explanations" of Christ's eucharistic presence:

> In the history of the Church there have been various attempts to understand the mystery of the real and unique presence of Christ in the eucharist. Some are content merely to affirm this presence without seeking to explain it. Others consider it necessary to assert a change wrought by the Holy Spirit and Christ's words, in consequence of which there is no longer just ordinary bread and wine but the body and blood of Christ. Others again have developed an explanation of the real presence which, though not claiming to exhaust the significance of the mystery, seeks to protect it from damaging interpretations.

The issue being addressed here is chiefly that of *confessional* differences, but it is interesting to wonder whether *culturally* different accounts could be accommodated. I am thinking, for instance, of what cultural anthropology has brought to light concerning African philosophies and experiences of personal presence which seem to have much in common with what biblical scholars have taught us about "extended personality" in the Scriptures.[17]

Returning to the confessional question, it is obvious that the recovery of church unity is an essential stage in the baptismal and eucharistic "dynamic" whose scope is no less than universal. In paragraph 7 of the Lima text baptism is presented as "the sign of the kingdom":

> Baptism initiates the reality of the new life given in the midst of the present world. It gives participation in the community of the Holy Spirit. It is a sign of the kingdom of God and of the life of the world to come. Through the gifts of faith, hope and love, baptism has a dynamic which embraces the whole of life, extends to all nations, and anticipates the day when every tongue will confess that Jesus Christ is Lord to the glory of God the Father.

And in references to the eucharist:

> The eucharist . . . signifies what the world is to become: an offering and hymn of praise to the Creator, a universal communion in the body of Christ, a kingdom of justice, love and peace in the Holy Spirit. (E # 4) The eucharist opens up the vision of the divine rule which has been promised as the final renewal of creation, and is a foretaste of it. (E # 22)

The exclusionary side of Pope Boniface VIII's *Unam Sanctam* and of the false ending of Mark is therefore *conditional*: excluded are those who refuse the offer of salvation. But insofar as it is—at least provisionally—exclusive at the soteriological level, this perspective is likely to place its proponents at the negative extreme of H. Richard Niebuhr's fivefold typology: Christ *against culture*.[18] The world lies in the evil one (1 Jn 5:19), and little can be expected from the culture of those who remain "without God in the world" (Eph 2:12). With, of course, Alexandrian exceptions, the Fathers of the pre-Constantinian church did not look for contributions from Athens to Jerusalem. Even the Apologist Justin, who held that good Greeks who had lived according to the *logos* were Christians *avant la lettre*, nevertheless attributed any similarities between the Christian sacraments and the mystery religions to diabolical counterfeiting on the part of the pagans.[19] When it is in opposition to the dominant culture, Christianity will produce its own culture which will be ideologically a counter-culture and sociologically a subculture. And such a culture, though it may be narrow, will not necessarily be unadorned: pentecostal glossolalia has been likened to great cathedrals of sound.

In a situation in which Christianity has achieved some historical weight, its oppositional thrust gets modified into Niebuhr's fourth type, the dialectical. Christ and culture are found in the kind of tension represented by Luther's doctrine of the *zwei Reiche*. Here the civil institution may play a part-way positive role in the order of preservation, holding the fort against the worst ravages of sin and thus creating a space for the proclamation of the Gospel.[20] In the former East Germany the Lutheran churches on the whole tried to see themselves in "critical solidarity" with the socialist society. Such a distinctly *post*-Constantinian condition was new to the church: Karl-Heinrich Bieritz has written on the worship life of the church in such a "nicht-mehr-Volkskirche" situation.[21] I once spoke with a former chaplain who told me that some university students in East Germany were committed to the Christian faith but saw no point in undergoing the antiquated rite of baptism. It was socially and culturally a costly act to receive baptism in the German Democratic Republic, but a healthily mixed practice of baptism for people of all ages was developing. Christian competition with Marxist-Leninist rites of passage raised some vital questions for liturgists and pastors.

Let me finish this predominantly baptismal part of this chapter with an example from the so-called younger churches. The commentary on paragraph 21 of the Lima text reads thus:

> In some parts of the world, the giving of a name in the baptismal liturgy has led to confusion between baptism and customs surrounding name-giving. This confusion is especially harmful if, in cultures predominantly non-Christian, the baptized are required to assume Christian names not rooted in their cultural tradition. In making regulations for baptism, churches should be careful to keep the emphasis on the true Christian significance of baptism and to avoid unnecessarily alienating the baptized from their local culture through the imposition of foreign names. A name which is inherited from one's culture roots the baptized in that culture, and at the same time manifests the universality of baptism, incorporation into the one Church, holy, catholic and apostolic, which stretches over all the nations of the earth.

I am reminded of spontaneously chosen baptismal names reported from Papua-New Guinea: "The Peace of God," which is Geoffrey, my own Christian name; "Property of the Lord," which is Dominic, my son's Christian name; "Royal Treasure," which is the Pearl of the Kingdom or Margaret, my wife's Christian name.

With that we are coming close to the transformationist character of the church's move into the world, corresponding to Niebuhr's fifth and final type; but before we end up there, we must now make the opposite journey, from the world to the church. After looking at the church as sacrament, let us in the second part consider the world as sacrament; and here the accent will be predominantly eucharistic.

THE WORLD AS SACRAMENT

Karl Rahner does not, so far as I remember, speak of the world as sacrament, though he does daringly call the world "God's body" in one of the later articles in which he describes the copernican revolution in his conception of the sacraments.[22] That shift of Rahner's may be summarized as follows:

> Rahner no longer wants to think primarily from the mental and spiritual reality of the sacramental event towards its "secular" effect; rather he wishes to make a spiritual movement which

leads from the world to the sacrament. In this view, sacraments, and therefore finally the Church itself, are no longer punctiliar interventions of God into the world from outside; rather the world, in its innermost root, in the personal center of knowing subjects, is always and permanently grasped by grace, carried and moved by God's self-communication. This inner dynamic of the normal, "profane" life of humanity always and everywhere has found in Jesus Christ its clearest expression. From that point out, the sacraments are epiphanies of the holiness and redemption of the secular character of humankind and the world. They are the manifestation, in the order of signs, of the liturgy of the world. In the sacraments, there occurs nothing that is not otherwise present in the world; rather they bring to conscious expression and cultic celebration what is taking place as God's saving act in the world and in human freedom.[23]

Taken alone, that vision poses considerable difficulties. In Rahner's "universalem Heilsoptimismus,"[24] sin often appears—even typographically—as a parenthesis. The work of Jesus Christ becomes more exemplary than redemptive; Christology becomes merely successful anthropology, and the hypostatic union forfeits somewhat its uniqueness. The *"non ponentibus obicem"* is interpreted so generously that it becomes very difficult to fail salvation. Rahner's "anonymous Christianity" may have started as a "limit-phenomenon" in his thinking, but it finally threatened to push the church from the center into the extraordinary, and evangelization risks being reduced to gnoseology, as though baptism did nothing new but simply put a name on something that was already there. Culturally, the consequence of such a soteriology is a swing to the far extremity, the second of Niebuhr's five types and the one with which Niebuhr himself rightly had the least sympathy: the Christ *of culture*. There Christ is absorbed by the culture and, chameleon-like, takes on its coloring. It is nevertheless possible to stop short of that extreme and adopt Niebuhr's third type, the synthetic. Niebuhr's star representative for that type is Thomas Aquinas: grace does not destroy nature or culture but, after a certain purification, perfects it.

Theologians who talk of the world as sacrament usually make the eucharist the dominant analogue. Let us look at two examples, one from an Orthodox theologian and of protological cast, the other from a Methodist theologian and of eschatological cast.

Under the title *The World as Sacrament*,[25] Alexander Schmemann (of blessed memory) reinterpreted in a biblical sense Feuerbach's materialist dictum, "Man is what he eats":

> [Man] is indeed that which he eats, and the whole world is presented as one all-embracing banquet table for man . . . In the Bible the food that man eats, the world of which he must partake in order to live, is given to him by God, and it is given as *communion with God* . . . All that exists is God's gift to man, and it all exists to make God known to man, to make man's life communion with God. It is divine love made food, made life for man. God *blesses* everything he creates, and, in biblical language, this means that he makes all creation the sign and means of his presence and wisdom, love and revelation. "O taste and see how gracious the Lord is" . . . The unique position of man in the universe is that he alone is to *bless* God for the food and the life he receives from Him . . . The first, the basic definition of man is that he is the *priest*. He stands in the center of the world and unifies it in his act of blessing God, of both receiving the world from God and offering it to God—and by filling the world with this eucharist, he transforms his life, the one that he receives from the world, into life in God, into communion. The world was created as the "matter," the material of one all-embracing sacrament, and man was created as the priest of this cosmic sacrament.

In its fallenness, humanity has switched from being the priest of the world to its slave, loving and worshiping the creature instead of the Creator. That way lies death. Through the God-Man Jesus Christ the redemptive transformation of humanity and the world has begun. The gates of paradise have been opened again. There the whole of life is praise and thanks to God, and human beings share in the divine life at the table of the Lord.

Among the advantages of this Orthodox vision must be reckoned the concreteness and the personalism which it draws from the liturgy. God is not only the mysterious horizon of human self-transcendence but the addressee of the eucharistic prayer. Conscious intentionality is of the essence. (Each November I wonder how profane Americans can celebrate Thanksgiving without a dative object.)

At the end of his book Schmemann offered a concise formulation of the eschatological perspective:

The Church is the sacrament of the Kingdom—not because it possesses divinely instituted acts called "sacraments," but because first of all, it is the possibility given to man to see in and through this world the "world to come," to see and to "live" it in Christ. It is only when, in the darkness of *this world*, we discern that Christ has *already* "filled all things with Himself," that these *things*, whatever they may be, are revealed and given to us as full of meaning and beauty. A Christian is the one who, wherever he looks, finds everywhere Christ, and rejoices in Him. And this joy *transforms* all his human plans and programs, decisions and moves, makes all his mission the sacraments of the world's return to Him, who is the life of the world.

For the Methodist theologian Theodore Runyon, the eschaton is the operative beginning of his idea of "the world as original sacrament."[26] He quotes the messianic vision of Isaiah 11:6-9:

The wolf shall dwell with the lamb,
and the leopard shall lie down with the kid,
and the calf and the lion and the fatling together,
and a little child shall lead them.
The cow and the bear shall feed;
    their young shall lie down together;
and the lion shall eat straw like the ox.
The suckling child shall play over the hole of the asp,
and the weaned child shall put his hand on the adder's den.
They shall not hurt or destroy in all my holy mountain;
for the earth shall be full of the knowledge of the Lord
as the waters cover the sea.[27]

Our author concludes from this passage:

No sharp demarcation is drawn between humanity and the rest of the created order, for the futures intertwine. As St. Paul later was to describe it, the creation itself will benefit from the redemption of humankind through Christ, just as it now suffers from human corruption [cf. Rom 8:19-21].

The turning-point was the work of Jesus Christ as the irruption of the divine kingdom through self-sacrificial love to God and humanity and the victory over the devil. Derivatively, the sacraments of the church become signs of the critical transformation of the world according to God's original design and the goal God has set for the world:

> In the hands of Christ the sacrament is presented to us as *the world in its original and eschatological form.* He takes the bread and wine, which are products of our ordinary world—and therefore related to the complexities of international grain cartels, embargoes, starvation, alcoholism, and all the other ways in which God's good gifts have gone awry—and turns them into signs of his kingdom of justice and love. He does this by identifying them with himself and his mission, just as he did the paschal bread and wine at the Last Supper. Having joined them with his life for the kingdom, he hands the bread and wine back to us to make us participants in that kingdom by sharing its first fruits which nourish us along the way.

The strength of this eschatological perspective lies in its apocalyptic coloration, which is quite lacking in Rahner. Even when he writes, in rather teilhardian fashion, of participation in the turmoil of the world, Rahner remains more or less in the wisdom tradition. But suffering and redemption belong to the conflict with evil. Runyon knows that Christ's kingdom is not of *this* world. For the new order, a radical transformation is needed; and that means, on the human side, conversion.

In protological, soteriological, and eschatological perspectives, the Lima text sees the eucharist as the church's representative act of praise and thanksgiving on behalf of the world:

> The eucharist, which always includes both word and sacrament, is a proclamation and a celebration of the work of God. It is the great thanksgiving to the Father for everything accomplished in creation, redemption and sanctification, for everything accomplished by God now in the Church and in the world in spite of the sins of human beings, for everything that God will accomplish in bringing the Kingdom to fulfillment . . .

> The eucharist is the great sacrifice of praise by which the Church speaks on behalf of the whole creation . . . This sacrifice of praise is possible only through Christ, with him and in him. The bread and wine, fruits of the earth and of human labor, are presented to the Father in faith and thanksgiving. The eucharist thus signifies what the world is to become: an offering of praise to the Creator, a universal communion in the body of Christ, a kingdom of justice, love and peace in the Holy Spirit. (E 3-4)

In a sentence which gave trouble at Lima even to the *Uni-*

versalgeschichtler Wolfhart Pannenberg, the text acknowledges present signs of salvation even outside the church:

> Signs of [the final] renewal [of creation] are present in the world wherever the grace of God is manifest and human beings work for justice, love and peace. The eucharist is the feast at which the Church gives thanks to God for these signs and joyfully celebrates and anticipates the coming of the Kingdom in Christ. (E # 22)

The church promotes the cause of the kingdom, first, by its *intercession*:

> In the memorial of Christ . . . the Church, united with its great High Priest and Intercessor, prays for the world; (E # 23)

> The Church, gratefully recalling God's mighty acts of redemption, beseeches God to give the benefits of these acts to every human being; (E # 8)

second, by its *witness*:

> Reconciled in the eucharist, the members of the body of Christ are called to be servants of reconciliation among men and women, and witnesses of the joy of resurrection; (E # 24)

> The eucharistic community is nourished and strengthened for confessing by word and action the Lord Jesus Christ who gave his life for the salvation of the world; (E # 26)

and third, by its *loving service*:

> All . . . manifestations of love in the eucharist are directly related to Christ's own testimony as a servant, in whose servanthood Christians themselves participate. As God in Christ has entered into the human situation, so eucharistic liturgy is near to the concrete and particular situations of men and women. In the early Church the ministry of deacons and deaconesses gave expression in a special way to this aspect of the eucharist. The place of such ministry between the table and the needy properly testifies to the redeeming presence of Christ in the world; (E # 21)

> As Jesus went out to publicans and sinners and had table-fellowship with them during his earthly ministry, so Christians are called in the eucharist to be in solidarity with the outcast and to become signs of the love of Christ who lived and sacrificed himself for all and now gives himself in the eucharist. (E # 24)

Karl Rahner mused: Must the eucharist be celebrated even in Alaska with wine from the grape?[28] In a carefully nuanced commentary to paragraph 28 on the matter of the eucharist, the Lima text raises the question of what the church can take up from the culture:

> Since New Testament days, the Church has attached the greatest importance to the continued use of the elements of bread and wine which Jesus used at the Last Supper. In certain parts of the world, where bread and wine are not customary or obtainable, it is now sometimes held that local food and drink serve better to anchor the eucharist in everyday life. Further study is required concerning the question of which features of the Lord's Supper were unchangeably instituted by Jesus, and which features remain within the Church's competence to decide.

Perhaps it is indeed ultimately a question of authority, but there is no mistaking the morally charged nature of the situation. In the Roman Catholic Church, Latin was for centuries valued as a sign of the universality of the church. In the emergent world church, Rahner hails the liturgical use of vernaculars as an instance of decentralization. At the same time, he speaks of an incipient world civilization, which can be of service to the Christian proclamation and has indeed arisen largely through technical means that originate in "Christian" countries. Yet the beginnings of this exportation are linked with colonialism, and in the Third World the values of the native cultures are being threatened and even replaced by problematic, and even downright evil, products from the North. That is the complex situation in which the world church must simultaneously attempt the cosmopolitanization and the inculturation of its theology and practice of the sacraments.[29]

THE PROMISE OF TRANSFORMATION

I have tried to show that in both soteriology and culture the two ways are needed: from the church to the world, and from the world to the church. The sequence of the dialectic is significant: the first move is baptismal, the second is eucharistic. I want finally to bring to the surface two underlying issues.

The first is the old one concerning the necessity of the sacraments for salvation. The Lima text at least make no exclusive claims for the church. Indeed it suggests that the gift of salvation brings with it awesome responsibilities, the failing in which may lead to judgment. Positively put, I would say that the Lima text contemplates the church and the sacraments as what may be called "non-exclusive promises." I think this rather Indian-style double negative gets the balance about right. Since I have enlarged upon this concept elsewhere,[30] I will say no more here.

The second, and related, issue I do want to dwell on rather more. Its old-fashioned name is sacramental causality. It should have become clear by now that, while at least four of Niebuhr's types have certain theological strengths that may vary with the historical circumstances (the exception is the abysmal second type, "the Christ of culture"), it is the *fifth* which has the most to commend it: Christ the *transformer of culture*. While maintaining the goodness of creation, it recognizes the radical character of the change or conversion which is needed for the salvation of a fallen race and world. It is the transformationist view which is most characteristic of the Lima document. With regard to baptism, BEM regrettably omitted to borrow Alexander Schmemann's insistence on the exorcisms and the renunciation of Satan in the rites of initiation;[31] but the following at least found its way into a commentary:

> As seen in some theological traditions, the use of water, with all its positive associations with life and blessing, signifies the continuity between the old and the new creation, thus revealing the significance of baptism not only for human beings but also for the whole cosmos. At the same time, the use of water represents a purification of creation, a dying to that which is negative and destructive in the world; those who are baptized into the body of Christ are made partakers of a renewed existence. (B # 18)

The main text is quite explicit about the transformative effect of baptism:

> By baptism, Christians are immersed in the liberating death of Christ where their sins are buried, where the "old Adam" is crucified with Christ, and where the power of sin is broken. Thus those baptized are no longer slaves to sin, but free. Fully identified with the death of Christ, they are buried with him and are raised here and now to a new life in the power of the resurrection of Jesus Christ, confident that they will also ultimately be one with him in a resurrection like his (Rom 6:3-11; Col 2:13; 3:1; Eph 2:5-6); (B # 3)

> Those baptized are pardoned, cleansed and sanctified by Christ, and are given as part of their baptismal experience a new ethical orientation under the guidance of the Holy Spirit. (B # 4)

In the eucharist Christ is anamnetically and epicletically present in the Holy Spirit,[32] in order to transform believers and the wider world:

> Christ unites the faithful with himself and includes their prayers within his own intercession so that the faithful are transfigured and their prayers accepted; (E # 4)

> It is in virtue of the living word of Christ and by the power of the Holy Spirit that the bread and wine become the sacramental signs of Christ's body and blood. They remain so for the purpose of communion; (E # 15)

> The Holy Spirit through the eucharist gives a foretaste of the Kingdom of God: the Church receives the life of the new creation and the assurance of the Lord's return; (E # 18)

> The world, to which renewal is promised, is present in the whole eucharistic celebration. The world is present in the thanksgiving to the Father, when the Church speaks on behalf of the whole creation; in the memorial of Christ, where the Church, united with its great High Priest and Intercessor, prays for the world; in the prayer for the gift of the Holy Spirit, where the Church asks for sanctification and new creation; (E # 23)

> As it is entirely the gift of God, the eucharist brings into the present age a new reality which transforms Christians into the image of Christ . . . (E # 26)

Now with regard to sacramental causality, the question is this: does all this really happen? In baptism and the eucharist more is taking place than meets the senses: God is present and active. However, the sign is not simply identical with the signified but rather tends towards it; in old-fashioned terms, the *sacramentum* tends towards its *res*. On the human side, a lack of in-tention can hinder the effect which God wills. Without becoming a cultural Donatist, one may affirm that, in its ministrations, the church must aim really to reach those to whom it offers the evangelical sacraments; celebrations will therefore be sensitive to questions of expressive form. On the side of the recipients, a believing openness is required, which for its part also surrenders itself to divine transformation. Whether the fault lie in the administration or in the reception, the celebration of a sacrament may in different ways fail to express the divine mystery or to produce fruit. Insofar as the sacrament remains inexpressive or unfruitful, it falls short of transparency.[33] The church, and indeed the world, are sacramental *insofar* as in and from them the philanthropy of God radiates and God's kingdom makes its way among people.

Notes

1. Note particularly K. Rahner, "Basic Theological Interpretation of the Second Vatican Council," and "The Abiding Significance of the Second Vatican Council," *Theological Investigations* XX (New York: Crossroad, 1981) 77-89, 90-102.

2. See "On the Presence of Christ in the Diaspora Community according to the Teaching of the Second Vatican Council," *Theological Investigations* X (New York: Seabury, 1973) 84-102.

3. For the privileged position of baptism and eucharist, see Y. Congar, "The Notion of 'Major' or 'Principal' Sacraments," *Concilium* 31 (1968) 21-32.

4. See his "Considerations on the Active Role of the Person in the Sacramental Event," *Theological Investigations* XIV (New York: Seabury, 1976) 161-184.

5. K. Rahner, *Kirche und Sakramente* (Freiburg: Herder, 1960); English translation, *The Church and the Sacraments* (New York: Herder, 1963). (But see below, note 11.)

6. In addition to the article mentioned in note 4, see "Zur Theologie des Gottesdienstes," *Schriften zur Theologie* 14 (Zurich: Benziger, 1980) 227-237.

7. *Baptism, Eucharist and Ministry* (Geneva: World Council of Churches, 1982). In what follows, the three parts are abbreviated respectively as B, E, and M.

8. *Lumen Gentium* 1; also 9, 48, and 59; see already *Sacrosanctum Concilium* 5 and 26, and further *Gaudium et Spes* 42 and 45, and *Ad Gentes* 1 and 5.

9. H. de Lubac, *Catholicisme*, 4th ed. (Paris: Editions du Cerf, 1947) 50; abridged English translation, *Catholicism* (New York: Longmans, 1950) 29.

10. E. Schillebeeckx, *Christus, Sacrament van de Godsontmoeting* (Bilthoven: Nelissen, 1957); English translation, *Christ the Sacrament of Encounter with God* (New York: Sheed and Ward, 1963). O. Semmelroth, *Die Kirche als Ursakrament* (Frankfurt am Main: Knecht, 1953).

11. The English translation of *Kirche und Sakramente* (see note 5) does not make it apparent that Rahner in the original had used *Ursakrament* of the church. For his later preference of *Grundsakrament* as an ecclesiological

term, see K. Rahner, *Grundkurs des Glaubens* (Freiburg: Herder, 1976) 396-398; English translation, *Foundations of Christian Faith* (New York: Seabury, 1978) 411-413. For Scheffczyk, see H. Luthe, ed., *Christusbegegnung in den Sakramenten* (Kevelaer: Butzon & Bercker, 1981) 9-61 ("Jesus Christus—Ursakrament der Erlösung"), 63-120 ("Die Kirche—das Ganzsakrament Jesu Christi").

12. See, briefly, J. Ratzinger, "Die Kirche als Heilssakrament," *Theologische Prinzipienlehre* (Munich: Wewel, 1982) 45-57.

13. W. Beinert, "Die Sakramentalität der Kirche im theologischen Gespräch," in *Kirche und Sakrament*, vol. 9 of *Theologische Berichte*, ed. J. Pfammatter and F. Fürger (Zurich: Benziger, 1980) 13-66. Beinert himself locates the (re)discovery of the sacramentality of the church in the history of ideas and of culture as a response to the problems and opportunities of secularization. At the end of his survey of the literature, he offers his own convincing systematic exposition of the theological value of the notion.

14. A. Harnack, *The Mission and Expansion of Christianity in the First Three Centuries*, 2d ed. (New York: Putnam, 1908) [1st German ed. 1902]). K.S. Latourette, *A History of the Expansion of Christianity*, 7 vols. (New York: Harper, 1937-1945).

15. P. Brunner, "Zur katholischen Sakramenten- und Eucharistielehre," *Theologische Literaturzeitung* 88 (1963) 169-186, in particular 175f. Among Protestants, vigorous opposition to "ecumenical" usage is maintained by E. Käsemann, *Kirchliche Konflikte*, vol. 1 (Göttingen: Vandenhoeck & Ruprecht, 1982) 46-61 ["Zur ekklesiologischen Verwendung der Stichworte 'Sakrament' und 'Zeichen'"]. E. Jüngel remains suspicious of an understanding of the church as "realsymbolische Repräsentation Jesu Christi" *to the extent that* it endangers the primarily *receptive* character of salvation on the side of the church: "Die Kirche als Sakrament?" in *Zeitschrift für Theologie und Kirche* 80 (1983) 432-457. Less guarded is W. Pannenberg in his contribution to the article "Kirche" in R. Scherer and others, eds., *Christlicher Glaube in moderner Gesellschaft*, vol. 29 (Freiburg: Herder, 1982) esp. 126-128.

16. H. Fries and K. Rahner, *Einigung der Kirchen—reale Möglichkeit* (Freiburg: Herder, 1983).

17. See G. Wainwright, *Eucharist and Eschatology* (New York: Oxford University Press, 1981) esp. 109f., 196.

18. H.R. Niebuhr, *Christ and Culture* (New York: Harper & Row, 1951).

19. Justin Martyr, *Apology* I. 46 and 66 respectively.

20. See. G. Wainwright, "Revolution and Quietism," *The Ecumenical Moment* (Grand Rapids: Eerdmans, 1983) 150-168.

21. K.H. Bieritz, "Der Oeffentlichkeitsanspruch des Gottesdienstes in einer 'Nicht-Mehr-Volkskirche'," *Jahrbuch für Liturgik und Hymnologie* 26 (1982) 67-78.

22. See Rahner, "Considerations on the Active Role" 172.

23. Borrowed from W. Kasper, "Die Kirche als universales Sakrament des Heils," in E. Klinger and K. Wittstadt, eds., *Glaube im Prozess: Für Karl Rahner* (Freiburg: Herder, 1984) 221-239, in particular p. 236.

24. As in Rahner, "The Abiding Significance" 99ff.

25. A. Schmemann, *The World as Sacrament* (London: Darton, Longman & Todd, 1965). The book was published in the United States under two other titles, *For the Life of the World* (1963) and *Sacraments and Orthodoxy* (New York: Herder, 1965).

26. T. Runyon, "The World as the Original Sacrament," *Worship* 54 (1980) 495-511.

27. One of the few occasions when Woody Allen's theological instincts have let him down was his remark that the lion might lie down with the lamb, but the lamb would not get much sleep.

28. As in Rahner, "Basic Theological Interpretation" 79.

29. K. Rahner, as in note 1, pp. 78f., 80f., 86, 92; also in the same volume p. 165, and "Aspekte europäischer Theologie," *Schriften zur Theologie*, XV (Zurich: Benziger, 1983) 84-103. See further G. Wainwright, "The Localization of Worship," *Studia Liturgica* 8 (1971-1972) 26-41; "Christian Worship and Western Culture," *Studia Liturgica* 12 (1977) 20-33; *Doxology* (New York: Oxford University Press, 1980) 357-398. Also A. Schnijder, "Cosmopolitization of Mankind and Adaptation of the Liturgy," *Studia Liturgica* 8 (1971-1972) 169-184; A.J. Chupungco, *Cultural Adaptation of the Liturgy* (New York: Paulist Press, 1982).

30. See especially Wainwright, *Doxology* 143-146.

31. A. Schmemann, *Of Water and the Spirit* (Crestwood, NY: St. Vladimir's, 1974) 20-30.

32. Out of the vast literature on anamnesis and epiclesis, see M. Thurian, *The Eucharistic Memorial*, 2 vols. (Richmond: Knox, 1960-1961), and J.H. McKenna, *Eucharist and Holy Spirit* (Great Wakering: Mayhew-McCrimmon, 1975).

33. For the notion of transparency, see L. Boff, *Die Kirche als Sakrament im Horizont der Welterfahrung* (Paderborn: Bonifacius, 1972), in particular pp. 125-130. The Vatican II Constitution on the Sacred Liturgy, *Sacrosanctum Concilium* 21 and 49, had underlined the importance of the expressive form of the signs at least at the level of *pastoral* efficacy; see F. Eisenbach, *Die Gegenwart Jesu Christi im Gottesdienst—Systematische Studien zur Liturgiekonstitution des II. Vatikanischen Konzils* (Mainz: Grünewald, 1982) 281, 305-316, 363f.

7

The Sacraments in
Wesleyan Perspective

To treat any matter in a Wesleyan perspective is not merely, for a Methodist, an act of piety toward John and Charles Wesley, the principal founders of our particular tradition, although such gestures certainly have their proper place for Christians who live in the communion of the saints. There is another reason why, in the late twentieth century, American Methodists should be looking to the Wesley brothers for guidance. Our own missionary situation bears an uncanny resemblance to the England of the eighteenth century in which the Methodist movement took its origins. For two centuries the American Constitution has forbidden any national establishment of religion of the kind the Wesleys knew in England and which still obtains there, even if in attenuated degree. Nevertheless, an often vague form of non-dogmatic, non-denominational Christianity has constituted the unofficial "civil religion" of the United States; and the "mainline" denominations have functioned in part as variant carriers of the civil religion—our own Methodism as much as any other body. And our church now takes on many of the features that marked the declining effectiveness of the Church of England in the Wesleys' days. If we look for renewal, we may find hints in what God did through the Wesleys.

We discover there a multifaceted movement which comprehensively united the dimensions of classic Christianity: evangelical and evangelistic preaching; adherence to the historic faith; an active social engagement on behalf of the needy; a tight network of fellowship and pastoral care (the "classes"); and a strong sacramental, and especially eucharistic, life. It is on this last point that I wish to concentrate, but it would be easy to show the connections between sacramental faith and practice, on the one hand, and all the other features of a thriving church.

In particular, I want to show that the sacraments are the place where the church discovers and rediscovers its own identity. Without the heartbeat of the sacraments at its center, a church will lack confidence about the gospel message and about its own ability to proclaim that message in evangelism, to live it out in its own internal fellowship, and to embody it in service to the needy. In baptism we are given a share in Christ's death and resurrection and made members of his Body, the church, which is charged with God's mission in the world. The Lord's Supper is, in the first place, a "confirming" ordinance, an ordinance for the community of the converted. Through their faithful observance of the ordinance, God offers Christians the power to reach out and win others for Christ. When it is thus celebrated by a vital community, the Lord's Supper will also have a greater chance of functioning as a directly "converting" ordinance in so far as that may in certain circumstances be appropriate.

THE LORD'S SUPPER FOR THE LORD'S PEOPLE ON THE LORD'S DAY

"I also advise the elders to administer the Supper of the Lord on every Lord's Day."[1] John Wesley's choice of terms in this injunction of 10 September 1784 to "our brethren in America" shows him establishing a theological, or more precisely a Christological, connection between Sunday and the Holy Communion, "the Supper of the Lord" and "the Lord's Day." To set forth a Wesleyan perspective on the sacraments, we may appropriately begin with a hymn by Charles Wesley "For the Lord's Day."[2]

1

Come, let us with our Lord arise,
Our Lord, who made both earth and skies;
Who died to save the world he made,
And rose triumphant from the dead;
He rose, the Prince of life and peace,
And stamped the day for ever his.

2

This is the day the Lord hath made,
That all may see his love displayed,
May feel his resurrection's power,
And rise again to fall no more,
In perfect righteousness renewed,
And filled with all the life of God.

3

Then let us render him his own,
With solemn prayer approach the throne,
With meekness hear the gospel word,
With thanks his dying love record;
Our joyful hearts and voices raise,
And fill his courts with songs of praise.

4

Honour and praise to Jesus pay
Throughout his consecrated day;
Be all in Jesus' praise employed,
Nor leave a single moment void;
With utmost care the time improve,
And only breathe his praise and love.

The third stanza can serve as our starting point. It offers the most direct reflection of *The Sunday Service*—"a liturgy little differing from that of the Church of England"—that John Wesley sent to the American Methodists in 1784:

1. To "render him his own" is the active intention of all Christian worship of God. "All things come from thee, and of thine own have we given thee," said David as the people brought their gifts for the construction of the Lord's house (1 Chr 29:14). *Ta sa ek ton son* is the exclamation of the eastern eucharistic liturgies. We offer our gifts and thanks to God, says John Chrysostom in commenting on the one grateful leper who was healed, not because God has need of them, but to bring us closer to God.[3] In point of fact, the worship of God is, in the words of Isaac Watts, both "our duty" and "our delight."[4] "The chief end of man," according to the Westminster Catechism, "is to glorify God and to enjoy him for ever." "The service of God," says the Anglican collect, "is our perfect freedom."[5] God gives, and we return with joy and thanks what we receive. It is for that loving communion that our Creator and Redeemer has made us and saves

us. Any theology of the sacraments has to be governed by that primordial and ultimate rubric.

2. The "solemn prayer" with which we "approach the throne" may refer to the service of morning prayer, which in Wesley as in The Book of Common Prayer, preceded the eucharist. Or perhaps it is the collect for purity at the beginning of the Communion Service ("Almighty God, unto whom all hearts be open . . ."), or the Greater Gloria ("Glory be to God on high . . . O Lord God, Lamb of God, have mercy upon us . . ."). According to Hebrews 4:14-16, we have through Jesus our great high priest access to the throne of grace, where we may find help in time of need. As creatures and as sinners, we are perpetually "standing in the need of prayer." It is God's pleasure to meet our need, for "the glory of God is humanity alive" (Irenaeus).[6] Again, any theology of the sacraments will stand under the rubric of God's mercy.

3. After our approach to the throne of grace, the next stage in the order of service reflected in the third stanza of "For the Lord's Day" is to "hear the gospel word." The "gospel word" is a favorite Wesleyan expression. In another hymn ("See, sinners, in the gospel glass") Charles sings:

> Sinners, believe the gospel word,
> Jesus is come your souls to save!
> Jesus is come, your common Lord;
> Pardon ye all in him may have;
> May now be saved, whoever will;
> This Man receiveth sinners still.[7]

This is the clue to the Christian reading of the Scriptures and the heart of all Christian preaching. According to Karl Barth in *The Knowledge of God and the Service of God*, the first *act* of the church in worship is to *listen*.[8] Truly to hear God is to obey God: a Greek prefix turns hearing into obedience; *akouē* becomes *hup-akouē*. We sit "under" the word. That is the "meekness" Wesley mentions. In yet another hymn, one that is based on the return of the prodigal, Wesley links obedience to the gospel word with participation in the eucharistic feast:

> Sinners, obey the gospel word;
> Haste to the supper of my Lord![9]

4. Charles Wesley shifts directly into eucharistic gear with the next line of our hymn: "With thanks his dying love record." Christ's

"dying love" is a phrase Wesley often uses in connection with the eucharist. Hymn 20 of the *Hymns on the Lord's Supper* (1745) begins with a variant formulation:

> Lamb of God, whose bleeding love
> We now recall to mind . . .[10]

The whole first section of that collection of 166 hymns, which was published in the joint name of the two brothers, is entitled the Lord's Supper "as it is a memorial of the sufferings and death of Christ." In his *John Wesley on the Sacraments* (1972), Bishop Ole Borgen has impressively expounded the strength of the eucharistic memorial in these hymns.[11] There is "a two-way suspension of time and place" (p. 92). In one direction, Christ is prayed to transport us back to the foot of the cross:

> Place us near th'accursèd wood
> Where thou didst thy life resign,
> Near as once thy mother stood;
> Partners of the pangs divine,
> Bid us feel her sacred smart,
> Feel the sword that pierced her heart.[12]

Or again:

> Endless scenes of wonder rise
> From that mysterious tree,
> Crucified before our eyes
> Where we our Maker see:
> Jesus, Lord, what hast thou done?
> Publish we the death divine,
> Stop, and gaze, and fall, and own
> Was never love like thine.[13]

In the other direction, the Holy Spirit, in images borrowed from the Fourth Gospel and the liturgy of *The Apostolic Constitutions*, is the Remembrancer or Recorder who brings "the sprinkled blood" of Christ into our present:

> Come, thou everlasting Spirit,
> Bring to every thankful mind
> All the Saviour's dying merit,
> All his sufferings for mankind;
> True Recorder of his passion,
> Now the living faith impart,

> Now reveal his great salvation,
> Preach his gospel to our heart.
>
> Come, thou witness of his dying,
> Come, Remembrancer divine,
> Let us feel thy power applying
> Christ to every soul and mine;
> Let us groan thine inward groaning,
> Look on him we pierced and grieve,
> All receive the grace atoning,
> All the sprinkled blood receive.[14]

5. The last two lines of the third stanza of our hymn "For the Lord's Day" echo the beginning of the eucharistic liturgy proper:

> Our joyful hearts and voices raise,
> And fill his courts with songs of praise.

The allusion is clearly to the *Sursum Corda* ("Lift up your hearts") and the *Sanctus* (". . . with angels and archangels and all the company of heaven, we laud and magnify thy glorious name, evermore praising thee and saying, Holy, holy, holy . . ."). As I emphasized in my *Eucharist and Eschatology*,[15] for the Wesleys the Lord's Supper is a "pledge," an "earnest," a "taste" of heaven:

> Whither should our full souls aspire,
> At this transporting feast?
> They never can on earth be higher,
> Or more completely blest.
>
> Our cup of blessing from above
> Delightfully runs o'er;
> Till from these bodies they remove,
> Our souls can hold no more.
>
> To heaven the mystic banquet leads;
> Let us to heaven ascend,
> And bear this joy upon our heads
> Till it in glory end.
>
> Till all who truly join in this,
> The marriage supper share,
> Enter into their Master's bliss,
> And feast for ever there.[16]

With that we have moved forward in the eucharistic liturgy to the communion itself, the eating and drinking. Our hymn "For the

Lord's Day" has already in the second stanza anticipated the ritual sequence. The last line can stand for all the rest when it speaks of being "filled with all the life of God." It is not exclusively in eucharistic contexts that the Wesleys use such language: it is one of the ways they describe salvation as such. But they do speak of sacramental communion in these terms, precisely because the sacraments are, for the Wesleys, *means* of grace and glory:

> O the depth of love divine,
> Th'unfathomable grace!
> Who shall say how bread and wine
> God into man conveys!
> How the bread his flesh imparts,
> How the wine transmits his blood,
> Fill his faithful people's hearts
> With all the life of God.[17]

It is precisely the eucharistic communicant who feels God's "closest love,"[18] drinks "larger draughts of God".[19] The change which God works in the believer through such means is described in terms similar to the second stanza of our Sunday hymn:

> We his image shall regain,
> And to his stature rise,
> Rise unto a perfect man,
> And then ascend the skies . . .[20]

The first stanza of our hymn "For the Lord's Day" has set forth the great events in salvation history which the Sunday liturgy commemorates, celebrates, and applies:

> Come, let us with our Lord arise,
> Our Lord, who made both earth and skies;
> Who died to save the world he made,
> And rose triumphant from the dead;
> He rose, the Prince of life and peace,
> And stamped the day for ever his.

This is the same dual grounding of Sunday worship in creation and redemption as was already given by Justin Martyr in the middle of the second century: "We assemble on Sunday because it is the first day, that on which God transformed the darkness and matter to create the world, and also because Jesus Christ our Savior rose from the dead on the same day."[21] The qualification for sharing in the worship of the new creation, as Justin describes it, is baptism. In a hymn drawn from Romans 6, Charles Wesley shows baptism as the basic sacrament of participation in Christ's death and resurrection, of power over sin and life unto God:

> Baptized into my Saviour's name,
> I of his death partake;
> Buried with Jesus Christ I am,
> And I with him awake.
>
> He burst the barriers of the tomb,
> Rose, and regained the skies;
> And lo! from nature's grave I come,
> And lo! with Christ I rise.
>
> A new, a living life I have;
> And, fashioned to his death,
> His resurrection's power receive,
> And by his Spirit breathe . . .
>
> I live to God, who from the dead
> Hath me to life restored,
> That I, from sin's oppression freed,
> Might only serve my Lord.[22]

It is the baptized people of the Lord who gather on the Lord's Day to celebrate and enjoy the Lord's meal.

SOME CONTROVERSIAL QUESTIONS

Our hymn "For the Lord's Day" has provided a structure for making clear the high appreciation which the Wesleys had for the two sacraments of the Gospel, and particularly perhaps for the Lord's Supper. Their "Sunday Service" was, in ideal and to a great extent in practice, a service of word and table. Within that positive perspective I now want, in the second half of this chapter, to face some questions that have been controversial in later Methodism, either because we have ignored or distorted John Wesley or found him difficult to interpret, or because relatively new issues or circumstances have arisen that were not foreseen by Wesley.

The Efficacy of the Sacraments

The Wesleys are very hesitant about explaining *how* the sacraments work; but *that* the sacraments work, they rejoice to confess.

They use the language of "mystery" and of the "operation of the Holy Spirit." For an example of Wesley's belief in the efficacy of the sacraments, let us examine an affirmation that many later Methodists have tended to deny: baptismal regeneration.

Wesley's words are often quoted out of context: "Baptism is not the new birth; they are not one and the same thing."[23] One only needs to read on in the same sermon on "The New Birth": "The reason of the thing is clear and evident . . . What can be more plain, than that the one is an external, the other an internal work; that the one is a visible, the other an invisible thing, and therefore different from each other?"[24] Wesley is here, as in several other places, endorsing the definition of a sacrament, given in the Church of England catechism and echoed in the Articles of Religion, as "an outward and visible sign of an inward and spiritual grace"; and he usually continues with the quotation: "and *a means whereby we receive* the same."[25]

In the sermon first quoted, Wesley refers explicitly to *adult* baptism, and he puts the condition for its efficacy: "if they repent and believe the Gospel." As he says in the *Explanatory Notes upon the New Testament*, at Acts 22:16: "Baptism, administered to real penitents, is both a means and a seal of pardon." By stating these biblical conditions, Wesley is wanting to oppose the automatism of what he understands as the Roman Catholic doctrine of "*ex opere operato*." In the case of infants properly brought to baptism—and Wesley's chief defense of infant baptism is a variant of the covenant argument—Wesley endorses the teaching of The Book of Common Prayer, that those "who are baptized in their infancy are at the same time born again."[26]

Bernard Holland, in *Baptism in Early Methodism*,[27] and Ole Borgen, in the work already cited, have convincingly demonstrated that Wesley never abandoned the doctrine of baptismal regeneration. Because God commanded the sacrament and promised his blessing, the sacrament will always be effective, whenever it is properly used, i.e., administered to people who have come to repentance and faith, or to the infants of believers who stand within the covenant. This is not to exclude God's working outside and beyond his sacraments. But it is to say that we are obligated to use them if we seek God's blessing. This is made very clear, for example, in Wesley's sermon on "Constant Communion."[28]

Baptism and the New Birth

Let us return to baptism and the new birth from another angle. We have already seen Wesley affirming the regeneration of baptized infants. This suffices for salvation unless and until a person should fall into actual sin and so *persist* in it as to die spiritually. The "principle of grace" infused by baptism "will not be wholly taken away, unless we quench the Holy Spirit of God by long-continued wickedness."[29] In the sermon on "The New Birth," it is to those who never had or *no longer have* the inward witness of the Spirit or the fruit of the Spirit in their lives that Wesley says, "You must"—baptized or unbaptized—"be born again."[30]

Now there is a problem here. Wesley certainly held to baptismal regeneration. Can then a man enter a *third* (or a fourth, or a fifth) time into his mother's womb and be born again? If a baptism is the sacrament of regeneration, then it might seem that multiple baptisms were in order, at every restoration from mortal sin. Happily, Wesley never said or practiced this; but, unfortunately, he did not adequately safeguard against it. Such a practice would run counter to the entire Christian tradition (even Baptists hold that what they see as a *real* baptism is not to be repeated!). St. John of Damascus went so far as to say that to undergo a "second" baptism was tantamount to crucifying Christ afresh, so close was the correspondence between baptism and the once-for-all death of the Savior.[31] It is therefore wise to make clear that any later restorations to life are made on a baptismal foundation and within a baptismal context. The once baptized and now *believing* person is right to be confident with Luther, "*Baptizatus sum.*" Restorations after lapses are properly made through penance, or through a renewal of baptismal vows, or through a "renewal of the covenant" in the Wesleyan tradition[32]—in all of which thanks should be given for baptism and God's continuing faithfulness; but baptism should not be *repeated*. The restored person may suitably also bear narrative testimony to the healing grace of God in a public way, surrounded by the supportive Christian fellowship.

Admission to the Table

Tensions arise between the poles of communion as a means of grace and the need to maintain the integrity of the celebrating community. To receive communion is to become part of the sign-enacting community, which is charged with the faithful steward-ship of God's mysteries in the world. Who, then, should be admitted to the table? The question arises in at least five contexts.

i. Evangelism

It is here that appeal is often made to Wesley's notion of the sacrament as a "converting ordinance." This phrase, which occurs but a very few times in John Wesley's writings, is one of the most abused of all his sayings. Wesley used the expression in the context of his controversy with Moravian quietism in the early 1740s. Whereas the Moravians held that earnest seekers should abstain from all the "means of grace" until God had favored them "out of the blue," Wesley held that those with some degree of repentance and faith should partake of the Lord's Supper. On 29 September 1740 (in a preface interleaved in the published *Journal* before the entry for 1 February 1738) he asserted (and indeed with appeal to Zinzendorf):

> (1) That a man may have a degree of justifying faith before he is wholly freed from all doubt and fear, and before he has, in the full, proper sense, a new, a clean heart;
>
> (2) That a man may use the ordinances of God, the Lord's Supper in particular, before he has such a faith as excludes all doubt and fear, and implies a new, a clean heart.[33]

When, in the *Journal* for 27-28 June 1740, Wesley affirms that "the Lord's Supper was ordained by God to be a means of conveying to men either preventing, or justifying, or sanctifying grace, according to their several necessities," the triple formula is explicated by the ensuing declaration that "the persons for whom it was ordained are all those who know and feel that they want the grace of God, either to restrain them from sin, or to show their sins forgiven, or to renew their souls in the image of God."[34] *All* that is required—but it *is* required—is "a sense of our state, of our utter sinfulness and helplessness" and "a desire to receive whatsoever [God] pleases to give." When, in the sermon on "The Means of Grace," Wesley encourages "unbelievers" (a designation he uses for the original disciples before Pentecost) to receive communion, he has in mind people who do not yet have *full assurance* of faith.[35] He recognized that there were "degrees of faith" that might precede assurance. In a later letter, of 25 July 1755 to Richard Tompson, Wesley wrote that "a man who is not assured that his sins are forgiven may yet have a kind or degree of faith, which distinguishes him not only from a devil but also from an heathen, and on which I may admit him to the Lord's Supper."[36]

In a Wesleyan perspective there can thus be no question of offering holy communion to all and sundry, in the vague hope that some may somehow be converted by it. But once the beginnings of conviction are there (which, for Wesley, includes "a willingness to know and do the whole will of God," "earnest desire for universal holiness," as he states in the letter of 17 June 1746 to Thomas Church, a letter entitled "The Principles of a Methodist Farther Explained"),[37] it is appropriate for a person to come expectantly to the Lord's Table.

ii. Baptism

I remember no place in which Wesley discusses baptism as a condition of admission to communion, except in an early insistence in Georgia that it be baptism by an episcopally ordained minister.[38] There is, however, no doubt that, in the situation of eighteenth-century England, Wesley could assume baptism on the part of that vast majority of those whom he exhorted to the Lord's Table. The eucharistic liturgy's "Ye that do truly and earnestly repent of your sins and are in love and charity with your neighbors" is an invitation to the baptized. Where a person needed baptism, Wesley administered it. As the "Treatise on Baptism" explains, baptism "is the initiatory sacrament": by it "we are admitted into the Church," and "from our union with the Church [proceeds] a share in all its privileges."[39]

While baptism is thus in Wesley, as in the whole classical tradition of Christianity, normally presupposed for admission to the Lord's Table, cases may arise, as in camp meetings or revivals, in which an "outsider," somewhat in the manner of 1 Corinthians 14:23-25, professes conversion to Christ. Should such a person immediately be admitted to holy communion? Without specific guidance from Wesley, my own inclination would be to say yes, on that occasion; and then the person should thereupon be put under instruction for a baptism that would be administered before too long. In discussing such an eventuality with a priest-theologian of the Orthodox Church, which is hardly lax in its communion policy,

I was surprised to find that he, too, hoped the presiding minister would be given a "charismatic judgment" in favor of admitting the sudden convert to a first communion. No more than in the case of Cornelius would that render a subsequent baptism superfluous.

iii. Discipline

For *entrance* into a Methodist society, Wesley's sole condition was "a desire to flee from the wrath to come, to be saved from [one's] sins." But the General Rules stipulate that more is required in order to *continue* in the societies: "doing no harm," "doing good," "attending upon all the ordinances of God."[40] In early Methodism, would-be communicants needed a class-ticket, a "note," or some other communion token—a practice long maintained in many parts of the overseas mission field.[41] The pastoral care and discipline of our members calls for attention to the communion roll.

It is not just a matter of confronting any who present themselves for communion but otherwise show no seriousness about their membership. There is also the reverse case of those members who feel themselves "unworthy" of communion. Short of some grave sin for which a period of penance and abstinence is appropriate, penitent and believing Christians seeking amendment of life should not let scrupulosity keep them from the table. The holy communion can "show sins forgiven." According to Wesley's sermon on "Constant Communion," neglect of the table is both the compounding of disobedience and the refusal of mercy.[42]

iv. Childhood

When children desired to partake of the Lord's Supper, Wesley's practice was to "talk with" them, to "examine" them first as to their "sense of the pardoning love of God."[43] Wesley apparently retained the medieval western and Reformation practice of not giving holy communion to the very youngest children. As the Lima text on *Baptism, Eucharist and Ministry* now recognizes, this raises questions as to the "completeness" of the baptism of infants.

v. Ecumenism

For all his "catholic spirit," Wesley refused his hand to Arians, Socinians, and Deists—precisely because "their heart was not right with his heart." With regard to such as Baptists and Roman Catholics, who might be presumed to have at least "the first elements of the Gospel of Christ," Wesley recognized that "a difference in opinions or modes of worship may prevent an entire external union," while it need not "prevent our union in affection."[44] The *Minutes* of the 1747 Conference recognize "the foreign Reformed Churches" to be "parts of the Church of Christ," and we may assume Wesley accepted the hitherto traditional practice of the Church of England regarding mutual eucharistic hospitality with such churches.[45]

From a Wesleyan perspective it seems entirely natural that as Methodism developed its distinct ecclesial identity, our denominations should seek to be "in communion" with all other bodies recognizably holding the historic Christian faith which we claim to share. Hopefully, the recognition would be mutual. But where another community cannot recognize us in this way, Methodist tradition commits us to pursue doctrinal discussion until agreement is reached in the truth of the Gospel. Meanwhile, from the Methodist side it is appropriate that our invitations should offer at least occasional communion to all members in good standing of churches in which we can see the faith.

Frequency of the Lord's Supper

In the sermon that he wrote in the 1730s for his Oxford students and then published fifty years later, Wesley refused even the word "frequency" and spoke rather of "Constant Communion."[46] To the objection that constant communion "abates our reverence for the sacrament," Wesley retorts that the "true religious reverence" shown in obeying the Lord's command will rather be confirmed and increased. To any who claim they have "not found the benefit" they expected from communion, Wesley replies that they will "find benefit sooner or later, perhaps insensibly." The canonical "three times a year" is a minimum against self-excommunication: the church "takes all possible care that the sacrament be duly administered, wherever the Common Prayer is read, every Sunday and holiday in the year." Even though the Church of England made such provision, it is well known that the service often never went beyond "Ante-Communion" because insufficient communicants had announced themselves. With that we come up against a longstanding problem.

Wesley was familiar with the patristic writers, and he believed that communion had been held daily in the primitive church (cf. Acts 2:46), and at least weekly in the early centuries.[47] In the passage we quoted earlier, Justin Martyr describes a service of word and table taking place every Sunday: the connection between "the Lord's Supper," "the Lord's Day," and "the Lord's People" was of the kind we saw Wesley establishing in his letter of 10 September 1784 to the brethren in America. Wesley lamented the decline of the church after the conversion of Constantine.[48] Imperial Christianity counted many lukewarm members who rightly or wrongly abstained from communion. In both east and west the eucharist became predominantly a clerical affair; and in the medieval west, in particular, the Mass turned into a placatory sacrifice whose benefits did not require reception of the sacrament for their appropriation. Luther, Calvin, and the English Reformers sought to reestablish a weekly communion of the people; but if not enough intending communicants announced themselves, the service was stopped before the eucharist proper. This is how the Protestant Churches acquired a "service of the word" as their "ordinary" service. Wesley tried to remedy this by exhortation and example: from periods throughout his life for which evidence is available, it has been calculated that Wesley received communion on average once every four or five days.[49] One of the factors in the eventual separation between English Methodists and the Church of England was the desire of the Methodists to receive the communion more frequently from their own preachers. Sadly, this zeal cooled in the succeeding century, and British Methodists became satisfied with an infrequency that almost matched that found in the frontier conditions of America.

In our century—when "constantinian" patterns of society are breaking down, and to be a Christian is again starting to be distinctive—there has been a remarkable growth in the frequency of communion. A far higher proportion of Roman Catholics who "go to Mass" now receive communion. A steady increase in the rhythm of eucharistic celebrations is observable in many parts of the Protestant world. None of this need or should detract from the importance of preaching. It is indeed interesting to note that, in the Roman Catholic Church, a revival of scriptural preaching has gone hand in hand with the renewal of communion.

Trinitarian Sacraments

Charles Wesley was very well aware of the "Unitarian foe": he wrote a collection of combative "Hymns on the Trinity," lauding "the divinity of Christ," "the divinity of the Holy Ghost," "the plurality and Trinity of persons," and "the Trinity in unity."[50] We have already observed that John Wesley did not embrace the antitrinitarians.[51] While Wesley was sometimes unwilling to impose the technical terms of "person" and "Trinity" since they were not directly taken from the Scriptures, he freely named Father, Son, and Holy Spirit, and called them the "Three-One God." This is how he envisioned final salvation in the sermon "The New Creation":

> And to crown all, there will be a deep, and intimate, an uninterrupted union with God; a *constant communion* with the Father and his Son Jesus Christ, through the Spirit; a continual enjoyment of the Three-One God, and of all the creatures in him.[52]

Today we have neo-Sabellians invoking "the Creator, Redeemer, and Sustainer," listing three external functions of an internally undifferentiated godhead, instead of naming the three persons of the Trinity. (In a letter of 3 August 1771 to Jane Catherine March, Wesley accurately perceives that "the quaint device of styling them three offices rather than persons gives up the whole doctrine."[53]) We have neo-Arians reducing the second and third persons to creatures when they invoke "the Creator, the Christ, and the Spirit." In point of fact, the best guidance for naming the God of the Christian revelation remains Jesus' address to "Abba, Father," his self-understanding as "the Son," and his promise of the Holy Spirit. The ecumenical councils of Nicea and Constantinople declared the distinctions, relations, and unity of the three persons in one God. Athanasius and Basil showed how our salvation is at stake in the work of the three persons invoked at baptism and operative in the eucharist. In his sermon "On the Trinity" John Wesley shows how all this is vital:

> I know not how anyone can be a Christian believer till "he hath" (as St. John speaks) "the witness in himself"; till "the Spirit of God witnesses with his spirit that he is a child of God"—that is, in effect, till God the Holy Ghost witnesses that God the Father has accepted him through the merits of God the Son—and having this witness he honors the Son and the blessed Spirit "even as he honors the Father." Not every Christian believer

adverts to this; perhaps at first not one in twenty; but if you ask any of them a few questions you will easily find it is implied in what he believes.[54]

The Wesleys' understanding of the sacraments was thoroughly trinitarian. Hear first a baptismal hymn:

> Come, Father, Son, and Holy Ghost,
> Honour the means ordained by thee!
> Make good our apostolic boast,
> And own thy glorious ministry.
>
> We now thy promised presence claim;
> Sent to disciple all mankind,
> Sent to baptize into thy name,
> We now thy promised presence find.
>
> Father, in these reveal thy Son;
> In these, for whom we seek thy face,
> The hidden mystery make known,
> The inward, pure, baptizing grace.
>
> Jesus, with us thou always art;
> Effectual make the sacred sign,
> The gift unspeakable impart,
> And bless the ordinance divine.
>
> Eternal Spirit, descend from high,
> Baptizer of our spirits thou!
> The sacramental seal apply,
> And witness with the water now.
>
> O that the souls baptized therein
> May now thy truth and mercy feel;
> May rise and wash away their sin—
> Come, Holy Ghost, their pardon seal![55]

And for the eucharist:

> Father, thy grace we claim,
> The double grace, bestowed
> On all who trust in him that came
> By water and by blood.
>
> Jesu, the blood apply,
> The righteousness bring in,
> Us by thy dying justify,
> And wash out all our sin.

> Spirit of faith, come down,
> Thy seal with power set to,
> The banquet by thy presence crown,
> And prove the record true:
>
> Pardon and grace impart;
> Come quickly from above,
> And witness now in every heart
> That God is perfect love.[56]

How should we ever know that the triune God of Scripture and Tradition was intended if, in our reading from the Bible, in our preaching of the Gospel, in our uttering of praise and prayer, in our administration of the sacraments, the name of Father, Son, and Holy Spirit were avoided or abandoned?[57]

Notes

1. *The Letters of the Rev. John Wesley*, ed. John Telford, vol. 7 (London: Epworth, 1931) 239.

2. First published in *Hymns for Children* (1763), the hymn is found in *The Poetical Works of John and Charles Wesley*, ed. George Osborn, vol. 4 (London: Wesleyan-Methodist Conference Office, 1869) 429. The hymn figures in the British Methodist hymnals of 1933 and 1983; it does not appear in twentieth-century American Methodist hymnals, although the Episcopal Church took it up in its *Hymnal 1982* (no. 49).

3. John Chrysostom, Homily XXV, 3 on Matthew (Migne: *Patrologia Graeca* 57:331).

4. From the hymn familiar as "I'll Praise My Maker while I've Breath," from Isaac Watts' *Psalms of David* (1719).

5. See the collect for peace in morning prayer in The Book of Common Prayer.

6. Irenaeus, *Adversus Haereses* IV.20.7.

7. First published in the anti-Calvinist *Hymns on God's Everlasting Love* (1741), the hymn is found in *The Poetical Works*, vol. 3 (1869) 20.

8. Karl Barth, *The Knowledge of God and the Service of God according to the Teaching of the Reformation* (London: Hodder and Stoughton, 1938) 210.

9. Having appeared in *Festival Hymns* (1746) and *Hymns and Sacred Poems* (1749), "Sinners, Obey the Gospel Word" was included in the definitive *Collection of Hymns for the Use of the People Called Methodists* of 1780 (no. 9). The text is found in *The Poetical Works*, vol. 5 (1869) 63-64.

10. A collection of 166 hymns, the *Hymns on the Lord's Supper* appeared in 1745 under the joint names of John and Charles Wesley and supplied

their innovative use of such singing at the eucharist. The text is found in *The Poetical Works*, vol. 3 (1869) 181-342 and in the work which launched the modern rediscovery of the collection, namely, J. Ernest Rattenbury, *The Eucharistic Hymns of John and Charles Wesley* (London: Epworth, 1948). These hymns constitute the principal testimony to original Wesleyan eucharistic theology, whereas the operative theology of the eucharist in later Methodism can be traced by their large-scale disappearance from liturgical use (some were doubtless in practice always unsingable) and their selective re-emergence (the British have done better than the Americans in this). "Lamb of God, Whose Bleeding Love" is no. 20 in the *Hymns on the Lord's Supper* (henceforth abbreviated as HLS).

11. Ole E. Borgen, *John Wesley on the Sacraments* (Zurich: Publishing House of the United Methodist Church, 1972).

12. HLS 22, verse 2.

13. HLS 21, verse 2.

14. HLS 16.

15. Geoffrey Wainwright, *Eucharist and Eschatology* (London: Epworth, 1971; New York: Oxford University Press, 1981).

16. HLS 99.

17. HLS 57, verse 1.

18. HLS 60, verse 1.

19. HLS 54, verse 5.

20. HLS 102, verse 3.

21. Justin Martyr, *Apology* I. 67.

22. First published in *Hymns and Sacred Poems* (1742), the hymn begins "Away, vain thoughts that stir within." The text is found in *The Poetical Works*, vol. 2 (1869) 246-247.

23. Sermon 23, "The New Birth" (1760), IV:1; in *The Works of John Wesley* (Bicentennial Edition), vol. 2 (Nashville: Abingdon Press, 1985) 196.

24. Ibid. 197.

25. See, for example, Sermon 16, "The Means of Grace" (1746), II.1; in *The Works of John Wesley* (Bicentennial Edition), vol. 1 (Nashville: Abingdon Press, 1984) 381.

26. "The New Birth," IV.2 (p. 197). Wesley's defense of infant baptism is found in a writing he borrowed in 1756 from his father's pen, "A Treatise on Baptism," included in *The Works of John Wesley*, ed. Thomas Jackson, vol. 10 (London: Wesleyan Methodist Book Room, 3rd ed., 1872) 188-201.

27. Bernard G. Holland, *Baptism in Early Methodism* (London: Epworth, 1970).

28. Sermon 101, "The Duty of Constant Communion," (1732; 1787); in *The Works of John Wesley* (Bicentennial Edition), vol. 3 (Nashville: Abingdon Press, 1986) 427-439.

29. "Treatise on Baptism," II:4 (*Works*, ed. Jackson, vol. 10, p. 192).

30. "The New Birth," IV.4 (pp. 199-201).

31. John of Damascus, *On the Orthodox Faith* IV.9 (Migne: *Patrologia Graeca* 94:1120).

32. See David H. Tripp, *The Renewal of the Covenant in the Methodist Tradition* (London: Epworth, 1969).

33. *The Works of John Wesley* (Bicentennial Edition), vol. 18 (Nashville: Abingdon, 1988) 220.

34. Ibid., vol. 19 (1990) 158-159.

35. Sermon 16, "The Means of Grace" (1746); in *The Works of John Wesley* (Bicentennial Edition), vol. 1 (1984) 376-397.

36. *The Works of John Wesley* (Bicentennial Edition), vol. 26 (Nashville: Abingdon, 1982) 575.

37. *The Works of John Wesley* (Bicentennial Edition), vol. 9 (Nashville: Abingdon, 1989) 183-184.

38. See *The Journal of the Rev. John Wesley*, ed. Nehemiah Curnock (London: Epworth, revised edition 1938), vol. 1, 370 (editorial note re Sunday, July 17, 1737); cf. John C. Bowmer, *The Sacrament of the Lord's Supper in Early Methodism* (Westminster: Dacre Press, 1951) 33.

39. "Treatise on Baptism," I.1 (*Works*, ed. Jackson, vol. 10, p. 188), II. 3 (p. 191).

40. *The Works of John Wesley* (Bicentennial Edition), vol. 9, 70-73.

41. See Bowmer, *The Sacrament of the Lord's Supper* 115-118.

42. "The Duty of Constant Communion," II.7-8 (p.433).

43. See *Journal*, ed. Curnock, vol. 5, 291 (editorial note re October 24, 1768), 525-526 (September 5 and 12, 1773); vol. 7, 23 (October 2, 1784).

44. Sermon 39, "Catholic Spirit" (1750), in *The Works of John Wesley* (Bicentennial Edition), vol. 2, 81-95. The "Letter to a Roman Catholic" of 1749 is found in *Works*, ed. Jackson, vol. 10, 80-86; for a modern edition with commentary, see *John Wesley's Letter to a Roman Catholic*, ed. Michael Hurley (London and Dublin: Geoffrey Chapman, 1968).

45. See Norman Sykes, *The Church of England and Non-Episcopal Churches in the Sixteenth and Seventeenth Centuries* (London: SPCK, 1949) and *Old Presbyter and New Priest* (Cambridge: Cambridge University Press, 1956).

46. "The Duty of Constant Communion" (pp.427-439).

47. See Ted A. Campbell, *John Wesley and Christian Antiquity* (Nashville: Abingdon/Kingswood, 1991) 96.

48. Ibid. 49-50.

49. Bowmer, *The Sacrament of the Lord's Supper* 49-58.

50. "Hymns on the Trinity" (1768), in *The Poetical Works*, vol. 7 (1870) 201-348.

51. See Geoffrey Wainwright, "Why Wesley Was a Trinitarian," *The Drew Gateway* 59:2 (Spring 1990) 26-43.

52. Sermon 64, "The New Creation," 18; in *The Works of John Wesley* (Bicentennial Edition), vol. 2, 510.

53. *Letters*, ed. Telford, vol. 5, 270.

54. Sermon 55, "On the Trinity" (1775), 17-18; in *The Works of John Wesley* (Bicentennial Edition), vol. 2, 385.

55. Published in *Hymns and Sacred Poems* (1749), this hymn figured in the definitive *Collection* of 1780 (no. 464). Missing from the British *Methodist Hymn Book* of 1933, it was restored to usage in *The Methodist Service Book* (1975) and *Hymns and Psalms* (1983; no. 580). It does not occur in twentieth-century American Methodist usage.

56. HLS 75.

57. See further chapter 14 in this book and G. Wainwright, "The Doctrine of the Trinity: Where the Church Stands or Falls," *Interpretation* 45 (1991) 117-132.

8

Renewing Worship:
The Recovery of
Classical Patterns

THE RECOVERY OF THE CLASSICAL SUBSTANCE AND FORMS OF CHRISTIAN worship was an aim, and to a considerable degree the achievement, of the modern liturgical movement in both its Catholic and its Protestant manifestations. Never an end in itself, the recovery subserved the active, intelligent participation of the people of God in worship that expressed the Gospel and the faith in their purity and their richness.

This pastoral concern marked already the event from which the twentieth-century liturgical movement in the Roman Catholic Church is conventionally dated: the address of the Belgian Benedictine priest Lambert Beauduin to the Malines conference in 1909 was inspired by the perception that corporate worship is where the lives and belief of the Christian people are shaped.[1] The German Benedictines of the abbey of Maria Laach quickly turned to the early church for the theological undergirding and concrete display of a liturgical practice that embodied the saving mystery of God in Christ. In many countries pastors sought to renew catechesis and to restore the vernacular in worship so that the instruction and active contribution of the faithful might take place under the same conditions as in the early centuries. The witness from such luminous points as St. John's Abbey (Collegeville, Minnesota) and the Centre de Pastorale Liturgique in Paris radiated throughout the Catholic Church, until finally the principles of the liturgical movement were consecrated by the Vatican II Constitution on the Sacred Liturgy, *"Sacrosanctum Concilium."* Normative rites were produced in accordance with that charter for liturgical reform, and the Order for the Christian Initiation of Adults (1972) and the Missal of 1969-1970 in particular put a clearer scriptural and patristic stamp upon patterns of worship that had been obscured by medieval and later developments.[2]

Meanwhile, many Protestant Churches had also been engaging in a liturgical movement. The starting points, themselves somewhat varied, were certainly different from the Roman Catholic. In Protestantism it was less a matter of scraping away ritual accretions than of recapturing the fullness of a sacramental celebration in which gesture and object allowed the word to be seen—and indeed handled (1 Jn 1:1) and tasted (Heb 6:4f. and 1 Pt 2:3)—as well as heard. In Protestantism the vernacular was already in use, even if there was to grow up a concern about the effects of cultural secularization upon ecclesial language and symbols. A first historical reference point for modern Protestant renewal was the liturgical intentions of the Reformers: Luther, Calvin, and the English had, for instance, all considered that Sunday worship properly included the communion of the people at the Lord's Supper. But in some respects the sixteenth-century Protestants had remained prisoners of the medieval system against which they were rebelling; so the twentieth-century revisers had to return as far back as the patristic period in order to discover the liturgical expression the earliest church had given to an apostolic Gospel and faith about whose expression in worship the canonical Scriptures say tantalizingly little. And here the Protestant scholars found Catholic colleagues already at work. The extent of their agreed conclusions finds striking expression in such landmark documents as the Episcopal Church's *Book of Common Prayer* (1976)[3] and *The Lutheran Book of Worship* (1978), and somewhat less stably in the "worship resources" produced by the United Methodist and the Presbyterian Churches in the 1970s and 1980s and their intentionally pluralistic *Book of Worship* (Methodist, 1992) and *Book of Common Worship* (Presbyterian, 1993).

In what follows, we shall concentrate on four areas in which the recovery of classical, patristic forms has taken effect: (1) the recapture of the paschal mystery of Christ's death and resurrection as the pivot of salvation history; (2) the restoration of a full pattern of

Christian initiation, including catechesis, baptism in water and the Spirit, and first communion; (3) the return to a service of word and table as the regular fare of Sunday worship; (4) the repossession of rite and symbol as means of communication in the dialogue between God and humankind. Each of these moves will appear not merely as backward-looking but as having a future orientation as well. Nevertheless we shall have cause to wonder whether they are in danger of fading before they have achieved lasting results.

THE PASCHAL MYSTERY

At a time when the history-of-religions school was making the most of the similarities between early Christian sacraments and pagan rites, Odo Casel's theology of the Christian mysteries came under suspicion of forfeiting their special character by attributing a hellenistic derivation to them.[4] But in fact, biblical theology did not have too far to seek for a deeper scriptural background to his notion that Christ's death and resurrection stand at the heart of the Pauline kerygma and that Christians are given through baptism and eucharist a saving share in the redemption gained by Christ's work. The "memorial" that the sacraments constituted of the original Easter mystery was foreshadowed by the Passover rites in which the children of Israel reappropriated the Lord's deliverance of their ancestors from Egyptian bondage. In the Old Testament a "memorial" is a divinely instituted object or action by which human beings call on God in their thankfulness or need in order that God may extend or renew the divine blessings to them. In the New Testament the Lord Jesus on eve of his passion instituted the eucharist as his memorial in order that his death be proclaimed until he come again. By that means, Christians continue to draw on the benefits of his redeeming work that are first sealed to them in their baptism into Christ according to the institution of the risen Lord.

The original paschal mystery of Jesus was a trinitarian event: "Christ through the eternal Spirit offered himself to God" (Heb 9:14). And "if the Spirit of him who raised Jesus from the dead dwells in you, he who raised Christ Jesus from the dead will give life to your mortal bodies also through his Spirit which dwells in you" (Rom 8:11). Correspondingly, baptism into Christ's death and resurrection is performed "in the name of the Father and of the Son and of the Holy Spirit" (Mt 28:19). And the Christian eucharist follows the pattern of Ephesians 2:18: "Through Christ we have access in one Spirit to the Father."

The WCC Faith and Order text on *Baptism, Eucharist and Ministry* sets out "the meaning of the eucharist" in its paschal and trinitarian dimensions with particular clarity.[5] The eucharist is presented as "thanksgiving to the Father," "memorial of Christ," "invocation of the Spirit," "communion of the faithful," and "meal of the kingdom." The official Roman Catholic response to this "Lima text" recognizes well the procedures of Faith and Order, which are in fact those learned in the liturgical movement right across the ecumenical board:

> The sources employed for the interpretation of the mystery of the eucharist and the form of celebration are scripture and tradition. The classical liturgies of the first millennium and patristic theology are important points of reference in this text ... It presents a strong christological dimension, identifying the mystery of the eucharist in various ways with the real presence of the risen Lord and his sacrifice on the cross ... The presentation of the mystery of the eucharist follows the flow of classical eucharistic liturgies, with the eucharistic theology drawing heavily on the content of the traditional prayer and symbolic actions of these liturgies. The text draws on patristic sources for additional explication of the mystery of the eucharist. There is strong emphasis on the Trinitarian dimension. The source and goal of the eucharist is identified as the Trinity ... There is a strong eschatological dimension. The eucharist is viewed as a foretaste of Christ's parousia and of the final kingdom, given through the Spirit.[6]

The appreciation shown by the churches' responses for the structure and content of the eucharistic section of the Lima text are in fact so overwhelmingly positive that we may confidently declare them to be in principle very close to a common mind on the matter. Such doctrinal and practical convergence is indisputably a fruit of the ecumenical liturgical movement and this movement's recovery of classical patterns.

Another excellent example of ecumenical convergence on the paschal and trinitarian character of a matching pattern of worship (*"lex orandi"*) and pattern of belief (*"lex credendi"*) occurs in the renewal of the Easter Vigil in the Roman Catholic Church (since

1951) and its introduction in many Protestant Churches. An order of service is found in the Episcopal *Book of Common Prayer* (1976) and in the minister's edition of the *Lutheran Book of Worship* (1978), in *The United Methodist Book of Worship* (1992) and in the Presbyterian *Book of Common Worship* (1993). The Easter Vigil liturgies bring out in its full scope the "mystery" of God's eternal saving purpose for the whole world, now revealed in Christ, and one day to be completed (Mk 4:11; Rom 16:25-27; 1 Cor 2:7; Eph 1:9-10; 3:1-12; Col 1:25-27; 2:2-3; 1 Tim 3:16; Rv 10:7). The Old Testament scripture readings display the mighty redemptive acts of God, especially through death-dealing and life-giving water as in the Exodus, looking forward to the "baptism" of Christ in his death and resurrection. "This night" (the *haec nox* of the Easter proclamation) is traditionally the preeminent occasion for the baptism of Christians, and so the waters of the font are blessed. If there are no candidates, then at least the faithful are invited to renew their baptismal profession. Easter communion follows, an anticipation (as always) of the feast in the messianic kingdom and especially appropriate at a season when the eschatological prospect of Christ's return has traditionally been strong.

CHRISTIAN INITIATION

Baptism is the climax of a more or less extended period of preparation for entry into the church and gives access to a continuing life of communicant membership. There is no doubt that the classical process of Christian initiation was constructed with intelligent and active subjects in view. Whatever the pros and cons of baptizing infants, it has always been in their case a matter of "retrieving" at a later date those elements which, whatever they were decided to be and with whatever nuances their lack was understood, could not in the nature of things be present at the baptism of an infant (catechesis? personal profession of faith? "confirmation"? communion?). From various starting points in the different churches, the modern liturgical movement has reverted to a classical ritual of initiation developed in the patristic period, stretching from (or at least presupposing) evangelization and catechesis, climaxing in baptism in water and the Spirit, and introducing the new Christian to eucharistic communion. The Roman Catholic Order for the Christian Initiation of Adults is the most complete example; and the "adaptation to the true condition of infants" which Vatican II called for in the case of their baptism was felt to be so extensive that a separate Order for the Baptism of Infants (1969) was also formulated. The tendency in most Protestant revisions has been rather the reverse one of bringing baptismal candidates of all ages and conditions into a single rite, with minimal rubrical adaptation to the case of those unable to answer for themselves.

Differences over the location of infants in relation to the church undoubtedly reflect tensions in ecclesiology, as the responses of the churches to *Baptism, Eucharist and Ministry* continue to show. Yet these responses also allow the hope that "the churches are coming to an understanding of initiation as a unitary and comprehensive process, even if its different elements are spread over a period of time." And substantively, "the total process vividly embodies the coherence of God's gracious initiative in eliciting our faith."[7]

Again, the Roman Catholic response to BEM pinpoints well the sources and methods of the section on baptism:

> It draws in a balanced way from the major New Testament areas of teaching about baptism; it gives an important place to the witness of the early church. While it does not discuss all major doctrinal issues that have arisen about baptism, it is sensitive to the effect that they have had on the development of the understanding of this sacrament and to the positive values of differing solutions that emerged; it appreciates the normative force that some forms of liturgical celebration may have and the significance of pastoral practice; within the ecumenical scope it sets for itself, it articulates the development of the Christian understanding of baptism with a coherent theological method.[8]

Since these are also the sources and methods of the ecumenical liturgical movement, it is not surprising that the Roman Catholic response should also note that the baptismal section of the Lima text "has many affinities, both of style and of content, with the way the faith of the church about baptism is stated in the Second Vatican Council and in the Liturgy of Christian Initiation promulgated by Pope Paul VI."[9]

With the varied qualifications already mentioned in connection with infants (which reflect differences among themselves over the role of personal faith), many churches would, according to their own responses to BEM, clearly subscribe to the substantial summary made in the Roman Catholic response:

(a) Baptism is confessed to be the gift and work of the Trinitarian God [1, 7, 17]. Faith in the Trinity allows the text to deal profoundly with the Christ-centredness of baptism and with the role correspondingly played in it by the Holy Spirit [4, 5, 7, 14].

(b) The practice of baptism is an integral part of God's plan to gather all into his kingdom through the church, in which the mission of Christ is continued through the Spirit [1, 7, 10].

(c) Baptism is a sacramental reality. The text calls baptism a sacrament [23 and Commentary 13]. But it deals with the question, not so much by using the word (which, because of its complex history, needs a great deal of explanation in inter-church conversations) as by affirming the principal features of baptism that the word sacrament has served to express. It says:

(i) Baptism is a sign [2, 18], with definite ritual requirements [17, 20], celebrated in and by the church [12, 22, 23]; it is a sign of the faith of the church [12], of its faith in Christ and in the new life that he inaugurated in his paschal mystery [2, 3, 4], of its faith in the gift of the Holy Spirit in whom this life is shared [5].

(ii) Participation in Christ's death and the gift of the Holy Spirit are both signified and effected by baptism [14].

(iii) The effective sign that is baptism was inaugurated by Jesus [1].

(iv) Baptism is both God's gift to us and our human response to that gift [8]. The gift that it signifies and effects is the washing away and overcoming of sin [2, 3], conversion, pardon, and justification [3, 4], incorporation into Christ [6], moral sanctity [4] of which the Holy Spirit is the source and seal [5], the making of men and women to be sons and daughters of God in Christ the Son [5], who will finally enter their full inheritance to the praise of the glory of God [5]. Our response is faith [8], confession of sin and conversion [4], life-long moral effort, under the transforming power of grace, to grow in the likeness of Christ [9], and work for the coming of the kingdom of God on earth as in heaven [7, 10].

(v) Baptism, in making us one with Christ, makes us one
with each other and "with the church of every time and
place" [6]; it signs and seals us in this common fellowship
[6] and is an unrepeatable act [13].[10]

These are precisely the themes that come through in modern
revisions of initiatory rites in Protestant Churches under the influence of the liturgical movement, often in considerable verbal enrichment, and certainly with ritual enhancement, in comparison with
the older Protestant services. They are indebted to the ancient
church order of the so-called *Apostolic Tradition* of Hipploytus as
well as to the various surviving series of catechetical lectures by
which bishops in the patristic age explained the rites of Christian
initiation to candidates or neophytes. One notes in particular three
examples. First, a fuller ritual expression of conversion is often
provided in the form of questions and answers concerning the
renunciation of sin and evil and the threefold interrogation that
invites profession of faith in the Holy Trinity in the words of the
traditional western baptismal creed, the Apostles' Creed. Second, a
prayer of thanksgiving over the baptismal water rehearses the
history of salvation and looks forward to the final consummation.
Third, a pneumatological sign is often provided in a prayer of
invocation, an imposition of hands, or an anointing that calls down
the Holy Spirit upon those being baptized.

Churches that practice initiation in such ways, and people who
undergo these rites, find brought home to them the particular place
which the church occupies in God's saving purpose, which yet is
comprehensive in scope. The privileges and responsibilities of adherence to the Christian faith are granted to the evangelized who in
turn become the evangelizing.

WORD AND TABLE

It is possible that the Emmaus story of Luke 24:13-35 reflects a
primitive Christian service of word and table: as on the first Easter
Sunday, the risen Lord expounds to his disciples the Scriptures
concerning him and then makes himself known to them in the
breaking of the bread. On "the first day of the week," the Christians
at Troas gather together "to break bread" and listen to the apostle
Paul (Acts 20:7-11). Certainly by the middle of the second century
Justin Martyr reports the regular Sunday assembly of the Christians
in Rome for the celebration of word and sacrament:

And on the day called Sunday an assembly is held in one place of all who live in town or country, and the records of the apostles or the writings of the prophets are read as time allows. Then, when the reader has finished, the president in a discourse admonishes and exhorts us to imitate these good things. Then we all stand up together and send up prayers; and as we said before, when we have finished praying, bread and wine and water are brought up, and the president likewise sends up prayers and thanksgivings to the best of his ability, and the people assent, saying the Amen; and the elements over which thanks have been given are distributed, and everyone partakes; and they are sent through the deacons to those who are not present . . .

And we all assemble together on Sunday, because it is the first day, on which God transformed darkness and matter, and made the world; and Jesus Christ our Savior rose from the dead on that day.[11]

In the first centuries, to be a Christian meant gathering for Sunday worship and receiving communion (the sick and the imprisoned were included through the ministry of the deacons), and only Christians were admitted to the assemblies. With the conversion of the Empire and then of the Germanic nations, things changed. Others were admitted at least to hear the Scriptures and the preaching, while many of the hastily baptized then refrained from communion. Into the Middle Ages Masses were multiplied as a propitiatory sacrifice, while lay communion declined to an annual event. Luther, Calvin, and the English Reformers sought to restore weekly communion, but the Lord's Supper was to be celebrated only if sufficient communicants announced themselves. The unhabituated could not be persuaded, and so the attempt to restore a primitive and early pattern of Sunday worship largely failed, leaving a service of Scriptures, sermon, and prayers as the regular fare for Protestants. Some knew better, but could not prevail. Thus, at a time when Anglican parishes held the communion service but four times a year, John Wesley in a letter of 10 September 1784 advised his North American elders to "administer the Supper of the Lord on every Lord's day," his choice of terms demonstrating the eschatological link between the resurrection, the sacrament, and the life of the Lord's people.

The most successful effort to encourage increased lay communion in the Roman Catholic Church began under Pope Pius X at the turn into the twentieth century. Belatedly, Catholics joined in the biblical revival, and by the time of the official liturgical reforms initiated by Vatican II they were in a position to produce a Sunday lectionary that restored an Old Testament lesson to the epistle and gospel of the Mass; and Vatican II's Constitution on the Sacred Liturgy declared the homily to be an integral part of the Mass. On the Anglican and Protestant side, it has been a matter of increasing the frequency of eucharistic celebrations, either through the "parish communion" movement or by seeking to include the sacrament in the "main service."

On almost all sides, official liturgical revisions in the second half of the twentieth century have recognized that Christian Sunday worship, in its fullness, includes both word and table. This is clearly stated in the Lima text on *Baptism, Eucharist and Ministry*, and in one way or another practically all church responses accept this, whatever their respective difficulties of implementation. It is not simply a question of an antiquarian return to early tradition (although even such an ostensibly unlikely instance as the Swiss Protestant Church Federation declares that "celebration [of the Lord's Supper] every Sunday is in line with biblical tradition"[12]). Rather, the ancient tradition is seen to have permanent theological advantages.

Here are but three examples. First, contemporary Orthodox theologians have taught us to recognize that the Sunday service is "the sacrament of assembly."[13] Vatican II's Constitution on the Sacred Liturgy calls the worship assembly "the principal manifestation of the Church" (*praecipua manifestatio ecclesiae*). Classical Protestants should have no difficulty with the idea that the church is "a congregation of faithful people in which the pure word is preached and the sacraments are observed according to the gospel" (cf. Augsburg Confession, 7, Anglican Articles, 19, etc.). Nor is recognition of the corporate, communal nature of the church any impediment to insistence on the dispersal of its members for evangelism, service, and holy living. Rather, Christians feed on word and sacrament for what the Orthodox have taken to calling "the liturgy after the Liturgy."

Second, the regular service of word and sacrament brings out, as the Roman Catholic liturgist Emil Joseph Lengeling has emphasized, the dialogical character of the relationship between God and the people of God.[14] To God's addressing us in the Scriptures and the sermon we respond by the confession of faith and prayers. In particular, the great prayer of thanksgiving for creation and redemption prepares for God to communicate to us again, through the eating of the bread and the drinking of the wine, every good and perfect gift and the blessings of salvation.

Third, the service of word and sacrament recognizes the theo-anthropological fact and incarnational confession that humans are intelligent, sensate beings destined in Christ for a final resurrection and the eternal praise of God and feasting in the divine kingdom. As the response of the United Methodist Church to *Baptism, Eucharist and Ministry* declares, in the eucharistic liturgy of pulpit and altar "God's effectual word is revealed, proclaimed, heard, seen and tasted"[15]—to which we may add "touched" (1 Jn 1:1) and "smelled" (2 Cor 2:14-16).

SIGNS AND SYMBOLS

In the twentieth century the human sciences have devoted sustained attention to the complex systems of symbols—words, gestures, objects, even institutions—by which people and communities explore, describe, interpret, and fashion reality, express and form their thoughts, emotions, and values, and communicate across time and space in ways that both build and convey traditions as well as both allowing and reflecting social relations in the present. Linguistic philosophy speaks of "performative language," or "how to do things with words" (to borrow the title of J.L. Austin's book). Hermeneutical theory emphasizes the importance of a tradition in the "reading" of "texts," broadly understood. Semiotics uncovers the structures and dynamics of the processes of signification. Ritual studies examine the consecrated ways by which groups of people define and maintain their identity and place in the world.

Now the Christian liturgy is a complex system of signs, a rich "speech-act" (*Sprachhandlung*), a locus of communication. Christians do not, of course, remain content with a purely humanistic account of the liturgy, since they believe it is God who invites its celebration, before whom it is performed, and from whom it receives its vital power. But, perhaps at first in rather an amateur fashion and then with increasing attention to the human sciences, Christian liturgists in the twentieth century have sought to improve the significant, communicative, and effective quality of the church's worship.

In Roman Catholicism it was a matter of laying bare again the main lines of rites whose sequence of principal moments had been obscured by the interpolation of many secondary and tertiary items and ceremonies, and of simplifying the postures and gestures of the ministers in particular (compare, for instance, the actions of the presider at the new eucharistic prayers with his performance in the pre-Vatican II missal). Catholics were helped to return to a pristine clarity and crispness in their ritual and ceremonial by reversing the secondary and tertiary developments described by Josef A. Jungmann in his "genetic explication" of the Roman Mass (*Missarum Sollemnia*).

With Protestants it has been more a matter of overcoming the suspicion of rite and ceremony that resulted from the overcorrection brought in the sixteenth century to the abuses of medieval liturgy. It was again to the patristic period that twentieth-century Protestants turned for the enrichment of the symbolic texture of their worship, in the reasonable trust that the early church had given appropriate expression to themes at which the apostolic Scriptures only hint. Thus the "kiss of peace" has been widely reintroduced (cf. Rom 16:16; 1 Cor 16:20; 2 Cor 13:12; 1 Thes 5:26; 1 Pt 5:14; Justin, *Apology* I. 65); a lighted candle may be presented to the newly baptized, or "enlightened" (cf. Eph 5:14; Heb 6:4; 10:32; 1 Pt 2:9; Justin, *Apology* I. 65); an anointing, or at least an imposition of hands, may betoken the unction of the Holy Spirit (cf. 2 Cor 1:21-22; Eph 1:13; 1 Jn 2:20, 27).

In this way, George Lindbeck's notion of doctrine as the "grammatical rules" of the church as a "cultural-linguistic" community can find its proper location in the more complex reality of an ongoing tradition in which the "*lex orandi*" and the "*lex credendi*" are more intimately related than Lindbeck brings out.[16] A deeper replunging into its own tradition will, in my judgment, be necessary if the church is to survive in recognizable form, particularly in our western culture.[17]

****

We have spoken of the saving purpose of the triune God—Father, Son, and Holy Spirit—for the world. We have spoken of a history of redemption focused on the paschal mystery of Christ's death and resurrection. We have spoken of initiation into the church as a distinct community, privileged with divine blessing and responsible for evangelization. We have spoken of a living dialogue and communion between God and God's assembled people. We have spoken of a particularistic Christian use of natural and cultural symbols. We have done all this in terms of the contribution of the liturgical movement, which joined in a remarkable confluence and interaction with several other movements in the life of the church that all reached their most significant development in the second third of the twentieth century: biblical theology, the return to the patristic sources, the ecclesiological renewal, the ecumenical movement. By the liturgical channel, these concerns passed into the life of the churches through the revised worship books of the 1970s.

If these things are not happening in your church, then either the liturgical movement has passed you by, or someone thinks your church has already outgrown it (there are disturbing signs of loss in, for instance, the 1986 *Book of Worship* of the United Church of Christ and the 1989 *Supplemental Liturgical Texts: Prayer Book Studies 30* of the Episcopal Church). My own hunch is that the liturgical movement of the twentieth century will have served, first, to make the Roman Catholic Church more biblically faithful and, second, to reintroduce many Protestants to the riches of the ancient tradition. When the next great testing of the spirits comes, the liturgical movement will thus have helped to maximize the number of those who stay with historic Christianity while others depart into doctrinally, morally, and institutionally unrecognizable forms.

Notes

1. See A. Haquin, *Dom Lambert Beauduin et le renouveau liturgique* (Gembloux: Duculot, 1976).

2. Annibale Bugnini, *The Reform of the Liturgy 1948-1975*, trans. Matthew J. O'Connell (Collegeville: The Liturgical Press, 1990).

3. See Thaddaeus A. Schnitker, *The Church's Worship: The 1979 American Book of Common Prayer in a Historical Perspective* (Frankfurt and New York: Peter Lang, 1989).

4. Casel was a monk of Maria Laach. Several of his important studies are assembled in his *The Mystery of Christian Worship* (Westminster, MD: Newman Press, 1962).

5. *Baptism, Eucharist and Ministry*, Faith and Order Paper no. 111 (Geneva: World Council of Churches, 1982).

6. In Max Thurian, ed., *Churches Respond to BEM*, vol. 6 (Geneva: World Council of Churches, 1988) 1-40, esp. 16-17.

7. *Baptism, Eucharist and Ministry 1982-1990: Report on the Process and Responses*, Faith and Order Paper no. 149 (Geneva: World Council of Churches, 1990), in particular 44-51, 112.

8. Thurian, *Churches Respond to BEM*, vol. 6, pp. 9-10.

9. Ibid.

10. Ibid. 10-11.

11. Justin Martyr, *Apology* I. 67.

12. Thurian, *Churches Respond to BEM*, vol. 6, p. 83.

13. Notably Nicolas Afanassieff, "Le Sacrement de l'assemblée," *Internationale Kirchliche Zeitschrift* 46 (1956) 200-213; then John Zizioulas, *Being as Communion* (Crestwood, NY: St. Vladimir's Seminary Press, 1985), and Alexander Schmemann, *The Eucharist* (Crestwood, NY: St. Vladimir's Seminary Press, 1987).

14. Emil Joseph Lengeling, *Liturgie: Dialog zwischen Gott und Mensch* (Freiburg: Herder, 1981).

15. In Max Thurian, *Churches Respond to BEM*, vol. 2 (Geneva: World Council of Churches, 1986) 188.

16. See George A. Lindbeck, *The Nature of Doctrine* (Philadelphia: Westminster Press, 1984).

17. For a compatible approach to the church as a liturgico-linguistic community, see Helen Kathleen Hughes, "Understanding the Nature and Function of Liturgical Language: A Narrative Approach," in *The Language of the Liturgy: Some Theoretical and Practical Implications* (Washington: International Commission on English in the Liturgy, 1984) 2-18, and Geoffrey Wainwright, "Divided by a Common Language? A Comparison and Contrast of Recent Liturgical Revision in the United Kingdom, the United States of America and Australia," *Studia Liturgica* 17 (1987) 241-255; reprinted and updated as Chapter 9 of this volume.

9

Divided by a Common Language?

A Comparison and Contrast of Liturgical Revision in the United Kingdom, the United States of America, and Australia

IN CHURCH AND LITURGY THE COMMONALITIES BETWEEN BRITAIN AND AMERICA are complex. The differences are complicated by independent developments and, particularly in the United States, by the intrusion of other-language factors. The ironies are subtle indeed. Moreover, the wit who spoke of Britain and America as two nations divided by a common language had not yet even heard of "Strine" (= Australian).

THE CONTEXTS

Britain itself underwent the Reformation in an English and in a Scottish form, and later the Church of England was not able to contain the Methodists. Following the American revolution, the Methodist Episcopal Church, though unestablished, became the largest Protestant Church in the country. The American Anglicans owe more to the Prayer Book of 1549 than to that of 1552/1662, and they got their first bishop and their liturgical tradition by way of the small Episcopal Church in Scotland.[1] Scots Presbyterians were the chief shapers of the Presbyterian churches in the United States. English Independents left their mark on New England Congregationalists, though these by now liberal Christians have been joined since 1958 in a problematic union—the United Church of Christ (UCC)—with the Evangelical and Reformed of German descent. The Evangelical and Reformed had been the cradle of the incarnational, sacramental, and liturgical Mercersburg Movement

141

in the nineteenth century, itself inspired by the Scots-Irish J.W. Nevin and indebted to the Irvingite Catholic Apostolics.[2] The Baptists, largely of English descent, have become a dominant force ecclesiastically and culturally in the southern states. In the Midwest, Lutherans from Scandinavia and the European continent settled large areas and, in the present century, they have overcome their linguistic isolation. Eastern and Oriental Orthodox of several jurisdictions have remained ecclesiastically unassimilated, although the English-speaking Orthodox Church of America is attracting members beyond its Russian origins. Black churches of a pentecostal type now have their counterparts in many British cities.

The Australian story stretches from the "triumphant nomads" of the Aboriginal culture, through first the settlement from those "distant" British Isles, both English and Celtic, then the inclusion of Mediterraneans in white Australia, and now to the immigrations from Asia and the multiculturalist policy that "Australia is for all."[3]

The Roman Catholic Church, shifting after Vatican II from Latin straight to the contemporary vernacular, has through its own ICEL (International Commission on English in the Liturgy) and the ecumenical ICET (International Consultation on English Texts) exercised great influence in all English-speaking countries on the language as well as the structures of revised liturgies in many Protestant Churches.

Church attendance throughout the United States is far stronger than anywhere in Britain, although a pluralistic atmosphere has greatly weakened particular denominational allegiances. More broadly, American church life tends to be divided between the "liberal," the "conservative," and the (now not so) "mainstream." The churches in Australia seem to be experiencing the secularization of society in a form more akin to the West European.

Having set this cultural and ecclesiastical context, let us now compare and contrast recent liturgical revision in Britain, America, and Australia, paying attention to "the language of the rite," i.e., not only the words but the whole communicative system that comes to expression in worship.[4] We shall chiefly draw on service-books, which at least serve to indicate official norms. The limitations of this method are that it puts the unbookish churches at a disadvantage and, in any case, leaves open the question of how books are actually used in churches that have them. Nevertheless, these constraints are required in order to make the available material even somewhat manageable.

THE TEXTS

To list the principal texts, first geographically. The Church of Scotland produced in 1979 a revised *Book of Common Order* (BCO) and then in 1994 a quite different and much expanded one. In the Episcopal Church in Scotland, the "Grey Bookie" of 1970 and *The Experimental Liturgy* of 1977 were succeeded by the "libretto azzuro"[5] of the *Scottish Liturgy* of 1982, authorized "for permissive use"; a new ordinal appeared in 1984; theological and practical variety regarding Christian initiation has, however, so far prevented the publication of unified new rites in that area. The Church of England worked through the alternative services of baptism, communion, and the daily offices in a series numbered from one to three, with various fractions in between, before arriving in 1980 at its *Alternative Service Book* (ASB). The United Reformed Church in England and Wales (URC) succeeded within eight years of its own inception in producing in 1980 a complete *Book of Services* and then in 1989 another *Service Book*. The Methodist Church completed a new *Methodist Service Book* (MSB) in 1975. The Church in Wales and the Church of Ireland produced modest revisions of their respective Prayer Books in 1984.

In the United States, the Episcopal Church ran through a series of blue, olive, and zebra covers before finally attaining to a revised *Book of Common Prayer* (BCP), substantially concluded in 1976 and definitively authorized in 1979. The *Lutheran Book of Worship* (LBW) of 1978 crowned the labors of the Inter-Lutheran Commission.[6] The *Methodist Book of Worship* of 1964 stood in the line of Cranmerian and Wesleyan renewal, whereas the 'seventies and early 'eighties saw a long series of "supplemental worship resources" (SWR) which partly resulted in *The Book of Services* for the United Methodist Church (1985) and then *The United Methodist Book of Worship* (1992). With its *Service for the Lord's Day* (SLD), the newly inaugurated Presbyterian Church, U.S.A.—together with the small Cumberland Presbyterian Church—started in 1984 to provide "supplemental liturgical resources" beyond the joint *Worshipbook* of 1972; the final result was a *Book of Common Worship* (BCW, 1993). In its swinging liberalism, the United Church of Christ has neglected the often excellent *Services of the Church* (1969) composed by such distinguished liturgists as Bard Thompson and Horton Davies and has produced instead a *Book of Worship* (1986) where the name of Father, Son and Holy Spirit has almost entirely disappeared.

In Australia revisions and experimentation in the 1960s and 1970s led the Anglican Church to *An Australian Prayer Book* (AAPB, 1978), which was intended as a "supplement" to the BCP. Its "first orders" conservatively update the archaisms of 1662 language, whereas its "second orders" are intentionally more "radical" in their changes of liturgical structure and formulation. These moves have been taken further in *A Prayer Book for Australia* (APBA, 1995). Since its inception in 1977, the Uniting Church in Australia (UCA)—of former Methodists, Presbyterians, and Congregationalists—has through its Commission on Liturgy produced several booklets for eucharistic worship and the occasional offices and finally *Uniting in Worship* (1988).

One could also run through these productions again, aligning them not on a geographical grid but rather a confessional: Anglican, Reformed, Methodist, Lutheran, United. Suffice it instead to add that the British Joint Liturgical Group (JLG), on which the Anglican, Methodist, and Reformed traditions as well as the Roman Catholic and the Baptist are officially represented, has since 1963 wielded considerable influence on revisions throughout the United Kingdom. The American Consultation on Church Union (COCU) put forth an *Order for the Celebration of Holy Baptism* (1973) and eucharistic orders in an *Order of Worship for the Proclamation of the Word of God and the Celebration of the Lord's Supper* (1968), *Word, Bread, Cup* (1978), and *The Sacrament of the Lord's Supper: A New Text* (1982; 1984). An unofficial ecumenical committee for a common eucharistic prayer in 1975 composed a text close to the eastern-style Eucharistic Prayer IV of the Roman Missal of 1969-1970 which has been taken up, with slight variants and varying degrees of authority, among Episcopalians, Methodists, Presbyterians, and Lutherans in the United States. Further, an American ecumenical Consultation on Common Texts has been working semi-officially on lectionary questions in particular, and its concerns have been made international in the English Language Liturgical Consultation (ELLC). In Australia, the Anglican and the Uniting Church went to a common source—Dr. Leatherland, I presume—for some of their eucharistic prayers. Finally, several churches in Britain, America, and Australia have begun to consider their liturgical life in light of *Baptism, Eucharist and Ministry* (BEM), the "Lima text" of the Faith and Order Commission of the World Council of Churches.

Those, then, are the materials which will allow us to examine contemporary liturgico-linguistic communities in Britain, the United

States, and Australia.[7] We shall treat, first, admission to the liturgico-
linguistic community, or the patterns of "Christian initiation"; second, the assembly of the liturgico-linguistic community, or the
ritual and personal structures of the Sunday service; third, the story
of the liturgico-linguistic community, or its use of the Scriptures;
fourth, the praise and prayers of the liturgico-linguistic community,
and principally the eucharistic anaphora; fifth, the experience of
time in the liturgico-linguistic community, or calendrical questions;
sixth and last, the interaction of the liturgico-linguistic community
with the surrounding culture, focusing on language questions in the
narrower sense.

THE LITURGICO-LINGUISTIC COMMUNITY

Admission to the Liturgico-Linguistic Community

When and where accession to the church cannot be taken for
granted, deliberate attention must be paid to the patterns of Christian initiation. The Roman *Ordo Initiationis Christianae Adultorum* of
1972 was perhaps the most carefully wrought of the post-conciliar
rites, reestablishing a patristic pattern that began with admission to
the catechumenate, reached its climax in baptism, confirmation,
and first communion, and went on to mystagogical catechesis. The
pattern has importance not only in new areas of evangelization but
also in situations where society at large is becoming dechristianized.
Infant baptism is practiced by all churches whose texts we are
surveying, but there appears to be a distinct trend towards a single
structure of initiation, and that primarily directed to the admission
of believers, with such deliberately minimal adaptations as are
necessary when the baptismal part is being administered to infants.
That is especially clear in the Church of England's ASB, in the
"second orders" of AAPB and in APBA, and in the English free
church rites of the URC and the Methodists, as well as among
American Episcopalians (BCP 1979) and Presbyterians (BCW, 1993).
In a curious counter-movement, the Roman *Ordo Baptismi Parvulorum*
of 1969 goes so far in following the instruction of Vatican II to
provide a rite that is "adapted to the true condition of infants" that
some have begun to wonder whether—as in some Protestant circles
in the recent past—there are not two rather distinct understandings
and practices of baptism, infant and believers'. The Uniting Church
in Australia seemed to hesitate between the two in its *Baptism and*

Related Services of 1981, and *Uniting in Worship* (1988) lays out two distinct services for "Baptism" and "The Baptism of a Child."

The national churches in England and Scotland are keener than the free churches there to use the full language of "membership" in reference to infant baptism, but they do not appear to contemplate the uninterrupted continuance of sacramental life in those thus sacramentally "regenerated" or "grafted into Christ." The American Episcopalian BCP moved earliest in bringing all the sacramental moments of initiation together even in the case of infants: it mandates a pneumatological prayer and imposition of hands, with optional unction, immediately after baptism, and it leaves open the possibility that infants also may be given communion.[8] (Historically, the BCP revisers accepted Marion Hatchett's thesis that Cranmer's post-baptismal consignation leaned towards confirmation[9]—a position that left their English confreres so unimpressed that in the ASB they allow the consignation to be shifted to a catechumenal place before baptism.) The LBW and now *The United Methodist Book of Worship* (1992) and the Presbyterian *Book of Common Worship* (1993) also provide for a rite of the Spirit to follow directly on water baptism. Among Episcopalians, Lutherans, Methodists, and Presbyterians in the United States, there is a practical tendency to lower the age at which communion may be regularly received, and the liturgical revisers in all four traditions sought to reduce later "confirmation" to one of a possible series of other affirmations or reaffirmations of the baptismal faith, although this reduction has met with episcopal or popular resistance.

All four traditions do, however, provide for specific and repeated renewals of the human side of baptism. Liturgically, they have been influenced by the "renewal of baptismal vows" which was introduced into the Roman Catholic service of the Paschal Vigil in 1951/1955. British Methodists retained the Wesleyan custom of an annual covenant service; and such a rite is now provided, with Reformed nuances, in the Scottish 1994 BCO. The English Anglican ASB also provides for a baptismal renewal at Easter or on other occasions. This growing movement responds to a felt need for individual support and ecclesial cohesion at a time when the faith is under threat. It may also supply proper ritual satisfaction for those who disturbingly seek a "second baptism" when they have come to a powerful experience of the new birth which had already been sacramentally signified to them earlier. The *experience* of being "born again" is not to be sneezed at when it occurs amid a culture in which Christianity has sunk into formality or even oblivion.

In *Uniting in Worship* the Uniting Church in Australia has not only provided a "covenant service" after the British Methodist pattern of 1975 and a "congregational reaffirmation of baptism" for use particularly at Easter and Pentecost; it has also supplied for individual or small-group cases of spiritual awakening a "celebration of new beginnings in faith" and a "personal reaffirmation of baptism"; opportunities are given for people to bear testimony before the congregation and to receive assurance of its encouragement and rejoicing. The baptismal character of the entire life of a Christian was stated in the aim of the North American Inter-Lutheran Commission "to restore to Holy Baptism the liturgical rank and dignity implied by Lutheran theology, and to draw out the baptismal motifs in such acts as the confession of sin and the burial of the dead."[10]

The Assembly of the Liturgico-Linguistic Community

There is a growing recognition among the Reformed and the Methodists of the propriety of celebrating (in Wesley's words to the American Methodists in 1784) "the Supper of the Lord on every Lord's Day."[11] The British *Methodist Service Book* declares that "the worship of the Church is the offering of praise and prayer in which God's Word is read and preached, and in its fullness it includes the Lord's Supper, or Holy Communion." The American Methodists present their Sunday service as "Word and Table" (1976). The Scottish 1979 BCO, in words we find echoed in the URC books of 1980 and 1989, declared "the normative character of the service of word and sacrament which . . . was undoubtedly recognized by the Reformers as it has been down the centuries by the universal Church." The American Presbyterians bring out the dominical and resurrectional accents of the service and the day that were probably implied in the phrase Wesley had used to the American Methodists in 1784. They write in BCW 1993:

> From its beginning, the Christian community has gathered on the first day of the week to hear the Scriptures read and proclaimed and to celebrate the Lord's Supper. This day has special significance since it was on "the first day of the week" that Jesus' followers discovered the empty tomb and met the risen

> Lord . . . Gathered on the Lord's Day, Christians celebrate the
> age to come, which was revealed in the risen Christ, by remem-
> bering the words and deeds of Jesus and celebrating the pres-
> ence of the Risen Christ among them in the Word proclaimed
> and in the bread and cup of the Eucharist.

This theological norm of both word and sacrament remains a long
way from practical recovery in any of the churches named, yet there
are promising local signs in all of them. The ecumenical potential of
this movement is great, as the Lima text indicates, particularly in
paragraphs 30-31 of the "eucharist" document.

As an interim step, the Methodist and Reformed Churches often
advocate for non-sacramental Sundays a kind of "dry mass," whose
defining feature is the placement of substantial prayers of thanksgiving and intercession after the sermon. In my experience, this
often meets resistance from the congregation on the ground that it
diminishes the importance of the sermon, which, after all, remains
the weightiest single item in a service limited to the word. Besides
the *missa sicca*, the LBW also provides an integral "Service of the
Word" and an order of "Morning Prayer with a sermon" as other
possibilities on non-eucharistic Sundays. This policy does not appear to have harmed the eucharistic renewal which is, in fact,
making greater progress among American Lutherans than among
Reformed or Methodists either in the United States or in the United
Kingdom. It is striking too that the outstanding recovery of the
eucharist among Anglicans or Episcopalians has largely not—despite ASB's provision for "Morning Prayer or Evening Prayer with
Holy Communion"—proceeded by annexing matins, but rather by
allowing matins to continue on its own as an alternative or supplement for those who wish it. My suspicion is that Lutherans and
Anglicans score over Methodists and Reformed by acknowledging
the sacramental specificity of the Holy Communion. Methodists
and Reformed need to rediscover the distinctiveness of the sacramental mode of grace over against a view that treats the sacrament
as a doublet of the preached word.

The ritual structure of the liturgy is performed by a community
whose personal structures find significant expression in the assembly. God addresses us, we address God, and the mediator of this
communicative encounter is Christ. The downward and upward
mediation of Christ is symbolized by his ministers, who in his name

both proclaim the Gospel and lead the whole assembly in its response. Christian pastors feed the flock of Christ through word and sacrament; they direct it in its praise and prayers. Their priestly ministry is in these ways "related," as the Lima text puts it,

> to the priestly reality of Jesus Christ and the whole community
> ... They fulfil a particular priestly service by strengthening and
> building up the royal and prophetic priesthood of the faithful
> through word and sacraments, through their prayers of inter-
> cession and through their pastoral guidance of the community.
> ("Ministry" 17 and commentary)

Ordained ministers are thus the "overseers" and "elders" of the whole community in Christ.

The dialogical structure of the liturgical assembly finds enhanced expression in the active participation which all recent revisions encourage from the various members of the Body and the whole congregation. Acclamations stud the scripture readings and the great eucharistic prayer. Litany forms are supplied for thanksgiving and intercession. Some prayers are said in unison. Yet the presidency remains with those whom the whole people have acknowledged as *axioi* at their ordination, or otherwise assented to.

The Story of the Liturgico-Linguistic Community

In her linguistic analysis of the prayers of the Roman Mass Helen Kathleen Hughes[12] finds the surface structure of thanks and supplication to rest upon a deep structure of God's having acted for humankind. What binds together the Godward and manward movements is the concept and reality of story. In distinction from standard narrative, Hughes finds the Christian story to have the following six characteristics:

(1) The storytellers are involved in the story; the heavy use of first and second person pronouns testifies to a dynamic covenantal relationship between God and the community.

(2) The language of Revelation is used; the biblical narrative supplies major paradigms and an indispensable frame of reference for the meaningful use of language in the liturgy.

(3) The story is told today; in a temporal immediacy past event is named as present promise.

(4) The story is unfinished, open-ended; liturgical prayer has an eschatological thrust as the community looks for the resolution of its "crisis" in the definitive establishment of the reign of God.

(5) The story invites transformation; prayer not only forms the community from one generation to the next but is potentially transformational in that it demands decision and summons people to conversion.

(6) The story is told in a context; prayer is proclaimed in a community gathered in praise of God and aware of its need.

In this section I shall concentrate on the movement of God towards us; in the next on our responsive movement towards God.

The condition for the merging of God's story and our story is that we hear "the story so far." This is why the Scriptures must be read and proclaimed. The choice and range of the biblical readings in the liturgical assembly become crucial matters. Protestantism is moving out of a period where the decision depended on the charismatic inspiration or private whim of the preacher. Great preachers such as Chrysostom or Calvin worked through whole books of the Bible "in course," at least in their preaching services.[13] Continuous or semi-continuous reading, extended over a season, has traditionally been a factor also in the Sunday liturgy of the church. There, however, it had to mesh with the desire to find correspondence among the various readings from different parts of the Bible. There have been signs of tension between British and American churches over these lectionary questions.

The British got their spoke in first, through the Joint Liturgical Group. The JLG's two-year Sunday lectionary of 1967 was, with some variants and with varying degrees of authority, very widely adopted in the Protestant Churches of Britain. Each Sunday had not only its "controlling lesson," which might be from the Old Testament, the Epistles, or the Gospels, but also its assigned "theme." Sharp criticism has been directed at the "didactic" character of this arrangement, as though the celebratory event of worship was being submerged in "Christian education." Another cause of concern has been that the JLG lectionary, unadopted elsewhere, is isolating the British Protestant Churches even in the English-speaking world.

Churches in the Commonwealth and in the United States, in fact, and again with variants and with varying degrees of authority, adopted rather the three-year Sunday lectionary of the post-conciliar Roman Catholic Church. Again, however, there are problems. The Roman years are named after the Gospels of Matthew, Mark, and Luke. Epistles are often left unassimilated, whereas the Old Testament, to the contrary, becomes a mine of what some see as strained typologies. This last worry led in the United States to an attempt by the Consultation on Common Texts to arrive at a more continuous reading of the Old Testament on the Sundays after Pentecost, with only a rough typological correspondence between the Pentateuch and Matthew, the Davidic narrative and Mark, the Prophets and Luke. The plan was elaborated with American Catholic participation, and it is hoped that its submission to Rome will eventually provide favorable results, perhaps even beyond the English-speaking world. This "Common Lectionary" is already being used by Methodists and Presbyterians in the United States, and by the UCA; it is gradually taking over also in Britain.

Ecumenical representatives from Britain, America, Australia, and elsewhere had started to tackle these problems at the first formal meeting of the English Language Liturgical Consultation (ELLC) at Boston in 1985: how to avoid "domesticating" the Scriptures while recognizing their unity; how to maintain the latreutic character of worship while acknowledging its role in teaching and formation; how to reach an optimal agreement in the liturgical use of Scripture internationally and ecumenically.

The Praise and Prayers of the Liturgico-Linguistic Community

The specialized area of hymnology must be omitted here, although the geographical spread, sometimes under other names, of *The Australian Hymn Book* (1977) is particularly noteworthy. A British Methodist cannot resist the temptation to mention also *Hymns and Psalms: A Methodist and Ecumenical Hymn Book* (1983). The interest and controversy which the production of a new hymn book aroused among our people indicate the unparalleled part hymns play in our worship and in our appropriation of the faith. The Wesleys are represented in a proportion which we do not expect those in other spiritual traditions fully to share, though we are gratified at the increasing appearance of Wesleyan hymns in sometimes unexpected places.

Let us concentrate rather on the eucharistic anaphora. Here British Methodists found themselves somewhat isolated by the 1975 provision of a single new prayer, fine though it is, in addition to the text of 1662/1936. Others have gone abundance. The United Methodist *At the Lord's Table* (SWR9, 1981) provided twenty-two eucharistic prayers in various styles for various seasons and occasions. The crop of new prayers produced within several traditions varies more in style and detailed content than in structure. There is, in fact, a remarkable ecumenical convergence at this point, resulting from the kind of historical research epitomized by W.J. Grisbooke's "Anaphora" in the Davies *Dictionary of Liturgy and Worship.*[14] The Scottish 1979 BCO offered three anaphoras, roughly corresponding to the linguistic styles of the Authorized Version, the Revised Standard Version, and the New English Bible, while the 1994 BCO reverts in new prayers to Genevan and Celtic patterns. In the *Holy Communion* (1980) of the UCA, rite one drew on "the ancient liturgies of the Church," whereas rite two reflected "insights of our reformed traditions." In *Uniting in Worship* (1988) the anaphoras rose to nine in number, including loans from the United Church of Canada, the British Methodists, and the American Presbyterians. The second of the URC's three anaphoras was the only adoption, so far as I know, of the JLG's *jeu d'esprit* with the *Te Deum* and the Lord's Prayer.[15] Of the eight "great prayers of thanksgiving" in the American Presbyterian SLD, "G" (which disappeared from BCW) was a redirection of Calvin's communion exhortation, whereas "D" (redesignated "G" in BCW) is a translation—based on the work of ICEL—of the anaphora from the so-called *Apostolic Tradition* of Hippolytus. Other rites have expanded that ancient prayer at various points, whereas others again have been content to include a few Hippolytan phrases in what are fundamentally new compositions. In England the obsessive question for the framers of the ASB was the formulation of the anamnesis-oblation, a battleground for Catholic and Evangelical Anglicans over the understanding of memorial and sacrifice. In the United States, the Episcopalian compilers made two particularly bold ventures. They wrote the "Star-Trek" preface in Prayer IIc (since echoed by a prayer in the Scottish 1994 BCO):

> At your command all things came to be:
> the vast expanse of interstellar space,
> galaxies, suns, the planets in their courses,
> and this fragile earth, our island home.

And they provided guidelines for an improvised eucharistic prayer. ICEL produced in 1984 "an original eucharistic prayer"—later adopted as prayer E by the Presbyterian BCW—whose imagery bears one or two feminine touches:

> When the times had at last grown full
> and the earth had ripened in abundance,
> you created in your image humankind
> . . .
> As a mother tenderly gathers her children,
> you embraced a people as your own . . .

An American Methodist prayer includes the phrase:

> You gave birth to your church . . .

The Experience of Time in the Liturgico-Linguistic Community

While the Roman Catholic Church has been uncluttering its calendar, the Protestant Churches have been recovering the riches of the liturgical year. In Britain the greatest single influence was the work of A.A. McArthur on *The Evolution of the Christian Year* (1953) with its thesis of the three originally unitive festivals of the Pascha (Good Friday/Easter), Ascension/Pentecost and Christmas/Epiphany. The JLG lectionary, fundamentally accepted by the British Protestant Churches, organized the entire year around those three foci. Whether "post-Pentecost" constitutes a coherent season is particularly controversial among liturgists. The strongly seasonal approach to much of the year was represented in America by the United Methodist *From Ashes to Fire* (SWR 8) and *From Hope to Joy* (SWR 15), the former being a series of services for Lent and Easter, the latter stretching from All Saints to Epiphany and the pre-Lenten Transfiguration. The Roman Catholic Church has gone to the opposite extreme in designating so many "ordinary Sundays" *per annum*. *Both* tendencies might be thought to threaten in their different ways the eschatological character of *every* Sunday.

On the other hand, an eschatological note is being struck as some Protestants develop a sanctorale. The most unexpected case may be the LBW, whose ecumenicity stretches to Calvin (27 May) though not to Zwingli. The Wesley brothers are commemorated on John's death-day (2 March); the United States Episcopalians and the Australian Anglicans move them to 3 March because the previous day has been preempted by St. Chad. In a gracious gesture, the English ASB follows Methodist logic rather than its own and places the Wesley commemoration on 24 May, the date of John's evangelical conversion. The Australian Anglicans not only show a new openness to the saints of the Orthodox East, but also commemorate John Fisher and Thomas More, "scholars and martyrs for conscience' sake" (6 July), Martin Luther "and the Continental Reformers" (30 October), and John Bunyan, "Independent preacher and spiritual writer" (31 August). In its new venture of a commemorative calendar found in *Uniting in Worship*, the UCA displays both a wide range of modern ecumenical figures and a regional flavor of Asia and the Pacific.

The American Lutherans deserve notice too, for the recapturing of a cosmic dimension through their services of morning and evening prayer. The themes of day and night, light and darkness, familiar in traditional Lutheran hymnody, set the new creation in relation to the first. While the Presbyterian BCW also introduces prayer of the hours, one may question how well the daily rhythms are being marked by prayer in any of the churches. *An Australian Prayer Book* openly addressed the very same question in its preface.

The Liturgico-Linguistic Community and the Surrounding Culture

The issue is one of tradition and modernity. A superficial symptom for Protestants, by no means decisive in itself (it has scarcely affected Roman Catholics), has been the question of "You" versus "Thou" in the address to God. Whereas Methodists and Lutherans have completely shifted to "You" in their recent liturgies, the English ASB, the American BCP and at first the Scottish BCO have all retained some services in the older form. This question is a small part of the problematic which the preface to the BCO phrased thus:

> It is clear that the language of today must be pressed into the service of the Church not just because it is modern but because it has a contribution to make to the worship and mission of the Church. It is equally clear, however, that traditional prayer language must be used and developed in the service of the Church, not just because it is traditional, hallowed by usage centuries-long, but because it has a contribution to make to the worship and mission of our Church, because it is an art-form of rare quality and part of our culture.

This can be taken as a perennial statement concerning the maintenance and evolution of tradition. But the sharper question is whether
the specifically "modern," i.e., the post-Enlightenment European,
can at all be reconciled with Christian identity.

In speaking of the perennial *"search* for language and for forms
that are appropriate at once to worshippers and to Christ," the BCO
could invoke a Reformed custom of providing directories rather
than imposing prayer books. But what is to account for the new-
found apophatism of hitherto book-bound Anglicans? The preface
to the ASB concludes thus:

> Words, even agreed words, are only the beginning of worship.
> Those who use them do well to recognize their transience and
> imperfection; to treat them as a ladder, not a goal; to acknowl-
> edge their power in shaping faith and kindling devotion with-
> out claiming that they are fully adequate to the task. Only the
> grace of God can make up what is lacking in the faltering words
> of men. It is in reliance on such grace that this book is offered to
> the Church, in the hope that God's people may find in it a
> means in our day to worship Him with honest minds and
> thoughtful hearts.

In our time such modesty hints, I think, at the crisis of the Christian
faith amid a godless secularism.

In contrast with Britain and Europe, and perhaps Australia, the
crisis in the United States is not with religion as such. It is in fact
frequently claimed that the United States is the most religious
country on earth. The crisis is rather with the Christian tradition as
a particular variant of religion. The crisis is epitomized linguistically by radical feminist attempts to "reconceive" and "reimagine"
Christianity, which affect liberal circles more generally. A striking
example was the *Inclusive Language Lectionary,* produced by an
administrative process within the National Council of Churches.
There canonical Scripture is subjected to barbarity, suppression,
and interpolation. An instance of each must suffice. In John 9 Jesus
and the man born blind are neutered in order to allow women
hearers to empathize with the story:

> Having found the one born blind, Jesus said: "Do you believe in
> the Human One?" The one born blind answered: "And who is
> that, so that I may believe in whoever it is?" Jesus said, "You
> have seen who it is, and it is the very one who speaks to you."

In John 4 the threefold *Kyrie* by which the Samaritan woman addresses Jesus (verses 11, 15, 19) is simply deleted. Finally, Sarah and even Hagar (despite Galatians 4:21-31) are attached to mentions of Abraham, and God the Father receives the extra epithet "and Mother." Behind the complaints of patriarchalism against the Bible stand, I sense, questions concerning the whole conception of divine sovereignty in Scripture and Tradition, whatever its linguistic expression.[16]

The differences in *cultural* situations are probably the strongest argument that John McHugh of Durham can advance in favor of different English-language versions of the Catholic liturgy, in his open letter to the bishop of Shrewsbury *On Englishing the Liturgy*. Probably only someone on the eastern side of the Atlantic would subjoin the *social* argument—allowing class to counter geography— that a Harvard congregation would have more in common with the Catholic chaplaincy at Oxford than either would have with the automobile workers of Cowley or Detroit.

One must hope that the Christian faith has already created a linguistic tradition that is both coherent and sufficiently broad to include people in a very great range of cultural and social circumstances. If that is the case, then we share George Lindbeck's emphasis in *The Nature of Doctrine*[17] that, rather than present experience being allowed to hold sway over the inherited tradition, the inherited tradition should shape and govern present experience. Only when the present remains isomorphic with the given past can it properly effect further transmission.

Notes

1. M.J. Hatchett, *The Making of the First American Book of Common Prayer, 1776-1789* (New York: Seabury Press, 1982).

2. Jack M. Maxwell, *Worship and Reformed Theology: The Liturgical Lessons of Mercersburg* (Pittsburgh: Pickwick Press, 1976).

3. These catchwords I have twisted from Geoffrey Blainey, *The Tyranny of Distance* (1966), *Triumph of the Nomads* (1975), and *All for Australia* (1984). The consequences for ecclesial sociology I find described in Hans Mol's *The Faith of Australians* (Sydney: George Allen and Unwin, 1985).

4. Roger Grainger, *The Language of the Rite* (London: Darton, Longman and Todd, 1974).

5. I intend this designation as a sincere, if whimsical, tribute to the work of Dr. Gianfranco Tellini, the chief drafter of the "little light blue book."

6. I always take the opportunity to explain to American Lutherans that the only significance the initials LBW can possibly possess in British and Australian English is "leg before wicket."

7. This way of access through worship to the doctrine and life of the church is the theological method employed in my *Doxology* (London and New York: Oxford University Press, 1980).

8. M.J. Hatchett, *Commentary on the American Prayer Book* (New York: Seabury Press, 1980) 271.

9. Ibid. 261-267.

10. *Lutheran Book of Worship* (Desk edition) 12.

11. Letter to the Brethren in America, 10 September 1784.

12. H.K. Hughes, "Understanding the Nature and Function of Liturgical Language: A Narrative Approach," in *The Language of the Liturgy: Some Theoretical and Practical Implications* (Washington, D.C.: I.C.E.L., no date but in fact 1984) 2-18.

13. R. Kaczynski, *Das Wort Gottes in Liturgie und Alltag der Gemeinden des Johannes Chrysostomos*, (Freiburg in Br.: Herder, 1974); H.O. Old, *The Patristic Roots of Reformed Worship* (Zurich: Theologischer Verlag, 1974).

14. The dominance of the West Syrian or Antiochene pattern has not gone entirely unquestioned. Note in particular David N. Power, "The Eucharistic Prayer: Another Look," in *New Eucharistic Prayers: An Ecumenical Study of Their Development and Structure*, ed. Frank C. Senn (New York: Paulist Press, 1987) 239-257.

15. R.C.D. Jasper, ed., *The Daily Office Revised, with Other Prayers and Services* (London: SPCK, 1978) 11-13.

16. The introduction to the Scottish 1994 BCO declares: "In addressing or speaking of God, male-dominated language has been avoided wherever possible. Traditional metaphors like *Father, Judge, King* remain, but they are used sparingly, as are references to God's might and power." Official denominational service books published since the 1980s have shown a marked reluctance to use the scriptural and traditional name of Father, Son and Holy Spirit. In my judgment, this normative trinitarian name is a separable issue from the 1995 APBA's desire to "use a range of forms of address for God which reflects the diversity and richness of biblical imagery." See chapter 14 in this book. Most English-language service books produced since 1980 now use gender-inclusive language in reference to human beings.

17. George Lindbeck, *The Nature of Doctrine* (Philadelphia: Westminster, 1984).

10

The Reconciliation of Divided Churches: A Witness to the Gospel

The Scriptural Base

THAT CHRIST WILLS HIS DISCIPLES TO BE ONE IS CLEAR BECAUSE, IN HIS HIGH priestly prayer of John 17, Jesus prayed to the Father for their unity. The stated purpose is that the world may believe in the divine mission of the Son, so that all those whom Christ will draw to himself through their witness may, to the glory of the Father and the Son, come to a knowledge of the truth and an enjoyment of eternal life. St. Paul declares in Romans 5:10f. that sinners have been reconciled to God by the death of his Son, and that believers, having received this reconciliation, now rejoice in God through the Lord Jesus Christ. In Romans 15:5f. the apostle goes on to pray that God may grant them to live in such harmony with one another, in accord with Christ Jesus, that they may with one heart and one voice glorify the God and Father of the Lord Jesus Christ. Their unity is necessary to the spreading of the Gospel among the Gentiles, who must also come to the praise of God's name (15:7-33). Because we have believed, says St. Paul in 2 Corinthians, we speak out; and as grace extends to more and more people, it will increase the thanksgiving—swell the eucharistic chorus—to the glory of God (4:13-15). And in the next chapter:

> If anyone is in Christ, he is a new creation; the old has passed away, the new has come. All this is from God, who through Christ reconciled us to himself and gave us the ministry of

> reconciliation; that is, God was in Christ reconciling the world to himself, not counting their trespasses against them, and entrusting to us the message of reconciliation. So we are ambassadors for Christ, God making his appeal through us. We beseech you on behalf of Christ, be reconciled to God. For our sake he made him to be sin who knew no sin, so that in him we might become the righteousness of God. Working together with him, then, we entreat you not to accept the grace of God in vain. (2 Corinthians 5:17-6:1)

The New Testament hymns sing the truly cosmic scope of this reconciliation to God:

> In [Christ] all the fullness of God was pleased to dwell,
> and through him to reconcile to himself all things,
> whether on earth or in heaven,
> making peace by the blood of his cross. (Col 1:19f.)

The result should be universal praise:

> ... Therefore God has highly exalted him,
> and bestowed on him the name
> which is above every name,
> that at the name of Jesus
> every knee should bow,
> in heaven and on earth and under the earth,
> and every tongue confess
> that Jesus Christ is Lord,
> to the glory of God the Father. (Phil 2:9-11)

So it should be. And so our creeds and liturgies declare it to be.

The Creeds and Liturgies

"Repent," said St. Peter in his sermon at Pentecost, "and be baptized every one of you in the name of Jesus Christ for the forgiveness of your sins" (Acts 2:38). And in the Nicene Creed, "we acknowledge one baptism for the remission of sins." "Drink from it, all of you," says the Matthaean Jesus at the Last Supper, "for this is my blood of the covenant, which is poured out for many for the forgiveness of sins" (Mt 26:28). And the fruits of communion prayed for in the classical eucharistic liturgies include the forgiveness of sins. "Christ is our peace" (Eph 2:14); and, as reconciled sons and daughters of God in him, we greet each other with a holy kiss, we exchange the *pax* in the assembly (cf. Rom 16:16; 1 Cor 16:20; 2 Cor

13:12; 1 Thes 5:26; 1 Pt 5:14). Reconciled with one another, we bring our gift to the altar (Mt 5:23f.), and there "because there is one loaf, we who are many are one body, for we all partake of the same loaf" (1 Cor 10:17). In a prayer which some ancient liturgies take up from the *Didachè* (9:4), the eucharistic bread becomes a model—and its sharing, implicitly, an instrument—of the gathering of God's people into the kingdom.

> As this bread which we have broken was once scattered on the mountains and then, gathered together, became one, so may thy church be gathered together from the ends of the earth into thy kingdom.

In each local assembly, then, of the one church, we find forgiveness of our sins, reconciliation with our neighbors, and a foretaste of God's universal kingdom. When the sacraments of baptism and eucharist are working "normally," it appears that they are being celebrated in and by an existing corporate body—the church with its many local instances—for the conveyance to its converts or members of the benefits of the Gospel. Certainly this is the picture drawn in the usual sacramental theology of the catholic churches.

The Sad Reality

Unfortunately, however, there were already signs in the New Testament that all was not working out quite like that. So Paul fulminates against the fractious Corinthians: "Is Christ divided? Was Paul crucified for you? Or were you baptized in the name of Paul?" (1 Cor 1:13). Admittedly, the reality of the one baptism into Christ appears to remain, for the apostle appeals to it as the ground of a unity to be lived:

> For just as the body is one and has many members, and all the members of the body, though many, are one body, so it is with Christ. For by one Spirit we were all baptized into one body . . . (1 Cor 12:12f.)

The same should perhaps be true of the eucharist (cf. 1 Cor 10:17), but in fact the apostle tells the Corinthians that they are turning the Lord's Supper into their own supper (1 Cor 11:20f.), and he warns them of the dangers they place themselves in by their unworthy participation in the Lord's sacramental body and blood (11:27-34). The truths and benefits of the sacraments cannot be so easily maintained through the distortions introduced by divisions in a local congregation. "Normality" is also called into question by divisions among local churches or along confessional lines. And this is the sad reality of Christian history with which a theology of the sacraments must try to cope, in the hope indeed of discovering possibilities that will further the restoration of unity.

Listen to the baptismal section of the Lima text on *Baptism, Eucharist and Ministry*.[1] First, the positive statement in paragraph 6:

> Administered in obedience to our Lord, baptism is a sign and seal of our common discipleship. Through baptism, Christians are brought into union with Christ, with each other and with the Church of every time and place. Our common baptism, which unites us to Christ in faith, is thus a basic bond of unity. We are called to confess and serve one Lord in each place and in all the world. The union with Christ which we share through baptism has important implications for Christian unity. "There is . . . one baptism, one God and Father of us all" (Eph. 4:4-6). When baptismal unity is realized in one, holy, catholic, apostolic Church, a genuine Christian witness can be made to the healing and reconciling love of God. Therefore, our one baptism into Christ constitutes a call to the churches to overcome their divisions and visibly manifest their fellowship.

Only after the hint in the penultimate sentence ("When . . .") and the explicit mention of "divisions" in the last do we come to the critical commentary:

> The inability of the churches mutually to recognize their various practices of baptism as sharing in the one baptism, and their actual dividedness in spite of mutual recognition, have given dramatic visibility to the broken witness of the Church . . . The need to recover baptismal unity is at the heart of the ecumenical task . . .

Similarly with regard to the eucharist. First, paragraph 19 of the eucharistic section states the matter entirely positively:

> The eucharistic communion with Christ who nourishes the life of the Church is at the same time communion within the body of Christ which is the Church. The sharing in one bread and the communion cup in a given place demonstrates and effects the oneness of the sharers with Christ and with their fellow sharers in all times and places. It is in the eucharist that the community

of God's people is fully manifested. Eucharistic celebrations always have to do with the whole Church, and the whole Church is involved in each local eucharistic celebration. In so far as a church claims to be a manifestation of the whole Church, it will take care to order its own life in ways which take seriously the interests and concerns of other churches.

This is then followed by the sharp challenge, and finally the blunt judgment, of paragraph 20:

The eucharistic celebration demands reconciliation and sharing among all those regarded as brothers and sisters in the one family of God and is a constant challenge in the search for appropriate relationships in social, economic and political life ... All kinds of injustice, racism, separation and lack of freedom are radically challenged when we share in the body and blood of Christ. Through the eucharist the all-renewing grace of God penetrates and restores human personality and dignity. The eucharist involves the believer in the central event of the world's history. As participants in the eucharist, therefore, we prove inconsistent if we are not actively participating in this ongoing restoration of the world's situation and the human condition. The eucharist shows that our behaviour is inconsistent in face of the reconciling presence of God in human history: we are placed under continual judgment by the persistence of unjust relationships of all kinds in our society, the manifold divisions on account of human pride, material interest and power politics and, above all, the obstinacy of unjustifiable confessional oppositions within the body of Christ.

An early draft was even more severe: it said our lack of reconciliation "makes a mockery" of the eucharist.

Again, the section on the ministry begins with a magnificent description of the calling and task of the church "in a broken world" (paragraphs 1-5). Fifty paragraphs of discussion and proposals are then needed towards what the final paragraph will call "the mutual recognition of churches and their ministries" (55)—regrettably the chance to use the word "reconciliation" was lost—which is needed if the calling and task is to be fulfilled.

One does not have to be a Donatist in order to hold that, at the very least, the existential efficacy of preaching, baptism, and the eucharist as testimony to, and conveyance of, the Gospel of reconciliation is diminished when the proclaiming and celebrating Body is divided. The direct reverse of the title of the present chapter is unfortunately just as true as the obverse: the division of the churches is a counter-testimony to the Gospel of reconciliation. Severely put: the reality of the Gospel itself is called into question by disunity among Christians, and *a fortiori* the reality of the church which claims to have been brought into being by the Gospel. In an extreme case: can the church proclaim and transmit a gift it shows no sign of possessing? The Donatist question would re-emerge: can it truly be the Lord's baptism and supper that are being celebrated here?

A Church Penitent?

Before we go too far in a Donatist direction, it is well to remember that pastoral wisdom, in both the catholic churches and the classical churches of the Reformation, decreed that the benefits of the sacraments to faithful recipients do not depend on the personal worthiness of the ministers. Could it be that the church, even corporately, needs and enjoys that provision in order to benefit from the sacraments of which it has itself become an unworthy steward? Is there some way in which the whole church, by the renewal of the baptism which in recurrent celebrations ever and again constitutes it, can be brought to a more profitable, more effective, and in the end worthier practice of the sacrament of its continuing life, the eucharist? The model of the individual Christian suggests that we look towards penitence and penance. Whether in the "grave penance" of the early centuries, or in the "penance of devotion" that lasted from the Celts through Trent to times within living memory, or in the collective penitence that occurs at the start of the Roman Mass or in the "general confession" of the Protestant liturgies, believers who have lapsed into greater or lesser sins and then repented have had the opportunity to participate again in the church's eucharist and communion. Could it be that even churches (whether local or denominational), repenting of their disunity, should and might undergo the "second baptism" that penance represented for individuals in the patristic church, in order that, reconciled to God and to one another, they may more fitly and profitably celebrate the eucharist and more credibly proclaim the Gospel?

This will appear a staggering suggestion to those in churches that see "*the* church" (predominantly or exclusively identified with their own) as somehow hypostatically distinct from its members. How can "the church," source and mother of holiness, itself need to repent? The Orthodox always object when Protestants speak of a sinful church. But at least such a Catholic as Karl Rahner was prepared to speak, in a somewhat mediating way, of *"die Kirche der Sünder"* (the title of a book of his, in 1948). According to the Roman *Ordo Paenitentiae* of 1973, penance is "a liturgy by which the Church continually renews itself" (paragraph 11).

In the perspective of ecumenical relations, it will be remembered that Pope Paul VI, at the opening of the second session of Vatican II on 29 September 1963, addressed these words to the observers "from the Christian denominations separated from the Catholic Church":

> If we are in any way to blame for this separation, we humbly beg God's forgiveness. And we ask our brothers' pardon for any injuries they feel they have sustained from us. For our part we willingly forgive whatever injuries the Catholic Church has suffered, and forget the grief she has endured as a result of the long years of dissension and separation. May the heavenly Father deign to honour our prayers and grant us true brotherly peace.[2]

In their "common declaration" of 7 December 1965, Pope Paul VI and Ecumenical Patriarch Athenagoras I expressed "regret for historical errors":

> They regret the offensive words, the reproaches without foundation and the reprehensible gestures which on both sides marked or accompanied the sad events of that period [i.e., 1054] . . . They deplore the troublesome precedents and the later events which, under the influence of various factors, among them lack of understanding and mutual hostility, eventually led to the effective rupture of ecclesial communion.[3]

On his visit to the land of Luther in 1980, Pope John Paul II said of the history of division:

> "We will not pass judgment on one another" (Rom 14:13). But let us mutually confess our guilt. With respect to the grace of unity also, it is a fact that "all have sinned" (Rom 3:23). We must recognize and acknowledge that fact in all seriousness and draw the appropriate conclusions . . . If we do not try to avoid the facts, we realize that human failings are to blame for the harmful division of Christians, and that our own refusals have

time and again hindered the steps that are possible and necessary to unity.[4]

The joint international commission between Roman Catholics and Lutherans, in its report *Einheit vor uns* (1985), declared that ecumenical reconciliation needs to find expression in liturgical celebrations that include "both penance and thanksgiving" ("*sowohl Busse wie Danksagung*") (paragraph 69; cf. 138).[5]

When it came to a constitutive service of reconciliation between divided Christian communities, certain profound ecclesiological presuppositions would be laid bare. Who, in a divided Christendom, may act for "the church"? Who has the authority to "hear" the confession of the communities and to pronounce absolution for the sins of disunity? Who will reconcile whom to whom or to what? On the one hand, Protestants will want to avoid an "ecumenism of return" whereby they would be reintegrated into a single Catholic and/or Orthodox fold that itself was presumed to have enjoyed an uninterrupted existence. On the other hand, those churches that have—with whatever accommodations of "economy" or pastoral charity—maintained a fundamentally Cyprianic ecclesiology will want to uphold their witness to the visibly indivisible character of the church, from which one may indeed separate but only at forfeiture of ecclesial status and peril of one's salvation. In any case, it must be and remain clear that all parties need and are seeking forgiveness for disunity, and there should be no question of a declaration "*de haut en bas*" by whoever imagines they have the upper hand. Any ministers who pronounced absolution in an ecumenical reconciliation would in the nature of the case be unworthy ones, on account of the sins of their own community. Later I will be making a concrete liturgical proposal that seeks to resolve these problems *coram Deo*.

Ecumenical Endeavors

The churches have indeed begun to show regret, and even to express penitence, for the divisions among Christians, but they will not be ready to enact reconciliation among themselves unless and until they have managed to settle those matters pertaining to the truth of the Gospel that have hitherto—either as the cause or as the effect of a division—been considered church-dividing. This is why the dogmatic interests of Faith and Order have been vital to the modern ecumenical movement. Hence the importance of the Lima text on *Baptism, Eucharist and Ministry*: mutual recognition and reconciliation in these areas is impossible without a sufficient measure of agreement as to the nature, meaning, and effect of these sacraments and structures. BEM is now being set in a wider dogmatic context by the Faith and Order project, "Towards the Common Expression of the Apostolic Faith Today."[6] This multilateral work is accompanied by the numerous bilateral dialogues that are taking place on doctrinal themes among the confessional families or "Christian communions."

In some cases entire confessional traditions, or denominational churches at a national level, have already entered into new relationships with one another. It would be fascinating to study the "orders of service" by which they have liturgically celebrated or enacted their reconciliation, say at the inauguration of the Church of South India (1947) or the Uniting Church in Australia (1977). The most I have been able to come up with in the way of liturgical materials are two proposals, one of which failed to be accepted, whereas the other remains under discussion; and each aimed or aims at a covenant among denominational churches rather than immediate structural unity.

i. The English Plan

The report of the English *Churches' Council for Covenanting* in 1980[7] included a service for "The Making of the Covenant," whose opening declaration, by "a presiding minister," went thus:

> By the grace of God, we gather before him as representatives of [the covenanting churches named]. In Christ we are already one, one by our baptism, and by our profession of one faith, but we have lived in separation from one another. God in his mercy has kept us in his love, accepting us when we refused to accept one another. Now, in repentance and faith, trusting in God's grace, we have come to accept one another as he has accepted us, and to make in his presence a Covenant which rests upon the eternal Covenant embracing all creation, which he has made with us in his Son.
>
> By our Covenant together each of our Churches will be bound to the others by solemn promise, sealed by the sharing of the body and blood of our Lord Jesus Christ. We shall recognize one another as Christian Churches in membership and minis-

try, and commit ourselves to grow together in counsel and in action. We shall seek a deepening unity with one another in faith and praise, in witness and service.

We bind ourselves also to work for a fuller unity in Christ with all who call upon his name, in this country and throughout the world, and especially with those Churches that have helped our preparation for this day but cannot yet join us in this Covenant.

Our purpose is that together we may be a more effective instrument of Christ's mission to his world. This cannot be, unless the Father consecrates us by his Holy Spirit. We pray now to the Father for this consecration as we hear the word of the Lord, as we confess our sins, as we make our Covenant vows in reliance upon God's grace, as we offer ourselves and our ministries to be united in his presence; as we greet each other with the sign of peace; and as we take up our common pilgrimage, fed together by the bread of heaven.

After the ministry of the word, the "confession [of sin] and declaration of forgiveness" were to have taken this form:

A penitential hymn is sung.

A presiding minister says: The Churches entering this Covenant now offer records of their resolve, to show that they together seek God's pardon for past disobedience and his help to fulfil their vows.

The attested records of the resolutions of the Churches to enter the Covenant are brought forward and placed upon the Lord's table.

A presiding minister says: God's word of grace stands for ever. Though we are faithless, he is faithful. We humble ourselves therefore, before God, that his forgiveness may lift us up. We repent of our sins, and today especially of living in separation from one another. We ask our Father to free us from our disobedience, and from the faults which as yet we do not see. Let us pray.

All pray in silence, saying in conclusion: Merciful Father, we confess the sins of pride and self-will that have sustained our divisions; we confess our lack of vision for your Church and for your world. Forgive us for not living as one body in Christ. Give us strength, O Father, not to fall from our repentance, nor to turn aside again from your way, but to share together the obedience of your Son our Lord. Amen.

A presiding minister says: Here are the words we can trust: Christ Jesus came into the world to save sinners. Hear, then, the word of grace to all who repent and put their faith in Christ: Your sins are forgiven.

All say: Amen. Thanks be to God!

The "act of reconciliation" was to have looked like this:

All pray in silence.

The presiding ministers say: All glory is yours, almighty and most gracious Father, for you have called us to share the heritage of your people, the royal priesthood established in Christ. We thank you that, though we have rejected one another, you have not rejected us, that in our separation you have given us your gracious presence, and led us to this day. Hear us now, therefore, as under your mercy we accept one another in this Covenant; we are not our own, but yours, and in you we belong to one another. Send down on us your Holy Spirit. Quicken us anew in faith, and hope, and love. Order our common life and ministry for the fuller unity of your universal Church. In all our worship, work and witness, glorify your name.

Representative groups of laypeople and ministers from each of the covenanting Churches say together: Send down on us your Holy Spirit as we give one another the sign of reconciliation; unite us in love in the confession of our faith, through Christ, who is our peace.

All say: Amen, amen. Lord, keep us true to our word.

All stand. The representative groups come forward. In turn each addresses the others. There follows in each case an affirmation by all the members present from the Church represented, and the representatives share, by shaking hands, the sign of reconciliation with the other groups.

Group: We, who represent the . . ., give you the right hand of fellowship and reconciliation, accepting you as partners in this Covenant and pledge that we will grow with you into that communion of peace which Christ wills for us, and go on with you to the full unity of all his people.

Members: We go forward with you in the name of the Lord.

A presiding minister says: Let us say with one voice.

All say: This is the Covenant which we make. We declare it before God. We are one in Christ. We go forward in the Spirit.

The presiding ministers say: Thanks be to God.

The Doxology.

Next the covenanting churches would "act together in the ordination of bishops" and "of presbyters." Then it was envisaged that "members of the covenanting Churches reaffirm their baptismal promises" and confess the Nicene Creed. Finally, "the covenanting Churches celebrate together the Lord's Supper."

ii. The American COCU

In the United States, the Consultation on Church Union (COCU) was aware of this English model. It too has proposed liturgical instruments for covenanting at national, regional, and local levels.[8] The national service is "for declaring covenant, reconciling ordained ministries, and celebrating the sacrament of the Lord's supper." The opening "declaration of purpose" is read by a presiding minister:

> We are gathered here as representatives of the churches we now name . . . Our purpose is to declare the unity of our faith, confess the brokenness of our common life, renew the covenant of grace by which we are bound to God and to each other, and seal this new experience of oneness by sharing together the Supper of our Lord. Already we have recognized each other's baptism in Christ's body. By the covenant which we now declare we enter into a new and visible form of unity among the churches which, though being many, are one body in Christ.

The confession of sin is in litany form, acknowledging that "the sinfulness of our division," besides being a transgression of God's commandments and a violation of God's perfect will, "has obscured our witness to the Christian faith, diminished the fullness of our worship, hindered the exercise of ministry, and limited the mission of justice and love in all the world."

The liturgy of the word follows, including the Nicene Creed. Then "declaring the covenant" is done in lengthy terms that expand the opening declaration and express the resolve to live more faithfully. The concluding words are sealed with the *pax*:

> The representatives of each church in turn make the following declaration in unison: In the peace of Christ, we who represent . . . give ourselves to you by this covenant of unity, and we

recognize you as members with us in Christ's body, the Church. We pray that God will draw our churches together, and knit us into one People so that the world may believe.

A leader then prays: God of peace and reconciliation, by your Holy Spirit free us to greet each other in the peace that only you can give. Grant this through Christ our Lord. Amen. Amen. Amen.

The representatives of the churches and all present exchange the peace with appropriate words and gestures.

Then the service proceeds to "reconciling ministries with ordaining responsibilities," "reconciling presbyteral ministries of word and sacrament," and "welcoming ordained deacons and ordained ministers of governance." Finally there will be a celebration of the Lord's Supper according to a rite proposed by COCU in 1984.

These services represent serious thinking on penitence and reconciliation among the English and American churches. Perhaps only the Anglicans involved maintain—in however attenuated a form—even a residually Cyprianic ecclesiology. It is no doubt significant that the failure of the first proposal took place in a country in which "the Church of England," itself a partner with the Methodists, the Moravians, and the United Reformed down to the last round of voting is (if the word is not too strong) "dominant."

A Liturgical Proposal

In the liturgy number of *Concilium* for 1987 I was myself bold enough to launch a *ballon d'essai* for a wider constitutive reconciliation (when the dogmatic conditions will have been satisfied) between Catholic, Orthodox, and Protestant ecclesial communities.[9] Largely omitting the systematic-theological rationale, I would like to reproduce the liturgical outline here:

1. Appropriate introit psalms would be Psalms 122 and 133 (Hebrew numbering).

2. The opening prayer might be borrowed from the prayer before communion in the Roman Mass: *"Domine Jesu Christe, qui dixisti apostolis tuis . . ."* The problematic of Christian and ecclesial existence—between the sad history of disunity, on the one hand, and the fundamental faith and eschatological nature of the church, on the other—is reflected in the tension, even the ambiguity, of the petition: "Look not on our sins, but on the faith of your church." The gift

of ecclesial peace and unity (*pacificare et coadunari*) can only be prayed for.

3. A suitable epistle and gospel would be Ephesians 4:1-16 and John 17. These should be expounded in a homily.

4. The response would come in the recitation of the creed. The character of this act as an "anamnesis" of baptism could be enhanced if, as in the renewal of baptismal vows at the Paschal Vigil, the confession of faith took the form of questions and answers. Theologically, it must be stressed that the common baptism is the basis on which the reconciliation would be taking place, if at all. The Vatican II decree *Unitatis Redintegratio* makes it clear that baptism, and the faith in Christ signified by it, is for the Roman Catholic Church the basis of its ecumenism. Believer-baptist churches have been largely unwilling to recognize baptism received without personal profession of faith on the part of the recipient. The Orthodox have had the greatest difficulty in recognizing as baptism any rite administered by others than themselves. (Anecdotally, I may perhaps recall the letter received at the Faith and Order Commission meeting in Bangalore in 1978 announcing the imminent withdrawal of the Church of Greece from the BEM project on those grounds. Addressed to the West Indian Methodist who was General Secretary of the World Council of Churches, the letter was signed "With love in Christ." Happily, the Greeks remained and even voted positively at Lima.)

5. It is upon this baptismal foundation that the "reconciliation of penitents" would then take place. First, representatives of each community would confess before the other communities, perhaps in words adapted from the penitential beginning of the Mass: "I confess to almighty God, and to you, my brothers and sisters . . ." Each time, the respective confessing community would hear from the other communities the assurance that—at least at the level of Christian brotherhood and sisterhood—their confession had been heard and their forgiveness granted. After this *mutual* confession and pardon, all the communities together would then make a *common* prayer of confession to God. This would at least be a collective, if not a corporate, confession of sin. The delicate question of who would pronounce the absolution has already been hinted at earlier. Perhaps the best solution, as we shall see, is to pass immediately into the "prayers of the people."

6. The prayers of the people could embrace three themes. First place would be occupied, in fact, by *supplications* for divine forgiveness. There is ancient support for the "absolution" taking this rhetorical form. J.A. Jungmann makes clear, from the Gelasian sacramentary, that the oldest material and "firm kernel" (*fester Kern*) of the reconciliation of penitents included three such *prayers* said by the bishop: "The bishop pronounced the reconciliation in deprecative form, or more accurately in supplicative form, in the form namely of the so-called *supplicationes*; these were orations in the ordinary style of the Roman oration, containing the petition directed to God (the *supplicatio*) that he forgive the sinner."[10] Second would come prayers for the internal renewal of the church and for the more authentic prosecution of its evangelical mission in the world. The third theme in the prayers would retrieve the positive elements in the past by a commemoration of significant figures in our common—and *divided*—histories, in such a way that even controversial characters became "transfigured" in an authentic communion of the saints, where their virtues were honored and their failings remembered no more.

7. The kiss of peace would complete the reconciliation of the communities among themselves and their common reconciliation to God.

8. The achieved reconciliation would be enjoyed in a concelebrated eucharist. The problem of the recognition of ministries is a thorny one. Let me suggest that at least one constitutive element in the reconciliation of ministries would be this concelebration of a eucharist—preferably *"in coena Domini,"* thereby recalling Christ's own institution and gift of the sacrament and ministry.

9. The most appropriate occasion for this entire service of "penitence and thanksgiving" by which the churches are to be reconciled would accordingly be Maundy Thursday, the Thursday in Holy Week. This is not only the day of the institution of the eucharist but also the day when, in broad areas of the ancient church, penitents were reconciled.

In case I have not already made enough "impossible" suggestions, let me conclude by recalling that the period of proximate preparation for reconciliation was the season of Lent.[11] In the year appointed for ecumenical reconciliation among the churches, the churches could make their final spiritual preparations during the

Lenten period. A sign of penitence would be abstention from celebrating the eucharist during these days—except (since the Lord is greater than his church) on Sundays, when the advice once given by Abbé Paul Couturier on a particular occasion could be generalized:

> If you are a priest, I beg of you to offer the most holy Sacrifice on the coming feast of St. Bartholomew, 24 August, asking God's pardon for the acts of violence committed by our fathers, entreating him to change the atoning blood once shed into a spring of living waters wherein the Lamb-Redeemer will enable us to find once more our profound brotherhood in him.[12]

When the churches have been constitutively reconciled among themselves in a great general service of penitence and thanksgiving on Holy Thursday, the Christians in every locality will be able to celebrate a joyful Easter together three days later (provided, of course, the dispute concerning *that* date has also been settled).

The Healing of the Sick

There is yet another traditional sacrament whose thematics may also be appropriate to the divisions of Christendom and their overcoming. I mean the unction of the sick. Without developing much of a concrete liturgical proposal, let me just try transferring a few features of its theology from the case of the individual to the case of the churches and the church as such.

At its gravest, schism dismembers the Body of Christ. Even on a more moderate view, divisions inflict wounds on the body. At the very least, Christian disunity is a sickness of the body, and even chronic illnesses can be life-threatening. The mood is well caught by the magnificent English prayer from the troubled seventeenth century which has found its way into several subsequent Books of Common Prayer:

> O God the Father of our Lord Jesus Christ, our only Saviour, the Prince of Peace: Give us grace to lay to heart the great dangers we are in by our unhappy divisions; take away all hatred and prejudice, and whatever else may hinder us from godly union and concord; that, as there is but one Body and one Spirit, one hope of our calling, one Lord, one Faith, one Baptism, one God and Father of us all, so we may be all of one heart and of one soul, united in one holy bond of truth and peace, of faith and

charity, and may with one mind and one mouth glorify thee; through Jesus Christ our Lord. Amen.

God's desire to heal is clear from the Gospels, where the ambivalent *sôzô* also means to save. With a little fanciful transposition from the individual to the ecclesial plane, we may think that the sprinkling of baptismal renewal may open or re-open the eyes of the blinded church, whether the sin of disunity belong to this or previous generations or the healing be simply for the glory of God (cf. Jn 9). To hear Christ's declaration of forgiveness may release a penitent church from paralysis (cf. Mk 2:1-12). A trusting touch of the hem of Christ's garment may arrest the drainage of the church's lifeblood (cf. Mk 5:25-34). God has at his disposal the oil and wine needed for the church's recovery (cf. Lk 10:34).

From the ancient Roman oil-blessing onwards (*"Emitte, Domine, Spiritum sanctum tuum Paraclitum . . ."*), E.J. Lengeling has shown that unction—of the sick as in other rites—is characteristically a pneumatological act.[13] Such an unction would provide an excellent opportunity to strengthen the pneumatological dimension of the reconciliation of the churches. The Roman *Ordo Unctionis Infirmorum Eorumque Pastoralis Curae* of 1972-1973 restores the appropriate sequence of penance, unction, and communion. The liturgical order suggested in the preceding section for the reconciliation of churches could at least include a prayer for the healing of the church in the second part of the prayers of the people; it might even include representative anointings between the peace and the start of the eucharist proper.

It is in any case clear that a penitent church has the wherewithal to respond to the taunt "Physician, heal thyself." The *medicina ecclesiae* should be understood as both a subjective and an objective genitive. Healed by the anointing Spirit, the church will be able to take for itself, and give to all who come and let themselves be baptized in repentance and faith, the "medicine of immortality, the antidote against death," which is the eucharist.[14]

The Church as Mystery and Prophetic Sign

Within the context of the regular Roman Catholic administration of penance and reconciliation, Pope John Paul II, in *Reconciliatio et Paenitentia* (1984), reaffirmed the importance towards the world of this aspect of "the mission of the church today." On the ecumenical plane, we find the reconciliation of the churches themselves perceived as belonging to the witness and mission of the church in the world. Faith and Order thinking is represented by the study on "The Church as Mystery and Prophetic Sign."[15]

In her address to the 1983 Vancouver Assembly of the World Council of Churches on "the unity of the church and the renewal of human community," Mary Tanner made some remarks which were widely seen as decisively expressing the perspective of "The Church as Mystery and Prophetic Sign":

> There has been the growing recognition that the Church can never be a "sign" for the world unless the renewal of the Church is itself a discovery of its own true identity. Although its calling is to be a sign to the world and open to the world, the Church can never take its identity from the world . . . The identity of the sign becomes sure only as the Church finds its unity in the fellowship of the Son with the Father into which the Holy Spirit takes it (John 17:21). As the Church participates more deeply in the life of the Trinity, as in the process of renewal it is drawn more deeply into the eternal divine fellowship, so the human face of the Church will be conformed to the Triune God and bear God's image for the world . . . The Church is only an authentic sign to the world when, overcoming brokenness and division, it allows itself to be drawn into and enfolded in the unity of Father, Son and Holy Spirit and discovers its true identity.

> It is in the eucharist that the Church is most truly at home with God, and learns to know most truly who she is. The Church's identity which allows her to be the true sign is pregnantly actualized in the eucharist, for Christian identity is stamped in mystical experience . . . If it is indeed in the eucharist that the Church gets hold of its identity at the profoundest level, that identity it is to sign to the world, then eucharistic division subverts its character as sign. It is only a church constantly being renewed into unity—one which gets hold of its identity most profoundly through living in the Tradition encountered in the eucharist—that can be a fitting sign for the world. It is not only as passive sign that the Church draws the world to itself, for it both draws the world into that eucharistic celebration in its prayers and is sent out from that feast into the world to work

actively for the renewal of human community. It is only the Church which goes out from its eucharistic centre, strengthened in its own identity, that can take the world onto its agenda. There will never be a time when the world ceases to be the agenda of the Church. The Church living ever more deeply in its own identity can go out to the edges of society, not fearful of being distorted and confused by the world's agenda but confident that God is already in the midst ahead.[16]

Another text from the Faith and Order study contains a fine passage which is of particular pertinence to our theme:

The broken relationship between Creator and creature is a universal reality. The Church proclaims its one Lord, one faith, one baptism, but the historical fragmentation of Christianity also reflects the brokenness of the world. The Church experiences, as did its incarnate and sinless Head and Lord, the consequences of cosmic brokenness. The sources of the Church's hope reside in the fact that God, for his part, has never let go of the world nor given up his saving design for it.

In their desperate search for wholeness, people and nations sometimes look in a wrong direction, seeking unity by totalitarian means. More positively, they strive for unity on the basis of the aspirations and common humanity which God has given to them. What distinguishes the Church's striving for greater visible unity is its basis in the forgiveness of God accomplished in Christ, and in the unity already given by Christ in communion with the Father and the Holy Spirit. Such unity in redemption is already experienced in the deep communion shared by Christians and is the basis for renewal and reconciliation among them.[17]

Eucharistic Fellowship

The constitutional purpose of the World Council of Churches is to help the churches advance to "visible unity in one faith and in one eucharistic fellowship." Part of the ecumenical exercise itself is to discern what unity in faith, order, and life is necessary and sufficient for eucharistic communion. Four broad positions may be detected.

1. I myself now reject a totally "open communion," allegedly practiced on missionary grounds; for that is to underplay the second half of the paradox that if *"l'eucharistie fait l'église,"* it is also the

case that *"l'église fait l'eucharistie."* The identity of the celebrating church—the church that both offers the thanks and receives the communion—has to be preserved.

2. I also reject promiscuous intercommunion among individual Christians or the separate communities to which they belong; for that is to minimize the gravity of unrepented continuing divisions. Although it is true that institutional unity would be a mere façade without spiritual unity, it is also true that the alternative to visible unity is not spiritual unity but visible *dis*unity. Bodies that are not seen to be united are seen to be disunited. A realistic indication of the inadequacy of the lax kinds of ecclesiology underlying these first two positions is the case of the joint campaign of evangelism or mission. Even supposing that different denominational communities can agree sufficiently on the Gospel they will preach, the contentious question quickly arises of the particular denominational body into which individual converts will be initiated, and of the particular table at which they will henceforth be admitted to the Lord's Supper.

3. In my opinion, however, there do come points at which, short of the achievement of the envisaged full unity towards which they are praying and working, ecclesial communities that are converging in faith, order, and life may practice intercommunion. They will do so both in order to celebrate the measure of unity already reached and in order to gain strength for future progress.

4. Nevertheless, I respect the stricter view that no eucharistic communion should be enjoyed before some kind of qualitatively complete unity in faith, order, and life has already been attained. However the case may be between the last two positions, eucharistic communion among and in penitent and (intentionally) reconciled churches can make a powerful witness to the Gospel of the kingdom.

For the eucharist is a sign of that justice, peace, and joy in the Holy Spirit which characterize the kingdom of God (Rom 14:17). A rightly celebrated eucharist exemplifies justice, because penitent believers are all equally welcomed there by the merciful God into his table-fellowship and all together share in the fruits of redemption and in the foretaste of the new heavens and the new earth in which right will prevail (see 2 Pt 3:13). It exemplifies peace, because those who are reconciled are there at peace with God and with one another. It exemplifies joy in the Holy Ghost, because the cup of blessing conveys to all who partake of it a taste of that "sober intoxication" which the Spirit gives (see Eph 5:18). Heaving learned and experienced this in the paradigm of the eucharistic meal, the church is committed to an everyday witness in word and deed which will give the opportunity for all the material resources of creation and all occasions of human contact to become the media of that communion with God and among fellow human beings which is marked by justice, peace, and joy in the Holy Ghost, and in which the kingdom of God consists.

All this is under the grace of God and to God's glory. None of it, of course, guarantees that the world will accept the Gospel. The witness will have been made. The rest does not lie in the church's hands.

Epilogue

After the preceding chapter had been written, I acquired a copy of the "Order of Service for the Inauguration of Church Union in South India." The Church of South India (1947) brought together the fruit of labors on the part of missionary societies belonging to separated churches in the home countries (Anglican, Presbyterian, Congregational, British Methodist). The litany of general confession in the inaugural service contained these clauses:

> We acknowledge, O Lord, our share in the sin and shame of divisions in Thy holy Church; we confess our prejudice and our pride, our lack of sympathy and understanding; and the feebleness of our efforts to secure all the riches of our inheritance in the saints.

The prayer at the heart of the inauguration of the Church of South India saw the union as a new and necessary stage in Christian witness to the land:

> Almighty and everlasting God, who alone art the author of unity, peace and concord, we thank Thee for the Churches in this our land and for Thy grace in choosing us to be members in Thy Church. We bless Thee for our fellowship, and for our rich inheritance. We praise Thee for Thy messengers from other lands who brought the gospel of Thy kingdom to this land, and for those who have faithfully proclaimed it to succeeding generations, and for all who have prayed and laboured for the union of Churches, especially in South India. Thou hast heard

the prayers of Thy people and blessed the labours of Thy servants, and hast brought us to this day for the glory of Thy name. In obedience to Thy will and led by Thy Spirit, as we accept one another as fellow members and fellow ministers, do Thou strengthen the bonds between us and unite us and make us one body, Thyself, O Christ, being its head. Make us all of one heart and of one soul, united in one holy bond of truth and peace, of faith and charity. Grant that this Church may ever be zealous in commending Thy glorious gospel to the millions in this land, that India may find in Thee the goal of all her seeking and the fulfillment of her noblest aspirations. Hasten the time, O God, when throughout the world there shall be one flock, one shepherd, and in the name of Jesus every knee shall bow, and every tongue confess that Jesus Christ is Lord. Amen.

Notes

1. *Baptism, Eucharist and Ministry*, Faith and Order Paper no. 111 (Geneva: World Council of Churches, 1982).

2. English translation from Y. Congar, H. Küng, and D. O'Hanlon, eds., *Council Speeches of Vatican II* (Glen Rock, NJ: Paulist Press, 1964) 96.

3. French text in *Acta Apostolicae Sedis* 58 (1966) 20-21.

4. *Papst Johannes Paulus II in Deutschland*, Verlautbarungen des Apostolischen Stuhls, vol. 25 (Bonn: Sekretariat der Deutschen Bischofskonferenz, 1980) 80 and 86.

5. Gemeinsame römisch-katholische/evangelisch-lutherische Kommission, *Einheit vor uns: Modelle, Formen und Phasen katholisch-lutherischer Kirchengemeinschaft* (Paderborn: Bonifatius; Frankfurt: Lembeck, 1985).

6. See H.G. Link, ed., *The Roots of Our Common Faith*, Faith and Order Paper no. 119 (Geneva: World Council of Churches, 1984); H.G. Link, ed., *Apostolic Faith Today: A Handbook for Study*, Faith and Order Paper no. 124 (Geneva: World Council of Churches, 1985); T.F. Best, ed., *Faith and Renewal: Commission on Faith and Order, Stavanger 1985*, Faith and Order Paper no. 131 (Geneva: World Council of Churches, 1986); H.G. Link, ed., *One God, One Lord, One Spirit*, Faith and Order Paper no. 139 (Geneva: World Council of Churches, 1988); and *Confessing the One Faith: An Ecumenical Explication of the Apostolic Faith as It Is Confessed in the Nicene-Constantinopolitan Creed (381)*, Faith and Order Paper no. 153 (Geneva: World Council of Churches, 1991)

7. *Toward Visible Unity: Proposals for a Covenant* (London: Churches' Council for Covenanting, 1980).

8. The proposals in *Covenanting Toward Unity: From Consensus to Communion* (Princeton: Consultation on Church Union, 1985) were modified in light of a rethinking (some would say a downscaling) of the structural implications of covenanting: "The churches will commit themselves to live henceforth in one covenantal communion *even though they continue to exist as distinct ecclesial systems*" (italics added); see *Churches in Covenant Communion* (Princeton: Consultation on Church Union, 1989), from where the above description of the service is taken.

9. G. Wainwright, "Confession of Fault and Reconciliation between the Church," *Concilium* 190 (1987) 117-126.

10. J.A. Jungmann, *The Early Liturgy* (Notre Dame: University of Notre Dame Press, 1959; details in his *Die lateinischen Bussriten in ihrer geschichtlichen Entwicklung* (Innsbruck: Rauch, 1932) 74-83, 238-242.

11. Jungmann, *The Early Liturgy* 245f.; details in his *Die lateinischen Bussriten* 44-74, where the author also treats "the reception of heretics" as "a kind of mitigated penance" (60; cf. 150).

12. M. Villain, *L'Abbé Paul Couturier, apôtre de l'unité chrétienne* (Tournai: Casterman, 1957) 208.

13. E.J. Lengeling, "'Per istam sanctam unctionem...adiuvet te Dominus gratia Spiritus Sancti': Der heilige Geist und die Krankensalbung," in *Lex Orandi - Lex Credendi*, Studia Anselmiana, vol. 79 (Rome: Editrice Anselmiana, 1980) 235-294.

14. Cf. Ignatius of Antioch, *Ad Eph.* 20:2.

15. See *Church, Kingdom, World*, Faith and Order Paper no. 130, ed. G. Limouris (Geneva: World Council of Churches, 1986); *Faith and Renewal*, Faith and Order Paper no. 131, ed. T.F. Best (Geneva: World Council of Churches, 1986) 192-207.

16. M. Tanner, "The Unity of the Church and the Renewal of Human Community: an Assessment of the Relationship of Unity and Renewal," *Mid-Stream* 23 (1984) 38-50, in particular 46f., 49.

17. *Faith and Renewal* 201f.

11

Reconciliation:
Irish and Ecumenical

A Topical Prologue

IF, WITHIN A HUMAN SPACE INHABITED BY PEOPLE FOR WHOM RELIGION counts, one group considers another idolatrous and is itself in turn regarded as apostate by the other (or vice versa), then you have a recipe for trouble. It might be Bosnia. The Muslims will view Orthodox Christians as close to idolaters because belief in a trinitarian God is an affront to Allah. Orthodox Christians may see Muslims as apostate because they have followed the later prophet Mohammed whereas the incarnation of the divine Word in Jesus Christ was unsurpassable. Now change the geography and locate the human space within Christendom, in a place where Catholics and Protestants live cheek by jowl. In Protestant eyes the Catholics may have apostatized from the biblical faith and, by their "breaden God" and their "worship of Mary," be committing idolatry. In Catholic eyes the Protestants may have quit the true church and turned, let us say, to a God so transcendent of the incarnate realities of the sacraments and the saints that he passes over into deism and no longer even attracts worship, though still allowing his adepts to do very nicely for themselves. In such a case you have a recipe for "the Troubles."

Perhaps my description would be caricatural if applied to Northern Ireland. But in attempting as a sympathetic outsider to address the Irish situation, I want to recognize that the conflict is at least in part theological, or even dogmatic. As a theologian, I ask what part

Christians in my profession or vocation can play in the process of reconciliation. This is not, of course, to deny that social, economic, political, and cultural factors have a role in the problem and its solution, for we still live in earthly history. But I wish to be explicitly ecclesiological in my approach, and to attempt a dogmatic analysis of the situation and to propose dogmatic hints towards a process of healing, grounding what I have to say in the Christian liturgy or the life of worship. Any useful work that theologians may accomplish in the area of reconciliation will need to percolate into the preaching and teaching of the churches and the everyday conversation of Christians.

Introduction: The Example of an Ancient Rite

An eighth- or ninth-century Irish penitential, preserved at the monastery of St. Gallen in Switzerland, instructs the minister regarding the questions he is to put to a person seeking admission to the process of penance. He is to ask:

> Do you believe in the Father and the Son and the Holy Spirit?
>
> Do you believe that these three persons, whom we have spoken of as Father and Son and Holy Spirit, are three, and that God is one?
>
> Do you believe that in the day of judgment you are to rise in the flesh in which you now stand and are to receive either good or ill according to what you have done?
>
> Are you willing to forgive those who have sinned against you, since the Lord has said, If you do not remit to men their sins, neither will your heavenly Father forgive you your sins?

A person who answers affirmatively will be admitted to penance and later, on Maundy Thursday, sacramentally "reconciled" to God and to the church, and therefore to the communion of both.[1]

My suggestion is that this early medieval form can, with necessary adaptations, supply both a theological understanding and a practical model for the reconciliation of divided Christians and their communities to one another and their common restoration to the favor of God which has at least been jeopardized if not forfeited by their divisions. First, as the approach of the penitent presupposes, the desire for reconciliation must be present. Then, as the questions concerning the Holy Trinity and the last judgement indicate, there must be an awareness of God and the history of sin and redemption. (An adjacent penitential requires that the minister "hold forth the word of salvation and give the penitent an explanation: how the devil through his pride fell from the angelic dignity and afterward through envy drove man out of paradise, and how Christ accordingly for human salvation came into the world through the virgin's womb and by his resurrection both conquered the devil and redeemed the world from sin and afterward gave the apostles the grace of baptism by which he should deliver man from his sin . . . and how in the end of the age he shall come to judge the living and the dead and to render to every man according to his work."[2]) In fact, the penitential interrogations, with their *"Credis?"* and the expected response *"Credo,"*, recall baptism and the faith it signifies—which are the basis of, and summons to, the life of communion in the Body of Christ. When divisions among believers nevertheless occur and disrupt the Body of Christ, there must be a willingness on all sides—for faults rarely if ever reside with a single party—to forgive (as the *"Vis dimittere?"* requires of the individual penitent) and to be forgiven. Mutual reconciliation then allows the parties to come before God with an open face and be embraced by God's peace, the threat of divine judgment removed, the promise of divine communion finally enjoyed, and witness borne afresh to the Gospel of grace.

Correspondingly, this chapter will have the following sequence and structure. First, the history of salvation and the preaching of the Gospel will be seen in terms of reconciliation. Second, baptism and the faith it signifies will be viewed as inclusion in that history and response to that proclamation—and *ipso facto* the constitution of membership in a new community. Third, the sad and grave fact of divisions among that community will be shown to require repentance by admission of fault, sorrow for sin, and resolution to amend; and the possibilities will be opened up for forgiveness and healing, with a view to the restoration of peace and communion. A conclusion will return to the witness made to a Gospel of reconciliation whose credibility has been impaired by obstinate divisions. The concrete cases and arguments will largely be presented on the explicit or implicit assumption of a Catholic/Protestant polarity, since this bipolar perception predominates in Ireland, although there are of course nuances—and differences!—to be recognized between the Church of Ireland (with its historic links to the Church of England), the Presbyterian Church of Ireland (with its historic links to the Church of Scotland), and the Methodist Church in Ireland (with its Wesleyan origins and tradition). The Orthodox Churches, so important in world ecumenism, will scarcely be mentioned.

THE DIVINE ACT AND MESSAGE
OF RECONCILIATION

In the canonical Scriptures common to Catholics and Protestants, an apostle equally beloved of Protestants and Catholics describes the atoning work of Christ in this way:

> If while we were at enmity with God we were reconciled to God by the death of his Son, much more, now that we are reconciled, shall we be saved by his life. Not only so, but we rejoice in God through our Lord Jesus Christ, through whom we have now received our reconciliation.

Thus writes St. Paul in Romans 5:10f.; and in 2 Corinthians 5:18-6:1 he enlarges upon the apostolic ministry and message of reconciliation that derives from God's reconciling act in Christ:

> God . . . through Christ reconciled us to himself and gave us the ministry of reconciliation; that is, in Christ God was reconciling the world to himself, not counting their trespasses against them, and entrusting to us the message of reconciliation. So we are ambassadors for Christ, God making his appeal through us. We beseech you on behalf of Christ, be reconciled to God. For our sake he made him to be sin who knew no sin, so that in him we might become the righteousness of God. Working together with him, then, we entreat you not to accept the grace of God in vain.

The initiative of the reconciliation is God's, and its scope is as wide as the world. In Ephesians 2:11-21 the apostle declares that in Christ, who "is our peace," a common reconciliation to God has been effected for both Jew and Gentile, "those who were far off" and "those who were near," which *ipso facto* "breaks down the dividing wall of hostility" *between them* also. Clearly, the history of reconciliation to God entails reconciliation among the beneficiaries of God's grace. The message of divine reconciliation requires that its witnesses live at peace with one another: such is the connection implicit in Romans 15 between the apostle's summoning of the church to unity and his evangelistic and missionary endeavors in the world. Division among Christians is bound to impair, if not nullify, their testimony to the Gospel.

Basic to the entire Christian faith, the atoning work of Christ and its consequences for believers are well recalled in the First Eucharistic Prayer for Reconciliation of the current Roman Catholic missal, at the point of the anamnesis-oblation-epiclesis:

> We do this in memory of Jesus Christ,
> our Passover and our lasting peace.
> We celebrate his death and resurrection
> and look for the coming of that day
> when he will return to give us the fullness of joy.
> Therefore we offer you, God ever faithful and true,
> the sacrifice which restores man to your friendship.
> Father,
> look with love
> on those you have called
> to share in the one sacrifice of Christ.
> By the power of your Holy Spirit
> make them one body,
> healed of all division.[3]

Acceptance of reconciliation to God sets one in a community where reconciliation among the members is the norm.

THE COMMUNITY OF FAITH AND BAPTISM

In the same context of 2 Corinthians previously cited, St. Paul declares that "if any one is in Christ, he is a new creation; the old has passed away, behold, the new has come" (2 Cor 5:17). By the grace of God one enters Christ by faith, of which baptism is the sacrament. In Christ the baptized believer can sing with Charles Wesley:

> My God is reconciled,
> His pardoning voice I hear;
> He owns me for his child,
> I can no longer fear;
> With confidence I now draw nigh,
> And Father, Abba, Father! cry.[4]

To become a child of the heavenly Father is to acquire other Christians as brothers and sisters. Ecumenically, the question arises of the extent of the family.

On the Roman Catholic side, the Second Vatican Council declared that, even in separation, people "who believe in Christ and have been properly baptized are put in some, though imperfect, communion with the Catholic Church," and "the separated churches and communities are by no means deprived of significance and importance in the mystery of salvation" (Decree on Ecumenism, *Unitatis Redintegratio* 3). The modern ecumenical movement has driven almost all Christian communities, whatever their fundamental ecclesiology, to recognize, and offer some account of, the existence of Christians beyond their own boundaries—whether it be along the lines of the "traces of the Church" (*vestigia ecclesiae*) still detected by Calvin in the Roman Church (*Institutes* IV.2.11f.), the "branch theory" of some Anglicans (as in Lancelot Andrewes' "Eastern, Western, British" or William Palmer's "Greek, Latin, Anglican"), or the "all true believers" of John Wesley.[5] Baptism and faith have figured among the evidences that allow for recognition, though regrettably not always in such a conjoint formulation as that of *Unitatis Redintegratio*.

Yet problems remain with regard to baptism and faith as elements in mutual recognition among Christian communities. Take, for example, the responses of the Irish Churches to the Lima text of WCC Faith and Order on *Baptism, Eucharist and Ministry*, and particularly its baptismal section.[6] The Methodist Church in Ireland notes an insufficient distinction "between a sign and that which it signifies." The Presbyterian Church in Ireland asserts "an indirect identity between grace and baptism" so that "baptism does not as such effectuate salvation" but is its—by no means "automatic"—sign. The (Anglican) Church of Ireland finds in the Lima text a "balanced and comprehensive" theology of baptism but regrets that the document is not clearer that the sacraments are "*effective* signs." The Roman Catholic response finds that the Lima text "has many affinities, both of style and of content, with the way the faith of the Church about baptism is stated in the Second Vatican Council and in the Liturgy of Christian Initiation promulgated by Pope Paul VI"; the gifts that Lima says baptism "signifies and effects" are endorsed, and yet "despite many important points made about the meaning of baptism, there seems to be lack of clarity on the full effect of baptism." The Irish Presbyterians appear to regret the absence of the word "sacrament," whereas the Roman Catholic response, acknowledging that this word "because of its complex history needs a great deal of explanation in interchurch conversations," finds that Lima affirms "the principal features of baptism that the word sacrament has served to express." The Irish Presbyterians suspect Lima of affirming "baptismal regeneration which we do not and cannot accept"; the Church of Ireland notes, apparently with regret, that "Anglicans will find little reference to baptism as the sacrament of regeneration." The Church of Ireland finds Lima "a very positive document, admirable in its comprehensiveness, its honesty of approach, and its economy of style. As an effort in reconciliation, it deserves our serious consideration. It does not attempt to cover over differences, nor is it superficial in searching for areas of agreement." On the other hand, the Presbyterian Church in Ireland, while finding in the Lima section on baptism "more evidence of Biblical and Reformed emphasis" than in the sections on eucharist and ministry, detects much that is "obscure," "unfamiliar," "unclear," and "ambiguous" and judges that "the Report in its main thrust presents us with a model and conception of the Christian faith with which we find it difficult if not impossible to identify. Briefly, it gives priority to the 'Catholic' over the 'Protestant' view, to historical continuity and tradition over the witness of Scripture, to the sacraments over the Word, to a view of the Church centred more on rites than on proclamation and witness."

Nevertheless, the Presbyterian Church in Ireland affirms what Lima says under the heading "Towards Mutual Recognition of Baptism": "Churches are increasingly recognizing one another's baptism as the one baptism into Christ . . . Mutual recognition of baptism is acknowledged as an important sign and means of expressing the baptismal unity given in Christ. Wherever possible, mutual recognition should be expressed explicitly by the churches."

The current promise and tension regarding mutual recognition is expressed in the comment of the Methodist Church in Ireland on the baptismal section of BEM: "The statement is to be welcomed as a means to greater understanding among the members of the WCC. And the inclusion within the commission of theologians of the Roman Catholic and other churches which do not belong to the WCC is both welcome and important, since it holds open the possibility of a coming together into one body of brethren at present separated." What measure of doctrinal agreement ("greater understanding") is necessary? And what else is needed for integration of/ into (the) "one body"? Paragraph 6 of BEM, and its internal commentary, are crucial:

> Through baptism, Christians are brought into union with Christ, with each other and with the Church of every time and place. Our common baptism, which unites us to Christ in faith, is thus a basic bond of unity ... When baptismal unity is realized in one holy, catholic, apostolic Church, a genuine Christian witness can be made to the healing and reconciling love of God. Therefore, our one baptism into Christ constitutes a call to the churches to overcome their divisions and visibly manifest their fellowship.

> *Commentary*: The inability of the churches mutually to recognize their various practices of baptism as sharing in the one baptism, and their actual dividedness in spite of mutual baptismal recognition, have given dramatic visibility to the broken witness of the Church ... The need to recover baptismal unity is at the heart of the ecumenical task ...

Clearly, baptism cannot be abstracted from its dogmatic and ecclesiological context. This is why baptism and *faith* must be considered concomitantly as factors in the reconciliation of Christian communities and the restoration of churchly unity.

In his open *Letter to a Roman Catholic*, written from Dublin in 1749, John Wesley made a plea for mutual affection and help, even though (as he would say in the more broadly addressed contemporaneous sermon on *Catholic Spirit*) differences in serious theological opinion, mode of worship, and church government "may prevent an entire external union."[7] In setting out the basis for what he proposes to the Roman Catholic, Wesley says first: "I think you deserve the tenderest regard I can show, were it only because the same God hath raised you and me from the dust of the earth and has made us both capable of loving and enjoying him to eternity; were it only because the Son of God has bought you and me with his own blood." And then Wesley continues with a "how much more," based on a large measure of *common faith*. He expounds what "a true Protestant" believes in the form of an expansion upon the Nicene-Constantinopolitan Creed. Taking up the Wesleyan precedent, the current Joint Commission between the Roman Catholic Church and the World Methodist Council, in its 1991 Singapore Report on *The Apostolic Tradition*, calls this creed, which is "used by both Catholics and Methodists in their liturgy and teaching," "a comprehensive and authoritative statement of Christian faith," which "constrains us to take very seriously the degree of communion that Catholics and Methodists already share."[8] On the multilateral ecumenical scene, the WCC Faith and Order study "Towards the Common Expression of the Apostolic Faith Today"' took the same creed as its "theological basis and methodological tool," working—by way of an exposition of its historical origin, its scriptural ground, and its contemporary relevance—towards an ecumenical recognition, explication, and confession of this classic summary of Christian belief.[9]

Would a solemn reaffirmation of the ancient ecumenical creed constitute sufficient dogmatic agreement for the restoration of full unity? Apparently not, given the kind of response made by the Vatican in 1991 to the 1982 "Final Report" of the Anglican-Roman Catholic International Commission.[10] Yet the real nub may finally prove itself to be, not so much the doctrine (say) of the eucharist or even of the Trinity, but rather ecclesiology—the doctrine of the church and the concrete claims and perceptions of ecclesial identity.[11]

Summing up the present section of this chapter, we may conclude that some kind of mutual recognition of baptism and some measure of agreement in the faith is *necessary* to reconciliation, and that some kind of mutual recognition of baptism and some measure of agreement in the faith make reconciliation *possible*. Can we now envisage a process that would in fact, perhaps by stages, *realize* reconciliation—starting from the basis of the kind(s) of mutual recognition of baptism and the measure(s) of agreement in the faith that have persisted or been attained, and moving towards the fuller communion that properly belongs to the church as the Body of Christ?

A PROCESS OF RECONCILIATION

Here I would like to suggest a process that moves from division through repentance and reconciliation to eventual communion. Maximizing whatever recognition of baptism and agreement in faith exist, let us contemplate a penitential procedure that should lead to peace and joy.

First, it is essential to register the gravity of the sin of division. Since dominical authority attaches to it, it may suffice to evoke the saying of Jesus at Matthew 5:23f., which has traditionally been employed to authorize and require an "exchange of peace" before participation in the eucharist:

> If you are offering your gift at the altar, and there remember that your brother has something against you, leave your gift there before the altar and go; first be reconciled to your brother, and then come and offer your gift.[12]

Insofar as baptism and faith have established brotherhood and sisterhood between Christians and their communities, there is a clear warning that offending parties who have not sought reconciliation after a division in the family approach God only at the risk of rejection. Disunity among Christians is thoroughly castigated in the apostolic writings, by St. Paul especially. In fact, it gives the lie to their baptisms (1 Cor 1:10-17); it turns the Lord's Supper into their own supper and brings the offenders under divine judgment (1 Cor 11:17-34). This disunity can only be overcome by drawing again on the one Spirit by whom they were baptized into Christ (1 Cor 12:12f.) and by whom they confess Christ as Lord (1 Cor 12:3).

But who is the offending party? A hint may perhaps be found in the text of St. James, which Catholics have seen as scriptural and apostolic support for a sacrament of penance (and healing): "Confess your sins to one another, and pray for one another, that you may be healed" (Jas 5:16). Certainly, hindsight usually reveals that the fault in any division—even though truth may have been at stake in a matter of doctrinal conflict—did not reside on one side alone. Even though one side rather than the other may somehow be "proved right" in a matter of faith, the responsibility for the disruption will usually have been complex—and shared. Mutuality in confession of sin may therefore be appropriate between divided Christians and their communities.

In the case of an individual Christian coming to confession, penance involves—after recognition of the gravity of sin—the admission of fault, contrition (or sorrow for the offense), and resolution to amend. Modern ecumenical history displays some striking examples of this by communities vis-à-vis divisions among them, and even of the mutual asking of forgiveness. The "sacramental" implications of such cases have not been fully appreciated, nor the full consequences drawn for reconciliation and the eventual restoration of communion.

Note the words addressed by Pope Paul VI, at the opening of the second session of Vatican II on 29 September 1963, to the observers "from the Christian denominations separated from the Catholic Church":

> If we are in any way to blame for this separation, we humbly beg God's forgiveness. And we ask our brothers' pardon for any injuries they feel they have sustained from us. For our part we willingly forgive whatever injuries the Catholic Church has suffered, and forget the grief she has endured as a result of the long years of dissension and separation. May the heavenly Father deign to honor our prayers and grant us true brotherly peace.[13]

In their "common declaration" of 7 December 1965 Pope Paul VI and Ecumenical Patriarch Athenagoros I expressed "regret for historical errors":

> They regret the offensive words, the reproaches without foundation and the reprehensible gestures which on both sides marked or accompanied the sad events of that period [i.e., 1054] . . . They deplore the troublesome precedents and the later events which, under the influence of various factors, among them lack of understanding and mutual hostility led to the effective rupture of ecclesiastical communion.[14]

In his visit to the land of Luther in 1980 Pope John Paul II said of the history of division:

> "We will not pass judgment on one another" (Rom 14:13). But let us mutually confess our guilt. With respect to the grace of unity also, it is a fact that "all have sinned" (Rom 3:23). We must recognize and acknowledge that fact in all seriousness and draw the appropriate conclusions . . . If we do not try to avoid the facts, we will realize that human failings are to blame for the harmful division of Christians, and that our own refusals have time and again hindered the steps that are possible and necessary to unity.[15]

What is being looked for here includes what was called, in an Irish School of Ecumenics study, the "reconciliation of memories,"[16] an idea taken up in the dialogue between the Roman Catholic Church and the World Alliance of Reformed Churches.[17] There is also an implicit recognition of the divine judgment under which as Christians we presently stand on account of our persistence in division. At its gravest, schism dismembers the Body of Christ. Even on a more moderate view, divisions inflict wounds on the body. At the very least, Christian disunity is a sickness of the body, and even chronic illnesses can be life-threatening. The mood is well caught by the moving prayer from the troubled England of the seventeenth century which has found its way into several subsequent editions and versions of the Book of Common Prayer:

> O God the Father of our Lord Jesus Christ, our only Saviour, the Prince of Peace: Give us grace to lay to heart the great dangers we are in by our unhappy divisions; take away all hatred and prejudice, and whatever else may hinder us from godly union and concord; that, as there is but one Body and one Spirit, one hope of our calling, one Lord, one Faith, one Baptism, one God and Father of us all, so we may be all of one heart and of one soul, united in one holy bond of truth and peace, of faith and charity, and may with one mind and one mouth glorify thee; through Jesus Christ our Lord.[18]

Repentance and reconciliation look finally to the future, where the amendment of life may take place.

A first step in the future may be the solemn exchange of peace. Dating from the "holy kiss" encouraged by St. Paul as a greeting (Rom 16:16; 1 Cor 16:20; 2 Cor 13:12; 1 Thes 5:26; cf. 1 Pt 5:14), Christian communities have included in their assemblies, under several forms and with various accompanying formulations, a gesture that liturgiologists call "the peace." In a recent study of *The Ritual Kiss in Early Christian Worship*, L. Edward Phillips identifies several themes that could be interesting if we were envisaging an exchange of peace on the part of Christian leaders and members as a regular feature, or a special stage, in a process of reconciliation among divided ecclesial bodies.[19] Phillips places the kiss in the context of the Pauline and Johannine notion of the church as a community of persons who both "share and communicate" the indwelling Spirit given by Christ, the Holy Spirit ("holy breath"). In line with this, the kiss is seen by patristic writers as both "a demonstration of union already present" and "a means of union": Cyril of Jerusalem, for instance, says that the kiss "joins souls together in search of complete forgiveness from one another"; it is "a sign of the fusion of souls, and of the expulsion of all resentment for wrongs"; it is "a reconciliation."[20] The kiss is not only given by the bishop to the newly baptized, who then share for the first time in the congregational kiss (thus in the so-called *Apostolic Tradition* of Hippolytus);

it is also given by the bishop at the reconciliation of penitents (so St. Cyprian of Carthage, for whom the kiss of peace indeed prefigures "the embrace and kiss of the Lord [*complexum et osculum Domini*]" in heaven).[21] According to the Byzantine liturgy of St. Chrysostom, the exchange of peace is a summons to "love one another in order that we may with one heart and mind confess the Father, Son and Holy Spirit, consubstantial and undivided Trinity"—a confession which is then immediately enacted in the recitation of the Nicene-Constantinopolitan Creed before the anaphora or great eucharistic prayer proper; but Phillips suggests, on the basis of geographically scattered hints, that the greeting at the kiss of peace may originally have constituted the opening exchange of the dialogue introducing the anaphora itself[22]—and the anaphora is the supreme doxological confession of the Holy Trinity. Taking into consideration the associated themes of the Holy Spirit, baptism, reconciliation, unanimous confession of faith and praise of God, and the anticipation of the consummation, it would appear that there is room for the imaginative and productive use of the "kiss" or exchange of peace by historically divided Christian communities on their way from mutual recognition of baptism to the joyful restoration of full eucharistic communion.

Conclusion: Witness in the World

The Joint Commission between the Roman Catholic Church and the World Methodist Council envisages its dialogue as working towards the goal of "full communion in faith, mission, and sacramental life."[23] Deepening mutual recognition of baptism and increasing agreement in the faith as a prelude to eventual eucharistic communion can allow already for some cooperation in mission. The progress of reconciliation can itself help to render more credible the witness made to the Gospel, for Jesus prayed "that they may all be one, that *the world may believe that thou hast sent me*" (Jn 17:21).

The Irish Church and churches have historically played a prominent part in the spread of the Gospel, from the early evangelization of Britain and continental Europe to the worldwide modern missionary movement. In modern times, India was a choice spot for their contribution; and so it may be appropriate to receive back from there a testimony from the Church of South India, which in 1947 brought together the fruit of labors on the part of missionary societies belonging to separated churches in the home countries (Anglican, Congregational, Methodist, Presbyterian). Here, then, is a prayer from the "Order of Service for the Inauguration of Church Union in South India." *Mutatis mutandis,* it might be prayed in Ireland:

> Almighty and everlasting God, who alone art the author of unity, peace and concord, we thank Thee for the Churches in this our land and for Thy grace in choosing us to be members in Thy Church. We bless Thee for our fellowship, and for our rich inheritance. We praise Thee for Thy messengers from other lands who have brought the gospel of Thy kingdom to this land, and for those who have faithfully proclaimed it to succeeding generations, and for all who have prayed and laboured for the union of Churches, especially in South India. Thou hast heard the prayers of Thy people and blessed the labours of Thy servants, and hast brought us to this day for the glory of Thy name. In obedience to Thy will and led by Thy Spirit, as we accept one another as fellow members and fellow ministers, do Thou strengthen the bonds between us and unite us and make us one body, Thyself, O Christ, being its head. Make us all of one heart and of one soul, united in one holy bond of truth and peace, of faith and charity. Grant that this Church may ever be zealous in commending Thy glorious gospel to the millions in this land, that India may find in Thee the goal of all her seeking and the fulfilment of her noblest aspirations. Hasten the time, O God, when throughout the world there shall be one flock, one shepherd, and in the name of Jesus every knee shall bow, and every tongue confess that Jesus Christ is Lord. Amen.

A Personal Epilogue

An earlier Yorkshireman, the Carolingian Alcuin, wrote to the Christians in Ireland on the obligation to preach the orthodox faith, on the Lord's command to love one another, and on the fruitfulness of confession and penance while this life lasts.[24] If I have dared to do the same in the cause of reconciliation, it is only because my own British Methodist Church is implicated in the sin of ecclesial division, and because the need for Christian unity, and the ecumenical search for it, are worldwide.

I have here deliberately treated the theme of "Reconciliation: Irish and Ecumenical" in confessional and ecclesiastical terms. This does not imply that one can ignore social, cultural, psychological, economic, and political differences and conflicts—what were, at an earlier stage in the modern ecumenical movement, exaggeratedly called *"non*-theological factors." My thesis, however, is that faith, sacraments, and ecclesiology engage human life at a more fundamental and decisive level than the social, cultural, psychological, economic, and political. They set us directly *coram Deo*. The divine revelation and redemption told in the canonical Christian story provide a framework in which penultimate differences can be discussed; and, as progress is made in reconciliation in matters of faith, sacraments, and church, there emerges a hope for the resolution of those other conflicts in a gospel light. In other words, my bet is that water, bread, and wine are more potent symbols than sashes, berets, and flags. Hands lifted in prayer or laid on heads in forgiveness and healing are closer to reality than hands that plant bombs or squeeze triggers. The kiss of peace is more significant than a political pact, for which, however, it may lay the ground. If these things are not the case, then ultimately we are all losers.

Notes

1. Latin in F.E. Warren, *The Liturgy and Ritual of the Celtic Church* (Oxford: Clarendon Press, 1881) 151f.

2. From the Poenitentiale Sangallense Simplex. Latin in Herm. Jos. Schmitz, *Die Bussbücher und das kanonische Bussverfahren—nach handschriftlichen Quellen dargestellt* (Düsseldorf: Schwann, 1898; reprint Graz: Akademische Druck- und Verlagsanstalt, 1958) 340, cf. pp. 177, 345. English translation from John T. McNeill and Helena M. Gamer, *Medieval Handbooks of Penance: A Translation of the Principal "Libri Poenitentiales" and Selections from Related Documents* (New York: Columbia University Press, 1938) 280f.

3. *Glenstal Bible Missal* (London: Collins, 1983) 1593.

4. From the "Hymns and Sacred Poems" of 1742, in *The Poetical Works of John and Charles Wesley*, ed. G. Osborn, vol. 2 (London: Wesleyan-Methodist Conference Office, 1869) 323f. The hymn "Arise, My Soul, Arise," number 368 in *The Methodist Hymn Book* (London, 1933), has regrettably been altered in *Hymns and Psalms: A Methodist and Ecumenical Hymn Book* (London: Methodist Publishing House, 1983), hymn number 217.

5. For Wesley, see Geoffrey Wainwright, *The Ecumenical Moment: Crisis and Opportunity for the Church* (Grand Rapids: Eerdmans, 1983) 207-209.

6. *Baptism, Eucharist and Ministry*, Faith and Order Paper no. 111 (Geneva: World Council of Churches, 1982). The official responses of the churches are gathered in *Churches Respond to BEM*, ed. Max Thurian, 6 vols. (Geneva:

World Council of Churches, 1986-1988). The Church of Ireland response is found in vol. 1, pp. 61-69; the Methodist Church in Ireland in vol. 2, pp. 230-235; the Presbyterian Church in Ireland in vol. 3, pp. 206-221; the worldwide Roman Catholic Church in vol. 6, pp. 1-40.

7. See *John Wesley's Letter to a Roman Catholic*, ed. Michael Hurley (London: Chapman; Belfast: Epworth House, 1968). Sermon 39, "Catholic Spirit," is found in the Bicentennial Edition of *The Works of John Wesley*, vol. 2, ed. Albert C. Outler (Nashville: Abingdon, 1985) 81-95.

8. Joint Commission between the Roman Catholic Church and the World Methodist Council, *The Apostolic Tradition* (Lake Junaluska, NC: World Methodist Council, 1991).

9. See *Confessing One Faith: Towards an Ecumenical Explication of the Apostolic Faith as Expressed in the Nicene-Constantinopolitan Creed (381)*, Faith and Order Paper no. 140 (Geneva: World Council of Churches, 1987); revised as *Confessing the One Faith: An Ecumenical Explication of the Apostolic Faith as It Is Confessed in the Nicene-Constantinopolitan Creed (381)*, Faith and Order Paper no. 153 (Geneva: World Council of Churches, 1991).

10. Text in *Origins* 21 (1991-1992) 441ff.

11. It was above all an *ecclesiological* insufficiency that the Roman Catholic response found in BEM; see Geoffrey Wainwright, "The Roman Catholic Response to *Baptism, Eucharist and Ministry*: The Ecclesiological Dimension," in *A Promise of Presence: Studies in Honor of David N. Power, O.M.I.*, ed. Michael Downey and Richard Fragomeni (Washington, D.C.: The Pastoral Press, 1992) 187-206. The international bilateral dialogues turned to the theme of the church in the 1980s—especially where the Roman Catholic Church was one of the partners, as with the Orthodox (*The Mystery of the Church*, 1982), the Methodists (*Towards a Statement on the Church*, 1986; *The Apostolic Tradition*, 1991), the Anglicans (*Salvation and the Church*, 1986; *The Church as Communion*, 1991), and the Reformed (*Towards a Common Understanding of the Church*, 1991).

12. *Didache* 14:1f. reads: "On the Lord's day come together, break bread, and give thanks, having first confessed your transgressions, that your sacrifice may be pure. But let none who has a quarrel with his companion join with you until they have been reconciled, that your sacrifice may not be defiled" (cf. *Apostolic Constitutions* II.57.16 and VIII.12.2). In Eastern Churches, the "peace" occurs before the eucharistic anaphora; and the following patristic writers appeal to Matthew 5:23f. in this connection: Irenaeus, *Adversus Haereses* IV.18.1; Cyril of Jerusalem, *Mystagogical Catecheses* V.3f.; John Chrysostom, *Baptismal Instruction* XI (Papadopoulos-Kerameus 3), 32-34 (see Paul W. Harkins, *St. John Chrysostom: Baptismal Instructions*, Ancient Christian Writers, vol. 31 [Westminster, MD: Newman Press, 1963] 171f.); Theodore of Mopsuestia, *Catechetical Homily* 15 = *Baptismal Homily* 4, 40 (see Edward Yarnold, *The Awe Inspiring Rites of Initiation: Baptismal Homilies of the Fourth Century* [Slough: St. Paul Publica-

tions, 1972] 234); Narsai, *Homily* 17 (R.H. Connolly, *The Liturgical Homilies of Narsai* [Cambridge: The University Press, 1909] 9). According to St. Augustine (*Sermon* 227; Migne: *Patrologia Latina* 38:1099-1101), in early fifth-century North Africa the *pax* occurred just before communion, perhaps having been attracted to that position by the petition in the Lord's Prayer said at that point ("Forgive us our trespasses, as we forgive them that trespass against us"); cf. perhaps already Tertullian, who also cites Matthew 5:23f. (*De Oratione* 11; Migne: *Patrologia Latina* 1:1269-1270). This eventually became the Roman order: eucharistic prayer, Lord's Prayer, (*Agnus Dei*), peace, communion.

13. English translation from *Council Speeches of Vatican II*, ed. Y. Congar, H. Küng, D. O'Hanlon (Glen Rock, NJ: Paulist Press, 1964) 146f.

14. French text in *Acta Apostolicae Sedis* 58 (1966) 20f.

15. German in *Papst Johannes Paulus in Deutschland*, Verlautbarungen des Apostolischen Stuhls, vol. 25 (Bonn: Sekretariat der Deutschen Bischofskonferenz, 1980) 80 and 86.

16. *Reconciling Memories*, ed. Alan D. Falconer (Dublin: The Columba Press, 1988).

17. *Towards a Common Understanding of the Church: Reformed/Roman Catholic International Dialogue: Second Phase, 1984-1990* (Geneva: World Alliance of Reformed Churches, 1991).

18. This "prayer for unity" was included in the 1878 and 1926 versions of the *Book of Common Prayer* of the Church of Ireland (in the latter it was indeed promoted to first place among the "prayers and thanksgivings [upon several occasions]"). Regrettably, no real equivalent is found in the *Irish Alternative Prayer Book* of 1984.

19. L. Edward Phillips, *The Ritual Kiss in Early Christian Worship*. Ph.D. dissertation, University of Notre Dame (Ann Arbor, MI: University Microfilms International, 1992).

20. Cyril of Jerusalem, *Mystagogical Catecheses* V.3; see Yarnold, *The Awe-Inspiring Rites* 88f.; cf. Phillips, *The Ritual Kiss* 239f., 263f.

21. See Phillips, *The Ritual Kiss* 99-110 with reference to *Apostolic Tradition* 18 and 21; and 131f. with references to Cyprian, *Epistles* 6, 37, and 55.

22. See Phillips, *The Ritual Kiss* 196-212.

23. As in note 11: *Towards a Statement on the Church* (1986) #20; *The Apostolic Tradition* (1991) #94.

24. Alcuin, *Epistula* 225 (*Ad fratres qui in Hibernia insula per diversa loca Deo deservire videntur*), Migne: *Patrologia Latina* 100:500-503; cf. Stephen Allott, *Alcuin of York* (York: William Sessions, 1974) 45-47. Alcuin himself, who "had shriving and being shriven very much at heart," was influential in the spread of the Irish practice of frequent penance in England and on the European continent; see Gerald Ellard, *Master Alcuin, Liturgist* (Chicago: Loyola University Press, 1956) 207-209.

12

Eucharist and/as Ethics

Prologue: A Play with Words

EUCHARIST AND/AS ETHICS: THE PREGNANT HESITANCY OF THAT GIVEN TITLE suggests that our topic is full of both problems and positive potential. Take first "eucharist as ethics." The danger is that we shall see the eucharist as a duty more than as a delight. Or in historic Lutheran terms: we may succumb to works-righteousness if, with the medieval west, we place worship or religion under moral theology and view the liturgy as a *"cultus debitus,"* the payment of what we owe to God. Nevertheless, that is a risk I believe we are obliged to take; and fortunately the Lutheran tradition contains a feature that helps correct our course: I mean the understanding of "ethics as eucharist," though here in turn we shall have to be on our guard against dissolving the concreteness of the ethical demand into a mere doxological intention. The first half of this study, then, will be divided into two: "eucharist as ethics" and "ethics as eucharist."

But now take the other formulation of the title: "eucharist and ethics." If the first formulation—"eucharist as ethics," "ethics as eucharist"—threatened to confuse the two to the advantage of one or the other, the difficulty with the conjunctive formulation, on its own, is that we may never be able to bring the two together: eucharist *and* ethics, ethics *and* eucharist. In the second half of this study, my aim will be to show that it is precisely the dialectical mutual inclusions of "eucharist as ethics," "ethics as eucharist," which allow us to state correctly the reciprocal relationship: eucharist and ethics, ethics and eucharist.

EUCHARIST AS ETHICS, ETHICS AS EUCHARIST

For each of the mutual inclusions there is a Christological foundation. "My meat," says the Jesus of the Fourth Gospel, in a word which has the ring of authenticity, "is to do the will of him who sent me, and to accomplish his work" (Jn 4:32-34). That will and work involved Jesus in giving his flesh for the life of the world (Jn 6:51c). Jesus is the bread come down from heaven; and those who partake of him, who eat of his flesh and drink of his blood, have the divine life in them and will be raised at the last day (Jn 6:47-59). Thus to believe in Jesus is to "be doing the works of God" (Jn 6:28f.). Or to put it another way: "Eternal life is this, that they know thee the only true God, and Jesus Christ whom thou hast sent" (Jn 17:3). To know God, biblically, is to walk in God's ways.[1] And to have been "created in Christ Jesus" is to have been created "for good works, which God prepared beforehand, that we should walk in them" (Eph 2:10). Believingly to receive the body and blood of Christ is to be set on the path of righteousness: the eucharist is the beginning of ethics.

Then in the other direction, too: for ethics as eucharist there is a Christological foundation also. In Hebrews 10:5-10 Christ is made to say, "upon coming into the world:

> Sacrifices and offerings thou hast not desired,
> but a body hast thou prepared for me;
> in burnt offerings and sin offerings
>   thou hast taken no pleasure.
> Then I said, 'Lo I have come to do
>   thy will, O God,'
> as it is written of me in the roll of the book."

And the passage goes on: "When he said above, 'Thou hast neither desired nor taken pleasure in sacrifices and offerings and burnt offerings and sin offerings' (these are offered according to the law), then he added, 'Lo, I have come to do thy will.' He abolishes the first in order to establish the second. And by that will we have been sanctified through the offering of the body of Jesus Christ once for all." As Joseph Ratzinger puts it, the incarnation, life, and cross of Jesus are thus seen as a "prayer-event" (*Gebetsgeschehen*) between the Father and the Son.[2] Our incorporation into Christ takes us up into the prayer and self-offering of Jesus, so that our words and acts are lifted before God. Since that happens solely by the grace of God, our ethics can only be eucharistic.

Having laid the Christological foundation for both "eucharist as ethics" and "ethics as eucharist," let us build each up in turn.

Eucharist as Ethics

Right at the outset I warned you that Lutherans are likely to find this difficult. Let me compound the difficulty by quoting a Lutheran, and then Luther himself, in my favor. Eilert Herms, a systematician formerly of Kiel and Munich and now of Mainz, has recently written this: "That faith is a gift of God and *not* a deed of man, is emphatically to be denied. It derives from an insufficient distinction between revelation, which is truly God's act alone, and faith, which is an *act of man and a good work*; and this without prejudice to the fact that faith is necessarily conditioned by God's act of revelation."[3] For myself, I am not sure whether, even when so relocated, the characteristically sharp Lutheran distinction between God and humanity is proper; but I am impressed by this recognition of the active, human side of faith. And Herms appeals to Luther for support: Christian faith is made possible by the revelatory occurrence of the word of God; and, as the trusting acknowledgment of the Creator who is manifest in Christ, it is the active and responsible fulfillment of the first commandment on humanity's part, and as such it is that good work which all other good works flow from, enter into, and are measured by, including the public worship of God according to the third commandment (the hallowing of the holy day). So Herms reads Luther's *Treatise on Good Works*.[4] And in the *Large Catechism* all the commandments are said to depend on the first, which pervades all the others.[5] This insight is already obscured, says Herms, when the Augsburg Confession speaks of good works as the *consequence* of faith (arts. 6 and 20), and the point is even further lost by Melanchthon in the *Apology*.

However controversial Herms' argument may be, Luther's location of worship as the human creature's primary obligation toward the Creator has been demonstrated historically by Vilmos Vajta[6] and developed systematically by Peter Brunner.[7] Or to put it negatively, the primal sin is unbelief, exchanging the truth of God for a lie. And as Paul further teaches in Romans 1:18-32, the failure to honor God as God and give God thanks expresses itself in worship of the creature rather than the Creator. Luther knew that human beings are worshiping beings; the only question is whether we worship the true God or an idol: "That to which your heart clings and entrusts itself is, I say, really your god" (*Large Catechism*, on the first commandment).[8] The apostle identifies idolatry with covetousness (Eph 5:5; Col 3:5): worship of the creature is ultimately worship of self; and the heart turned in upon itself (*cor in se incurvatum*) is, as Luther also knew, doomed.

The worship of the Creator is, then, the first and last condition of appropriate human being: "Man's chief end is to glorify God, and to enjoy him for ever" (Westminster *Shorter Catechism*). Redeemed in Christ, we are now exhorted "through Christ to offer up continually to God a sacrifice of praise, the fruit of lips that acknowledge his name" (Heb 13:15). The *sacrificium laudis* became a name for the Christian eucharist. In the sacrifice of praise the emphasis is not so much on the praise as such, as though God needed our flattery; the accent falls rather on the offering of ourselves in Christ. St. John Chrysostom writes this: "God does not need anything of ours, but we stand in need of all things from God. The thanksgiving itself adds nothing to God, but it brings us closer to God."[9] For St. Augustine, the heart of sacrifice resides in this: "to adhere to God in holy fellowship."[10] The kingdom of God includes human salvation. "The glory of God is the human person alive," says St. Irenaeus, "and the life of the human person is the vision of God."[11]

That, then, is how eucharist may be viewed as ethics. In grateful worship, redeemed creatures are fulfilling the destiny for which their Creator and Redeemer made them and set them free. The will of God is being done. Our duty is also our delight. Let us now see how ethics may be viewed as eucharist.

Ethics as Eucharist

After speaking of the sacrifice of praise, the writer to the Hebrews immediately goes on: "To do good, and to distribute, forget not; for with such sacrifices God is pleased" (Heb 13:16). Thus Christian behavior is set in a liturgical context and interpreted in liturgical terms. So also St. Paul: after eleven chapters of what God has done for us in Christ, culminating in an outburst of praise, the apostle exhorts the Roman Christians: "I appeal to you therefore, brothers and sisters, by the mercies of God, to present your bodies as a living sacrifice to God, which is your reasonable worship" (Rom 12:1). This sequence is taken up into Cranmer's *Book of Common Prayer* (1552/1662); after the reception of God's gift in the holy communion, the following prayers are said: "O Lord and heavenly Father, we thy humble servants entirely desire thy fatherly goodness mercifully to accept this sacrifice of praise and thanksgiving . . . And here we offer and present unto thee, O Lord, ourselves, our souls and bodies, to be a reasonable, holy, and lively sacrifice unto thee . . ." Or in the alternative prayer: "Almighty and ever-living God, we must heartily thank thee, for that thou dost vouchsafe to feed us, who have duly received these holy mysteries, with the spiritual food of the most precious Body and Blood of thy Son our Saviour Jesus Christ . . . And we most humbly beseech thee, O heavenly Father, so to assist us with thy grace, that we may continue in that holy fellowship, and do all such good works as thou hast prepared for us to walk in . . ."

As grateful response to what God has already done for us, and as thankful cooperation with what God continues to do in us, our self-offering to God is removed from Pelagianism or works-righteousness. Luther's ethics was profoundly eucharistic. One quotation must suffice: "A Christian who lives in this confidence towards God knows everything, is capable of everything, dares to do everything that needs to be done, and does everything joyfully and freely, not in order to amass merit and good works, but because it is a pleasure to him to please God in this way; and he serves God wholly gratuitously, content that it pleases God."[12]

The clearest of all biblical texts in favor of a eucharistic ethic is Colossians 3:17: "And whatever you do, in word or deed, do everything in the name of the Lord Jesus, giving thanks to God the Father through him" (cf. Eph 5:20). Let us look at this in a little more concrete detail, still sticking with the Pauline writings.

In 1 Corinthians 6, St. Paul treats personal morality in the governing conceptuality of worship: "Do you not know that your body is a temple of the Holy Spirit within you, which you have from God? You are not your own; you were bought with a price. So glorify God in your body." It is, incidentally, under this last rubric that St. Benedict sets the whole of the *opus Dei*: the monks "magnify the Lord who is at work in them" (*operantem in se Dominum magnificant*) (prologue to the Rule). But to return to the apostle; he is being quite explicit about individual conduct: "Do you not know that the unrighteous will not enter the kingdom of God? Do not be deceived;

neither the immoral, nor idolaters, nor adulterers, nor sexual perverts, nor thieves, nor the greedy, nor drunkards, nor revilers, nor robbers will inherit the kingdom of God. And such were some of you. But you were washed, you were sanctified, you were justified in the name of the Lord Jesus and in the Spirit of our God." Nevertheless, he needs to remind them: "Do you not know that your bodies are members of Christ? Shall I therefore take the members of Christ and make them members of a prostitute? Never!"

Concrete doxological holiness is extended to the Christian community as a whole in 2 Corinthians 6: "What agreement has the temple of God with idols? For we are the temple of the living God; as God said,

> 'I will live in them and move among them,
> and I will be their God,
> and they shall be my people.
> Therefore come out from them,
>   and be separate from them, says the Lord,
> and touch nothing unclean;
> then I will welcome you,
> and I will be a father to you,
>   and you shall be my sons and daughters,
> says the Lord Almighty.'

Since we have these promises, beloved, let us cleanse ourselves from every defilement of body and spirit, and make holiness perfect in the fear of God." That passage has lost none of its relevance. There are certain practices current in our North Atlantic society in which we cannot ourselves indulge doxologically; which simply cannot be done with thanks to God and in the name of the Lord Jesus. The apostle has specified them plainly enough in the passages quoted above and in many others. No amount of sophisticated wriggling will put us in a position to share in them acceptably *coram Deo*.

Equally, there remains a definite and positive conduct which, as a Christian community, we are called to practice if our praise and thanks are to rise acceptably before God. The challenges of the Old Testament prophets remain in force (for example, Is 1:10-17; Am 5:21-24; Hos 6:6). But to take one fundamental example from the New Testament, in Romans 15:5f. St. Paul expresses this wish and prayer: "May the God of steadfastness and encouragement grant you to live in such harmony with one another, in accord with Christ Jesus, that with one mind you may glorify with one voice the God and Father of our Lord Jesus Christ."

In the Byzantine liturgy, before the creed and the anaphora the people are summoned in this way: "Let us love one another, that with one mind we may confess the Father, the Son, and the Holy Spirit." This applies at the level of personal relations in the local congregation. In our sadly divided Christendom we are also institutionally under an obligation to work for the time when "all in each place," that is to say "local churches which are themselves truly united," will "once again live as brothers and sisters in one undivided Church," each local church in fellowship with all the others and recognized as "belonging to the same Church of Christ and guided by the same Spirit."[13]

Here we end the first half of this study. So far, it has been shown that eucharistic worship is the fulfillment of the first and primary commandment of the Creator, now renewed in Jesus Christ: "This do in remembrance of me." Having this ethical character from the beginning, the liturgy properly spills over in a eucharistic ethic, calling for doxological living. Conversely, all our life in this world is meant to be a grateful response to God's gifts in creation and redemption; it will come to appropriate liturgical expression in an ethically responsible eucharist. Having dialectically located ethics at the heart of eucharist and eucharist at the heart of ethics, we can now formulate the positive relations between the two in their distinctness: ethics and eucharist, eucharist and ethics.

ETHICS AND EUCHARIST, EUCHARIST AND ETHICS

We may begin generally with a reflection on the reciprocal relationship implied by those "ands." To characterize the relation between "the company of Christians" and "the company of citizens," Karl Barth used the term "analogy."[14] The values known by the church in an "internal" and "definitive" way are to be realized in society at least in an "external" and "provisional" way. The mission of the church is to bear witness before the world to life, freedom, justice, peace, love, humanity, and all the other marks of God's kingdom. If this sounds too Calvinist to Lutheran ears, we might try to put the matter more sacramentally; and this could also help some of the rest of us who have difficulties from another angle with Lutheran doctrine on the two kingdoms.

The title of the 1983 Valparaiso Liturgical Institute was "The Eucharist: The Life of the Church." The theme of the Vancouver Assembly of the World Council of Churches in August 1983 was

"Jesus Christ: The Life of the World."[15] Put those two together sacramentally, and one gets a clue to the relationship between eucharist and ethics, ethics and eucharist. The eucharist is the sacrament of the Savior, and the church is the sacrament of the world's salvation. In the eucharist the church experiences salvation at the hands of the Savior in the mediated directness of the rite. What is there received and enjoyed in reality-filled symbols has to be discerned and enacted in everyday life, both among Christian believers and, so far as they are able, in the affairs of society at large. Christians come from the world, bearing (as it were) the raw materials for the eucharist, which is then celebrated in the assembled church. From the liturgical gathering they return to recognize and translate the eschatological reality—there experienced under signs— in quite mundane decisions and deeds which are part of the history of a human race that is an object of God's loving purpose. This oscillating movement, made possible by the mutual inclusion which enabled us to speak of "eucharist as ethics" and "ethics as eucharist," is now to be taken as the form of the dynamic reciprocal relationship between "ethics and eucharist," "eucharist and ethics."

Ethics and Eucharist

How, then, do we come from our daily life to the eucharist? I want to suggest an approach that combines six attitudes: anguish and confidence, repentance and resolve, intercession and thanksgiving.

First, anguish. The forms and degrees of existential anxiety vary with times and places, with cultures and with individuals; but death, dread, and despair are never far away from fallen humanity. They set the mood of many in our society today, threatened by global disaster and by the collapse of a civilization which had at least paid lip service to evangelical values. Like Jehoshaphat in the face of the invading enemy, "we are powerless against this great multitude that is coming against us; we do not know what to do" (2 Chr 20:12). Nevertheless, we have "a house in which the name of the Lord dwells"; indeed we *are* that house (Eph 2:19-22; 1 Pt 2:4f.); and so we foregather: "We do not know what to do, but our eyes are upon thee."[16]

Second, then, we come with confidence. We echo the Psalmist:

> I lift up my eyes to the hills.
> From whence does my help come?

My help comes from the Lord,
    who made heaven and earth.

That is true already at the level of physical preservation:

The eyes of all look to thee,
    and thou givest them, their food in due season.

These same Psalms, 121 and 145, make clear, moreover, that it is the matter of a Lord who by his mighty deeds saves his people in the very depths of their spiritual existence. He did this to the ultimate in Christ, and so we now await only the final manifestation of his triumph: "Look up and raise your heads, because your redemption is drawing near" (Lk 21:28). "Our citizenship is in heaven, from whence we await a Savior" (Phil 3:20). So "Lift up your hearts": "We lift them to the Lord." Ephesians 2:18 lays down the pattern of the classical eucharistic prayer: "Through Christ we have access in the one Spirit to the Father." "And now as our Savior Christ hath commanded and taught us, we are bold to say: Our Father . . . Thy kingdom come" (Book of Common Prayer, following the Roman Mass). Or with the *Didachè*: "Let grace come and this world pass away . . . Maranatha."

But, third, we come in repentance; for we know that we ourselves are part of the threat to ourselves. I know of no stronger confession of sin than that in the *Lutheran Book of Worship* of 1977: "Most merciful God, we confess that we are in bondage to sin and cannot free ourselves . . ." Charles Wesley prefers to confess: "He breaks the power of cancelled sin"; but, whatever the nuances in the process of redemption, so much of "the world," in the negative apocalyptic sense, still remains in us that even our eucharists may be disfigured. The Sri Lankan Catholic theologian, Tissa Balasuriya, observes that the golden vessels of the Mass are the spoils of colonialist robbery.[17] According to the Peruvian Gustavo Gutierrez the tension in contemporary Latin American Christianity between the political and economic oppressors and the politically and economically oppressed is such that "participation in the Eucharist, as it is celebrated today, appears to many to be an action which, without an authentic Christian community underlying it, becomes an exercise in make-believe."[18]

So, fourth, we come with resolve, hoping for "time for amendment of life" (Book of Common Prayer). This requires discernment.

The apostle knew the condition of our offering ourselves in reasonable worship: "Do not be conformed to this world but be transformed by the renewal of your mind, that you may prove what is the will of God, what is good and acceptable and perfect" (Rom 12:2). In the last section I shall be suggesting how the eucharist supplies us with paradigms to assist our discernment and action.

The good works of humans in the world can never be other or more than cooperation with God's will and activity. And so we come, fifth, in intercession, asking for the primary agency of God in the fulfillment of the divine purpose for the world. When Paul, through Timothy, urges that prayers be made for all people, he sets that request in the framework of God's universal saving will (1 Tim 2:1-7).

In the same passage the apostle also urges that thanksgivings be made for all people. Again, this can only be on account of their potential, of what they are called to as objects of God's will for their salvation in the one mediator between God and humankind, Christ Jesus. Our sixth attitude, then, in approaching the eucharist is precisely that of thanksgiving. The context is creation, but a world for which Christ has now done his redeeming work and which can therefore look forward in faith and hope to a final destiny in God's kingdom. The offering of creation and of ourselves for transformation is beautifully expressed in the new Roman prayers at the preparation of the gifts: "Blessed are you, Lord, God of all creation. Through your goodness we have this bread to offer, which earth has given and human hands have made. It will become for us the bread of life." "Blessed are you, Lord, God of all creation. Through your goodness we have this wine to offer, fruit of the vine and work of human hands. It will become our spiritual drink." This is the very specific focus from which to apply in everyday existence the general principle set forth in 1 Timothy 4:4: "Everything created by God is good, and nothing is to be rejected if it is received with thanksgiving; for then it is consecrated by the word of God and prayer."

All that, then, is how we come from our daily lives to the Lord's meal, from ethics to eucharist. The other side of the reciprocal relationship is expressed in the movement from eucharist to ethics.

Eucharist and Ethics

Here I want to suggest that the eucharist provides enabling paradigms for our ethical engagement in the world: the eucharist allows us to learn, absorb, and extend the values of God's kingdom.

At their ordination Roman Catholic priests are told, in a phrase of striking density, *"Imitamini quod tractatis"*: "Imitate what you handle. In as much as you celebrate the mystery of the Lord's death and resurrection, endeavor to mortify all sin in your members and to walk in newness of life." The prayers of the great fifty days of Eastertide indicate that the same is expected of all Christians: "Grant that the sacraments we have received at Easter may continue to live in our minds and hearts." "Grant that we may imitate and achieve what we celebrate and profess." "Grant that we who have celebrated the Easter ceremonies may hold to them in life and conduct."[19]

Let us look more precisely at the eucharist in these terms, beginning perhaps in a somewhat paradoxical place. In Romans 14:17 St. Paul declares: "The kingdom of God is *not* food and drink but righteousness and peace and joy in the Holy Spirit."[20] The context of the apostle's remark is disputes over meat-eating and wine-drinking: he rebukes those who, "for the sake of food, destroy the work of God." According to St. Luke, the Lord will at the judgment reject the claim of the "workers of iniquity" to have eaten and drunk in his presence (Lk 13:25-27). Yet the kingdom of God is pictured as a feast: "And people will come from the east and the west, and from the north and south, and sit at table in the kingdom of God" (Lk 13:29). It would capture the gist of biblical teaching concerning the messianic banquet if we were to paraphrase the apostle thus: "The kingdom of God is food and drink *only insofar as* eating and drinking express justice, peace, and joy in the Holy Spirit."

When any creature of God is received with thanksgiving (cf. 1 Tim 4:3-5), its use thereby becomes an occasion and medium of communion with God. In what it does with the bread and wine over which it has given thanks, the eucharistic liturgy makes exemplary use of all food and drink as a medium of communion with God which cannot make abstraction of communion with fellow humans (cf. 1 Jn 4:7-21). Moreover, the general way in which people use all food is itself a test of the way in which they are living before God and among themselves. Since the eucharist is representative of all meals, and since all food and drink is representative of the totality of human life, the sacrament should be so celebrated that it shows the kingdom of God to be food and drink, *only upon condition that* their use embodies justice, peace, and joy in the Holy Spirit.

Let us look at those three in turn. First, justice. A responsibly celebrated eucharist exemplifies justice because grateful people are all equally welcomed there by the merciful Lord into his table fellowship, and all together share in the fruits of redemption and in the foretaste of the new heavens and the new earth in which right will prevail (cf. 2 Pt 3:13). Second, peace. The eucharist, responsibly celebrated, exemplifies peace because reconciled people are there at peace with God and with one another (cf. Mt 5:23f.). Third, joy. The eucharist, responsibly celebrated, exemplifies joy in the Holy Spirit because there we "do not get drunk with wine" but rather the cup of blessing conveys to all who partake of it a taste of that "sober inebriation" which the Spirit gives (cf. Eph 5:18).[21]

Having learned and experienced all this in the paradigm of the eucharistic meal, the church is committed to an everyday witness in word and deed which will give the opportunity for all the material resources of creation and all occasions of human contact to become the medium of that communion with God and among human beings which is marked by justice, peace, and joy in the Holy Spirit, and in which the kingdom of God consists.

In terms of ethical theory, the eucharistic paradigm points us in the right direction: it sets the vector within which the difficult concrete decisions and actions of everyday life have to be taken and performed if they are to be authentically Christian; it excludes the choices which would fall out of the range indicated by the values of the kingdom there expressed in symbolic form.

But the eucharist does not only draw the pattern: it also gives the power and conveys a promise. The postcommunion prayer in the Church of England's *Alternative Service Book* (1980) reads thus:

> Almighty God,
> we thank you for feeding us
> with the body and blood of your Son
> 　Jesus Christ.
> Through him we offer you our souls and bodies
> to be a living sacrifice.
> Send us out
> in the power of your Spirit
> to live and work
> to your praise and glory.

Christ's pattern is not only to be observed but, by his grace, entered into; and for that we are given the power of the Holy Spirit. The resultant doxological living is supported by the divine promise that one day God's kingdom will be complete. It is this eschatological prospect which also contains the witnessing character of Christian behavior: "Let your light so shine before others, that they may see your good works and glorify your Father who is in heaven" (Mt 5:16). "Maintain good conduct among the Gentles, so that in case they speak against you as wrongdoers, they may see your good deeds and glorify God on the day of visitation" (1 Pt 2:12). What we receive in the eucharist, we are to do and to recognize in the world: we are to initiate and join in the works that bespeak the kingdom of God. In this context, "whoever is not against us is for us" (Mk 9:38-41).[22]

Epilogue: An Eschatological Game

Jean-Jacques von Allmen once characterized Christian worship as "an eschatological game."[23] It cannot do without rules; it profits from tried techniques; it calls for skilled improvisation; and the point, moreover, is the game itself. Christian ethics may be said to share that same character: only an antinomian would deny the rules; a body of traditional wisdom is there to guide us; the freedom of the Christian calls for inspired spontaneity; and there is about the whole thing a sheer gratuity: good works, as Luther said, are done for God's delight and ours. When Romano Guardini spoke about "the playfulness of the liturgy," he more precisely likened it to the *serious* play of children.[24] Never has ethics been a more serious business than today. In the past we have been able to upset the pieces and start over. Now we risk destroying pieces and board together. But even if that were to happen, the eucharist teaches us this: that God would still have gathered to himself a company of saints to delight in, and with whom he will enjoy eternity.

Notes

1. This is one of the strong points in the often problematic thesis of F.G. Downing, *Has Christianity a Revelation?* (London: SCM Press, 1964).

2. J. Ratzinger, *Theologische Prinzipienlehre: Bausteine zur Fundamentaltheologie* (Munich: Wewel, 1982) 20.

3. E. Herms, *Theorie für die Praxis: Beiträge zur Theologie* (Munich: Kaiser, 1982) 26f.

4. *Luthers Werke* (Weimar: Böhlau, 1883ff.), vol. 6 (1888) 202-276 ("Von den guten Werken"); note particularly pp. 204f., 209f., 217-220, 229-237,

243f. American edition: *Luther's Works* (Philadelphia: Fortress, 1966) 21-114; note particularly pp. 23f., 30, 39-42, 54-63, 71-73.

5. T.G. Tappert, trans. and ed., *The Book of Concord: The Confessions of the Evangelical Lutheran Church* (Philadelphia: Fortress, 1959) 408-411.

6. V. Vajta, *Die Theologie des Gottesdienstes bei Luther*, 2d ed. (Stockholm: Svenska Kyrkans Diakonistyrelses Bokförlag, 1954); abbreviated and translated as *Luther on Worship* (Philadelphia: Muhlenberg, 1958); see also V. Vajta, "Creation and Worship," *Studia Liturgica* 2 (1963) 29-46.

7. P. Brunner, "Zur Lehre vom Gottesdienst der im Namen Jesu versammelten Gemeinde," in K.F. Müller and W. Blankenburg, eds., *Leiturgia*, vol. 1 (Kassel: Stauda, 1952) 83-364; translated as *Worship in the Name of Jesus* (St. Louis: Concordia, 1968).

8. *The Book of Concord* 365.

9. Homily 25:3 on Matthew (Migne: *Patrologia Graeca* 57:331).

10. See *The City of God* 10:6 (*"sancta societate inhaerere Deo"*).

11. See *Against the Heresies* 4, 20, 7 (*"Gloria enim Dei vivens homo, vita autem hominis visio Dei"*).

12. Again from the "Treatise on Good Works" of 1520 (*Luthers Werke*, vol. 6, p. 207; *Luther's Works*, vol. 44, p. 27).

13. These phrases are taken from the New Delhi (1961) and Nairobi (1975) Assemblies of the World Council of Churches; see G. Wainwright, "Conciliarity and Eucharist," *Midstream* 17 (1978) 135-153.

14. K. Barth, *Christengemeinde und Bürgergemeinde* (Munich: Kaiser, 1946); translation in *Against the Stream* (New York: Philosophical Library, 1954).

15. See John Poulton, *The Feast of Life: A Theological Reflection on the Theme "Jesus Christ the Life of the World"* (Geneva: World Council of Churches, 1982).

16. Luther sees that turning to God in adversity is already a work honoring God's name: "The third work of this [second] commandment is to call upon God's name in every need. God considers his name hallowed and honored when we name it and call upon it in adversity and need." "Treatise on Good Works," *Luthers Werke*, vol. 6, p. 223; *Luther's Works*, vol. 44, p. 46f.

17. T. Balasuriya, *The Eucharist and Human Liberation* (New York: Orbis, 1979).

18. G. Gutierrez, *A Theology of Liberation* (New York: Orbis, 1973) 137.

19. In the Missal of Pius V these prayers comes respectively from the postcommunion of Easter Tuesday, the collect of Easter Friday, and the collect of the Sunday after Easter. In the Missal of Paul VI the material has been redistributed.

20. I first expounded the eucharist in this perspective in G. Wainwright, *Eucharist and Eschatology* (London: Epworth, 1971; New York: Oxford University Press, 1981) 59.

21. See Paul Lebeau, *Le Vin nouveau du royaume* (Paris-Bruges: Desclée de Brouwer, 1966).

22. The interweaving of "worship, doctrine and life" is characteristic of my systematic theology: see G. Wainwright, *Doxology* (London: Epworth; New York: Oxford University Press, 1980). In connection with our present theme, particular relevance attaches to chapter 12 of that work (399-434). The doxological coincidence of "duty" and "delight" is so formulated in a hymn of Isaac Watts, based on Psalm 147: "Praise ye, the Lord! 'Tis good to raise/ Your hearts and voices in his praise:/ His nature and his works invite/ To make this duty our delight." In the Church of Scotland's *Book of Common Order* (1979) the third service of Holy Communion attractively takes up the phrase at the *"Vere dignum"*: "It is indeed our duty and delight always and everywhere to give you thanks and praise . . ."

23. J.J. von Allmen, *Prophétisme sacramentel* (Neuchâtel: Delachaux & Niestlé, 1964) 287-311; cf. "Worship and the Holy Spirit," *Studia Liturgica* 2 (1963) 124-135.

24. R. Guardini, *Vom Geist der Liturgie* (Freiburg: Herder, 1918); translated as *The Spirit of the Liturgy* (London: Sheed & Ward, 1930).

13

Praying for Kings:
The Place of Human Rulers in the
Divine Plan of Salvation

THE PLACE OF THE CIVIL RULER IN GOD'S PLAN OF SALVATION IS RAISED BY AT least four New Testament texts that are of liturgical interest: 1 Peter 2:11-17, 1 Timothy 2:1-8, Titus 3:1-2, and Revelation 13:1-10. Taken in themselves or in literary context, all four passages also raise broader questions concerning the content of salvation, its extension, and the nature of the church. The civil ruler has to be seen in relation to these other matters, all of which have been of ecumenical concern both historically and in our times. The first three texts envision a benign role for the civil ruler in the larger drama; the fourth text, with perhaps an anticipation in the penumbra of the third, presents an altogether darker picture. That the themes of worship and prayer are present or close to all these four passages concerning civil rule is not surprising if we hold, with the *Westminster Catechism*, the implicitly political belief that "man's chief end is to glorify God and to enjoy him for ever."

1 Peter 2:17 reads: "Honor all men. Love the brotherhood. Fear God. Honor the king." This single verse thus brings into play the nature of the right relationship to God; it broadens the human horizon to universal dimensions; it characterizes the life of the church as a community of love; and it hints that the civil ruler has somehow a contribution to make to the proper state of affairs.[1] The passage from which it comes is therefore a good starting-point for our considerations.

I.

> [11]Beloved, I beseech you as aliens and exiles to abstain from the passions of the flesh that wage war against your soul. [12]Maintain good conduct among the Gentiles, so that in case they speak against you as wrongdoers, they may see your good deeds and glorify God on the day of visitation. [13]Be subject for the Lord's sake to every institution, whether it be to the king as supreme, [14]or to governors as sent by him to punish those who do wrong and to praise those who do right. [15]For it is God's will that by doing right you should put to silence the ignorance of foolish men. [16]Live as free men, yet without using your freedom as a pretext for evil; but live as servants of God. [17]Honor all men. Love the brotherhood. Fear God. Honor the king.
>
> (1 Peter 2:11-17; RSV, reading *king* for *emperor*)

Most modern commentators appear to recognize baptismal associations to 1 Peter. There is no need to follow in detail either the Anglo-Catholic reconstruction of F.L. Cross or the German Protestant reconstruction of H. Preisker.[2] Admitting the futility of such attempts to reconstitute from 1 Peter a primitive baptismal liturgy and even to distribute passages in the epistle to places in the rite, it is nevertheless hard to miss the echoes that the letter makes to the process of initiation. The Christians who receive the epistle have heard "the preaching of the good news" (1:12, 25). They "have been born anew through the living and abiding word of God" (1:23), "begotten again to a living hope through the resurrection of Jesus Christ from the dead" (1:4). They "have tasted the kindness of the Lord" (2:3). "Like living stones," they are to "be built into a spiritual house, to be a holy priesthood, to offer spiritual sacrifices to God through Jesus Christ" (2:5). As "a chosen race, a royal priesthood, a holy nation, God's own people," they are to "declare the wonderful deeds of him who called [them] out of darkness into his marvellous light" (2:9).[3] There is no knowing how active a missionary proclamation this was to be: it may be that the simple telling and showing of God's praises by God's people will be testimony enough, so that a doxology aimed directly at God will indirectly serve to invite other people into the praising community.[4] The persecution under which the addressees of 1 Peter were suffering may have hampered their ability to spread the Good News. In the former Soviet Union where the churches were forbidden to evangelize, the radiant witness of the liturgy attracted people to the Christian faith.

Coming specifically to our appointed text, we find the writer first characterizing his addressees as "aliens and exiles." Similar terms are found elsewhere in the New Testament as a designation for the faithful "in this world" (Eph 2:19; Heb 11:13; cf. 1 Pt 1:1, 17). The primary and contrasting reference point is their implied eschatological citizenship in the kingdom of God (Phil 3:20; Heb 13:14; cf. *Epistola ad Diognetum* 5:9). Persecution will doubtless heighten their present sense of being aliens and exiles. The author of 1 Peter draws consequences for behavior: "Abstain from the passions of the flesh . . . Maintain good conduct . . ." (cf. 4:1-3).

It is "among the Gentiles" that the Christians are to maintain good conduct. The first thought of 2:12 in this connection appears to be the eschatological confusion of the heathen, their conviction at the last judgment for having failed to recognize the true quality of Christians (cf. 4:4-5). Other New Testament texts suggest the possibility that unbelievers may, through the ethical testimony of Christians, be converted in time. Thus Matthew 5:16, a sentence used at the alms-giving in the Anglican communion service according to the Book of Common Prayer: "Let your light so shine before men, that they may see your good works, and glorify your Father which is in heaven." This more generous outcome—the bringing of converts to the worship of God—may even be at the back of the writer's mind when he comes, in 1 Peter 2:13-17, to locate Christian conduct in relation to civil society.

What, theologically, can be the ground of the injunction to "honor all men" (2:17) other than the fact that humankind is made in the image of God, and that the Creator offers a chance of salvation to all (cf. perhaps 4:19 and 4:6)?[5]

According to verse 16, the liberty brought by the Gospel does not carry antinomianism as a concomitant. As the Anglican collect puts it, it is in "the service of God" that we find our "perfect freedom."[6] Such free service bears implications for our relations to fellow human beings. In Luther's words: *"Ein Christenmensch ist ein Herr über alle Dinge und niemandem untertan. Ein Christenmensch ist ein dienstbarer Knecht aller Dinge und jedermann untertan."*[7] Towards Christians it appears that kings and governors still have the divinely given function—which is why *they* are to be "honored" as institutions—that they have towards humankind at large: "to punish those who do wrong and to praise those who do right" (2:13-14). Thus civil law, benignly understood, is a guide and encouragement also to Christians.

By "doing right" the Christians will "put to silence the ignorance of foolish men" (2:15). As Luther—along with other expositors of the Lord's Prayer—recognized, the first way to "hallow God's name" is to cease profaning it by blasphemies, lies, and evil deeds. The positive way is to speak and do God's praises.[8] It may be that by their worship and by the witness of their good deeds, Christians will bring at least *some* others to glorify God.

"Fear God" (2:17) is a reminder that God is God. The noun "fear" also occurs at 1:17 where Christians are told that the God they invoke as Father remains universal Judge. God is judge, even of the church (4:17a), from which he requires a holiness corresponding to his own (1:15-16). Some, perhaps even Christians, may finally fail salvation:

> What will be the end of those who do not obey the gospel of God? And "if the righteous is scarcely saved, where will the impious and sinner appear?" (4:17b-18)

Yet the dominant note of the Epistle is the comfort, hope, and joy that come from the redemption God has given and the glory he will bestow. These are for believers (1:7-9, 21; 5:9), and there is no reason to think that the number of believers may not be increased.

In reference to our special theme of church and state, a special question remains regarding the respect enjoined toward king and governor at a time of persecution. Several historians have argued that the civilian authorities would have been likely to investigate Christianity only if popular hostility could cast the Christian community in the light of a disturber of the public peace. If Christians were brought before the magistrates, their case would be improved, 1 Peter seems to argue, if their conduct were such as rightfully to win the praise of properly constituted authority; nevertheless, the possibility of unjust suffering is not excluded, any more than it was for Christ (3:14-18; 4:12-16). Even the closing (and perhaps later) reference to "Babylon" (5:13) is not yet evidence that the Roman emperor has forfeited his divine commission to rule.

II

[1]First of all, then, I urge that supplications, prayers, intercessions, and thanksgivings be made for all men, [2]for kings and all
who are in high positions, that we may lead a quiet and peace-
ful life, godly and respectful in every way. [3]This is good, and it
is acceptable in the sight of God our Savior, [4]who desires all
men to be saved and to come to the knowledge of the truth. [5]For
there is one God, and there is one mediator between God and
men, the man Christ Jesus, [6]who gave himself as a ransom for
all, the testimony to which was borne at the proper time. [7]For
this I was appointed a preacher and an apostle (I am telling the
truth, I am not lying), a teacher of the Gentiles in faith and truth.
[8]I desire then that in every place the men should pray, lifting
holy hands without anger or quarrelling . . .
(1 Timothy 2:1-8; RSV)

In his commentary on the Pastoral Epistles, G. Holtz finds extensive traces of the eucharistic liturgy in the letters. He considers 1
Timothy 2:1-7 to contain quotations from prayers at the eucharist.[9]
More modestly, A.T. Hanson heads the section "How to conduct
public prayer."[10] The passage is invoked by "the whole tradition" as
the scriptural foundation for the "universal prayer" that figures in
the patristic liturgies between the reading and exposition of Scripture and the eucharist proper.[11] The first formulator of the *lex orandi,
lex credendi* principle, Prosper of Aquitaine (c. 440), appeals to our
passage to make a precise point against semi-Pelagianism: the
apostolic injunction to *pray* for the whole human race—which the
church obeys in its intercessions at Mass—proves the obligation to
believe that all faith, even the beginnings of good will as well as
growth and perseverance, is from start to finish a work of grace.[12] In
tabulating the results of his examination of the "universal prayer"
(*oratio fidelium*) in the Latin rites up to the sixth or eighth century,
Paul de Clerck shows that prayer for "emperors and kings," especially with an eye to peace, is, with prayer for the church and clergy,
the most frequently recurring of all themes: it figures in nine cases
out of ten, whereas prayer for "pagans" sinks to two.[13]

Our passage begins with the exhortation to pray[14] and give
thanks "for all men." What is the sense of *hyper*? For the benefit of?
On account of? In place of? The question pales when we look ahead
at what verses 4-6 say precisely about "all": God "desires all men to

be saved," and Christ "gave himself as a ransom for all." Believers may not only "pray" but also even "give thanks" for all precisely as all are the objects of saving love;[15] they are thus hastening and anticipating the day when they will no longer need to speak vicariously for a world that, as Karl Barth says, "is not yet" ready and willing for God.[16] That God desires all to be saved is not, except in a Calvinistic universe, a *guarantee* that all will in fact let themselves be saved; but then, Calvinists do not like 1 Timothy 2:4-6. At least for an apostle (2:7), the mission is an active one of preaching and teaching.

Next, prayers and thanksgivings are to be made "for kings and all who are in high positions." In an article written in the Hitler year of 1933 and when he himself was still a Lutheran, Heinrich Schlier pointed out that such prayer is both a recognition of the *divine source* of civil authority—and thereby of the *limitations* of that authority also.[17] The civil authority is not autonomous, and its task is restricted to ensuring a civic peace in which a pious and moral life is possible. An interesting shift takes place in 1 Clement 61:2, where it is prayed that the rulers may "piously administer in peace and mildness the authority granted them by thee." There remains cause to pray for bad rulers, as Calvin argues:

> If the question is raised whether we ought to pray for kings from whom we do not receive these advantages [mentioned in 1 Timothy 2:2], my answer is that we ought to pray that, under the guidance of the Holy Spirit, they may begin to grant us these blessings they have up till now failed to provide. Thus we should not only pray for those who are already worthy, but we should ask God to make wicked rulers good. We must always hold to the principle that magistrates are appointed by God for the protection of religion and of the public peace and decency, just as the earth has been ordained to produce food.[18]

At times the motivation for praying for civil rulers has taken on a sharper formulation than the peace and quiet needed for a decent life. In face of the charges of political disloyalty made against the "atheistic" Christians for not praying to the Roman gods, Tertullian replies—and indeed with appeal to 1 Timothy 2:2—that Christians do in fact pray for regular civic peace, not least for the sake of their own tranquility; and he continues:

There is also another and greater necessity for our offering prayer in behalf of the emperors, nay, for the complete stability of the empire, and for Roman interests in general. For we know that a mighty shock impending over the whole earth—in fact, the very end of all things threatening dreadful woes—is only retarded by the continued existence of the Roman empire. We have no desire, then, to be overtaken by these dire events; and in praying that their coming may be delayed, we are lending our aid to Rome's duration.[19]

Or, more tersely:

We pray, too, for the emperors, for their ministers and for all in authority, for the welfare of the world, for the prevalence of peace, for the delay of the final consummation.[20]

Whatever may be the apocalyptic calculations that occupy part of the background to this argument,[21] there need be no conflict here with O. Cullmann's rather less outlandish exegesis of 2 Thessalonains 2:6-7: "what is delaying" the End is—in extension and transformation of the Jewish notion that the delay in the Messiah's coming is due to "the still unfulfilled repentance of Israel"—the missionary preaching of the Gospel to the Gentiles (cf. Mk 13:10; Mt 24:14); the interval is a time of God's patience and grace.[22] Now this would fit nicely with the idea, as old as Origen and Eusebius, of the *pax Romana* as providential circumstances for the spread of the Gospel.[23] The connection of political peace with the spread of the Gospel was maintained by the classical Protestant Reformers: they expected the princes to provide "room" for the Gospel to have free course.[24] The "political use" of the law—to check the ravages brought by sin to the social life—belonged to the order of preservation, which itself was a divine "holding operation" to maintain fallen humanity in earthly existence with a view to bringing it from sin to salvation.

In 1 Timothy 2:8 we see the church at its liturgical duty and delight—lifting holy hands in prayer.[25] The phrase "in every place" recalls Malachi 1:11, whose "pure oblation" is applied by several early Christian writers to a eucharist that is offered *semper et ubique*.[26] As 1 Timothy 2:8 says that the worshipers should be "without anger or quarrelling," so *Didachè* 14:2 enjoins fraternal reconciliation, "that your sacrifice may not be defiled." The church is a community reconciled in God's love; and the entail of that, as 1 Peter 2:17 said, is "love the brotherhood."

III

> Remind them to be submissive to rulers and authorities, to be obedient, to be ready for any honest work, to speak evil of no one, to avoid quarrelling, to be gentle, and to show perfect courtesy toward all men. (Titus 3:1-2; RSV)

Looking ahead to 3:5 ("God saved us . . . by the washing of regeneration and renewal in the Holy Spirit"), H. Schlier argues that obedience to civil authorities is here grounded in regeneration.[27] The rebirth into Christ which baptism signifies, relativizes the old creation and allows, even requires, submission to earthly rulers as conduct appropriate in a world that is for the moment still being divinely preserved although its form is passing. Believers know themselves to be in the hands of God, come what may; they draw their true life from a new world and belong to a city which they do not themselves have to build.[28] Schlier argues that Romans 13 is similarly governed by Romans 12:1-2, and that obedience to civil authorities in 1 Peter 2:13-17 instantiates the general principle of abstinence from the passions of the flesh (v.11) that is appropriate to eschatological "aliens and exiles."[29]

We notice that this passage, again, urges at least "courtesy toward all men."[30] In the previous chapter it has been declared that "the grace of God has appeared for the salvation of all men" (2:11).

A.T. Hanson argues that Titus 3:1-2 is embedded in liturgical, specifically baptismal, material that deliberately opposes Christianity to the imperial cult (2:11-14; 3:3-7), and that the insertion may be a way of implying "You must not join in emperor worship, but that does not mean that you should not be obedient to the emperor."[31] Hanson's notes on the vocabulary of the imperial cult and the Pastoral Epistles are certainly interesting:

> One can find in the Pastorals a whole battery of terms which were also used in the imperial cult: *sōtēr* ("savior"), *epiphaneia* ("appearance," "epiphany of a god"), *makaria elpis* ("blessed hope"), *megas theos* ("great god"), *philanthrōpia* ("humanity"), *chrēstotēs* ("kindness"), the suggestions that with the advent of the god a new aeon has begun for mankind—all these features of the Pastorals can also be paralleled in the imperial cult . . . Most of all when we read Titus we are driven to conclude that the author was trying to counter the imperial cult. Such phrases

as *hē Gaiou Kaisaros charis* ("the grace of Gaius Caesar"), and *tou epilampsantos hēmin epi sōtērai tou pantos anthrōpou genous euergetou* ("he who has lightened upon us, the benefactor for the salvation of the entire human race") which [was said] of the emperor Galba (who ruled only three months), make it seem very probable that the author of the Pastorals was consciously attempting to present Christ as the true savior of the human race over against the false savior Caesar . . . Coins from Crete dating from Domitian's reign bear the image of his baby son, who died in A.D. 83 and was immediately deified.[32]

With that, we come very close to the fourth and last of our scriptural texts.

IV

[1]And I saw a beast rising out of the sea, with ten horns and seven heads, with ten diadems upon its horns and a blasphemous name upon its heads. [2]And the beast that I saw was like a leopard, its feet were like a bear's, and its mouth was like a lion's mouth. And to it the dragon gave his power and his throne and great authority. [3]One of its heads seemed to have a mortal wound, but its mortal wound was healed, and the whole earth followed the beast with wonder. [4]Men worshiped the dragon, for he had given his authority to the beast, and they worshiped the beast, saying, "Who is like the beast, and who can fight against it?"

[5]And the beast was given a mouth uttering haughty and blasphemous words, and it was allowed to exercise authority for forty-two months; [6]it opened its mouth to utter blasphemies against God, blaspheming his name and his dwelling, that is, those who dwell in heaven.

[[7]Also it was allowed to make war on the saints and to conquer them.] And authority was given it over every tribe and people and tongue and nations, [8]and all who dwell on earth will worship it, every one whose name has not been written before the foundation of the world in the book of life of the lamb that was slain. [9]If any one has an ear, let him hear:

[10]If any one is to be taken captive,
to captivity he goes;
if any one slays with the sword,
with the sword must he be slain.

Here is a call for the endurance and faith of the saints.
(Revelation 13:1-10; RSV)

The exegesis of the Book of Revelation is notoriously difficult, and its results are correspondingly varied.[33] I will largely follow another powerful and poignant essay, written in 1935, by Heinrich Schlier.[34]

Satan stood on the sea shore (Rv 12:17), and the beast which arises from the waters (13:1) is Satan's reflection, given its power, rule and authority by him, the old dragon (13:2b; cf. 12:9). The sea is in the west, where Rome lies. For the seer's generation of Christians, which believed itself to be the last, the Roman Empire had become the manifestation of the Antichrist. But it is the whole of human history which is in fact being uncovered and judged in Revelation.[35] "Men *worshiped* the beast" (13:4), and "all who dwell on earth [except for the saints] *will worship* it" (13:8): "The beast claims the obedience of everybody at all times. The worship of the beast is universal in time and place."[36] The beast is, as Schlier wrote in a previous essay, *"der Grenzfall des möglichen Staates . . . die äusserste Möglichkeit der selbstherrlichen Welt."*[37]

Let us with Schlier look more closely at the rule exercised, and the worship claimed, by this mythical beast, concretely identified at the end of the first century with the Roman Empire, and the perennial limit-possibility of an autonomous world. First, at the level of words: the beast arrogates to itself divine titles (the "blasphemous names upon its heads" [13:1] will in the Roman case include *"divus Augustus"* and *"dominus ac deus"* [compare and contrast John 20:28!]) and attributes to itself divine achievements (compare and contrast the *megala* of 13:5 with the *megaleia tou theou* of Acts 2:11). The beast thus rivals God and even, in the worship it attracts, outstrips God: "Who is like the beast, and who can fight against it?" (such incomparability is reserved in the Scriptures for the Lord God: Exodus 15:11; Psalm 35:10; Isaiah 45).

Second, the beast not only speaks, it acts: it wages war against "the saints" (13:7a). Those whose "dwelling is in heaven," themselves the "tent" of God (*skēnē*, 13:6), are "metaphysically the archenemies" of the beast, which exercises its finally impotent rage upon them (12:12). It will fail to gain the worship of those whose name has been written in the Lamb's book of life (13:8). In face of persecution, the saints are meanwhile called to "patience and faith" (Rv 13:10).

Third, the beast is allowed "power over every tribe and people and tongue and nation" (13:7). In the Roman case the emperor is called *"potens terrarum dominus," "terrarum gloria"* (cf. Mt 4:8-9 = Lk 4:5-6!). "In the beast the historical cosmos finds its unity."[38] Here "all differences are finally removed," and yet "the people never become, as they innocently dream, 'free'." There is Another to whom "all authority in heaven and on earth has been given" (Mt 28:18). "On earth" this is still a matter of faith. There is a choice: *"Entweder ist Christus der Herr im gegleiderten und geordneten Leibe der Kirche aus allen Völkern, oder der Antichrist im entarteten, tierische Leibe seines Imperiums aus allen Nationen."*[39]

The manifestation of Satan is not yet done. In Revelation 13:11-18 a "second beast" arises "from the earth" to join the dragon and the first beast in what Jung-Stilling called "a satanic trinity." The origin of the second beast, says Schlier, is Asia Minor, the land of prophets and cults, and in particular of "apotheoses of the emperor." Lamb-like (13:11), this beast apes *the* Lamb.[40] He is, says Schlier, the false prophet, the propagandist priest (cf. 16:13; 19:20; 20:10). The sacral power in the service of the administrative, his function is to lead people to worship the first beast (13:12). He employs three tricks: he performs miracles (13:13), arousing misplaced faith (contrast Mt 4:3-6 = Lk 4:2-4, 9-11); he builds up a deceitful "image" of the "immortal" beast (13:14-15),[41] and makes worship of it a test of religio-political loyalty (the *"crimen laesae Romanae religionis"* was a *"crimen laesae maiestatis,"* and that was the *"dolus"* needed for the condemnation of Christians, the "atheists" who did not deserve to live in such a religious empire): for, finally, the priestly propagandist of the Antichrist's power makes religious belief a matter of permanent public control, stamping the worshipers of the beast with its mark (13:16-17), a "reappropriation" of the (invisible) seal of baptism.

Let me now briefly, independently of Schlier, come to a fundamental systematic reflection upon worship of the State. My inspiration this time is a Catholic who turned Lutheran, namely, "Dr. Martin" himself. "That to which your heart clings and entrusts itself is," says Luther, "really your god."[42] In that sense, worship is a phenomenon universal to humanity. The grounds of its universality reside in the fact that humankind was created in the image of God, for reverential communion with its Maker ("to glorify God and to enjoy him for ever"). If we do not worship the Creator, we shall inevitably worship the creature (cf. Rom 1:18-32). And the creature most "like" God is, of course, the human being. Idol-worship is ultimately worship of self. The *homo in se incurvatus* determines its own supreme values.

Idolatry of the State has to be seen in the perspective of the *imago dei*. One theme in traditional Christian interpretations of the creation of humankind in God's image concerns the political task of humanity. By analogy with the custom of ancient near eastern rulers to erect statues of themselves in distant provinces in order to assert their claim to sovereignty over the country, humankind is considered as God's viceroy upon the earth.[43] If the introduction of the monarchy into Israel was controversial, the danger lay in the risk that a single ruler might more easily usurp the primary place of Yahweh. Good kings, in the subsequent history of Israel, were those who ruled by the divine values of justice and mercy and kept the nation faithful to the Lord. In the New Testament we have seen that even "secular" rulers have the divine ministry at least to promote what is right and good, while restraining what is evil. At least as long as they do that, Christians are to obey them.

The need to hold evil in check is a recognition of the Fall. So radical and pervasive is human fallenness, however, that no exemption can in fact be made for the institutions of government, administered as they are by human beings. *Quis custodiet ipsos custodes*? (Juvenal). "Power tends to corrupt, and absolute power corrupts absolutely" (Lord Acton). "Those who are supposed to rule over the Gentiles lord it over them . . ." (Mk 10:42). Whether it need be so among the followers of Jesus is a question that became delicate with the developments outlined in the next paragraph. But meanwhile we pick up again the note from Revelation 13, that even the badly ruled may unfortunately but willingly comply with the evil rulers: "for people imagine that life is better under the rule of the beast than under the rule of Christ."[44] This is the measure of perversion in fallen humanity. That is why God's kingdom is such a saving alternative. Those who belong to God's kingdom will refuse to acquiesce in imperial or popular idolatry.

V

Since the fourth century, interpreters of the New Testament have had at their disposal at the contemporary end of the hermeneutical ellipse a possibility that was not envisaged by the apostolic writers nor seriously contemplated by the immediately intervening generations. Perhaps the most unlikely event in the history of Christianity was the "conversion of Constantine." For Tertullian (in part, perhaps, on account of his understanding of the restraining role of the Roman Empire in the eschatological drama), the conversion of an emperor had been *institutionally* unthinkable: Pontius Pilate, a "Christian in his own conscience" (cf. perhaps Jn 19:22), sent word to Tiberius, "and the Caesars too would have believed in Christ, if either the Caesars had not been necessary for the world, or if Christians could have been Caesars."[45] Alistair Kee has revived the thesis, more commonly found in minority churches than in the Church of Scotland, that what took place in the early fourth century was in fact Constantine's *sub*version of Christianity: "Why it has been previously thought that Constantine was a Christian is not because what he believed was Christian but because what he believed came to be called Christian."[46] In particular, says Kee, Constantine overturned the notions of power that go with a servant Messiah. Yet the church *did* hail Constantine as "the equal of the apostles" and a "great" emperor. For the fifteen or sixteen centuries of Christendom, theocracy became both an ideal and a temptation, sometimes in a more caesaropapist shape, sometimes in a more papocaesarist shape.

For post-Constantinian interpreters of the "political" texts of the New Testament, the full range of Niebuhr's "types" of relation between "Christ and culture" is available for bringing to the reading.[47] The extreme attitude of "Christ against culture" will be attracted by Revelation 13 and find confirmation there of the perennially demonic character of the State. The extreme "Christ of culture" attitude will have to maximize the positive correspondence between the Petrine "fearing God" and "honoring the king" and emphasize the new possibilities that became historically present through the acceptance of Christianity by rulers and nations. The moderate "dualist" or "synthetist" types will be encouraged by the exhortation in 1 Timothy to pray for civil authorities, so that at the least they may secure a civil peace that allows free course to the Gospel (so the dualist), or even (on a synthetic understanding) so that the civil authorities may promote religious and ethical values that the grace of God can perfect rather than destroy. Niebuhr's "transformationist" type will remember "the washing of regeneration and renewal in the Holy Spirit" of Titus and look for signs of the baptismal life in the community of believers in whom conversion to God's kingdom has begun.

VI

We were asked to examine the assigned New Testament texts in the perspective of our own discipline. I am a (Methodist) systematic theologian who holds that Christian faith begins and ends in worship, which is therefore a constant reference-point for theology.[48] The tendencies of my approach to the texts were gently indicated at the outset and will have emerged at various points along the way, and in return several "messages" from the texts have been picked up as we went along. What, then, with the aid of expert and sympathetic exegetes, have I seen, and perhaps helped the reader to see, in our texts when they are read in a systematic perspective colored by the liturgy? Briefly, I return from my reading this time with the following picture.

1. Humankind is a worshiping animal. The only and all-important question is whether it glorifies and enjoys the living God—or rather idolizes itself and finally dies.

2. In Christ God has provided means for the salvation of all. This is a cause for thanksgiving and a source of hope.

3. Civil rulers have a divine commission at least (a) to mitigate the ravages of sin sufficiently to preserve a social order while the Gospel can be preached; perhaps also (b) to further, or at least protect, a natural or civic piety and virtue that grace can come to perfect; and maybe even (c) to function still for believers in terms of the "third use" of the law that Calvin and Wesley allowed, in order to exhort and encourage Christians in the way of sanctification.

4. Perversely, civil leaders are in perpetual danger of coming to embody that very will to "self-rule" in which rebellion against God consists. They are then apt to attract the worship of a compliant populace, which may indeed have cast their leaders in that role in the first place. Even under persecution, the New Testament writers—perhaps because success was historically inconceivable—offer no advice to Christians on active resistance to authorities who have apparently ceased to carry out the minimal divine commission to rule according to right and wrong. Calvin concluded that "no command has been given us except to obey and suffer"—and even to suffer all the more, if obedience to God entails, in extreme cases, disobedience to the king.[49] It seems equally beyond the historical horizon of the New Testament writers that Christians or the church should have any participatory influence upon "public policy."[50]

5. The church is the company of those who have been reconciled in the love of God. It adumbrates and anticipates the final salvation in God's kingdom. Drawing its life from that future, this church is by word and deed, in its liturgy, its proclamation, and its conduct, a sign to the world of what is promised to all who, by the power of the Holy Spirit, come to believe in the God and Father of our Lord Jesus Christ. It prays and hopes for all as the objects of God's love. It prays for civil rulers in the official execution of their God-given responsibilities. It should pray for them as human beings also, to whom salvation is offered as to all.

Notes

1. It will be seen that, with the overwhelming exegetical tradition, I take 1 Peter 2:17 as four distinct clauses, rather than allowing the first clause to govern the other three, as the New English Bible does ("Give due honor to everyone: love to the brotherhood, reverence to God, honor to the sovereign").

2. F.L. Cross saw in 1 Peter an incomplete text of the celebrant's part in the paschal Vigil Service of baptism in I *Peter, a Paschal Liturgy* (London: Mowbray, 1954). In his revision of H. Windisch's commentary on the Catholic Epistles, H. Preisker detected in 1 Peter the elements of a baptismal service composed largely of hymns, prayers, and sermons.

3. "Enlightenment" was an early term for baptism: Justin, Apology I, 61; cf. Ephesians 5:14; Hebrews 6:4, 10:32.

4. Behind *ex-angello* at 1 Peter 2:9 stands the Old Testament *higgid* (from *ngd*; LXX *an-angello, ap-angello*), which is used for a solemn declaration, a recitation of faith before God (Dt 26:3-10), a publication of God's name and deeds among the nations (Ps 9:11; 40:5, etc.). In the New Testament *kat-angello* is used for proclaiming Christ (Acts 17:3; Phil 1:17-18; Col 1:28), the Gospel (1 Cor 9:14), the word (Acts 13:5, 15:36, 17:13); at 1 Corinthians 11:26 it refers to the eucharistic proclamation of the Lord's death until he comes.

5. "*Honor all men* - As being made in the image of God, bought by His Son, and designed for His Kingdom" (John Wesley, Explanatory Notes upon the New Testament, ad loc.). Wesley takes "the day of visitation" in verse 12 as "the time when God shall give them fresh offers of His mercy."

6. The second collect of morning prayer: "O God, who art the author of peace and lover of concord, in knowledge of whom standeth our eternal life, whose service is perfect freedom . . ." The sources in the Gelasian and Gregorian Sacramentaries even use the formulation "*cui servire est regnare.*"

7. Luther, WA 7, 21 (1-4).

8. Luther, Large Catechism, first petition of the Lord's Prayer.

9. G. Holtz, *Die Pastoralbriefe*, Theologischer Handkommentar zum NT, vol. 13 (Berlin: Evangelische Verlagsanstalt, 1965) 52-63, 95.

10. A.T. Hanson, *The Pastoral Epistles*, New Century Bible Commentary (Grand Rapids: Eerdmans, 1982) 66. In *Studies in the Pastoral Epistles* (London: SPCK, 1968), pp. 62-64 Hanson argues in more detail that our passage provides an "outline," almost a "blueprint," perhaps rather a "common tradition," on which 1 Clement 59-61 drew for a full text of apparently public prayer.

11. Paul de Clerck, *La "Prière universelle" dans les liturgies latines anciennes*, Liturgiewissenschaftliche Quellen und Forschungen, vol. 62 (Münster: Aschendorff, 1977) 4.

12. G. Wainwright, *Doxology* (New York: Oxford University Press, 1980) 224-227.

13. de Clerck, *La "Prière universelle"* 298-302. Whereas the earliest texts were *"très universalistes, suite à 1 Tim. 2:1, d'ailleurs,"* the later formularies *"reflètent un monde clos." "On constate, plus on avance dans le temps, un rétrécissement des perspectives ... On perçoit l'effondrement culturel de l'époque"* (p. 302).

14. Most commentators take *deēseis, proseuchai*, and *enteuxeis* as virtually synonymous, despite nuances.

15. "We may *give thanks for all men*, in the full sense of the word, for that God 'willeth all men to be saved,' and Christ is the Mediator of all" (John Wesley, *Explanatory Notes upon the New Testament*, ad loc.).

16. K. Barth, *Prayer*, 2d ed. (Philadelphia: Westminster, 1985) 44, 65.

17. H. Schlier, "Die Beurteilung des Staates im Neuen Testament," reprinted in his *Die Zeit der Kirche* (Freiburg: Herder, 1956) 1-16, in particular 11 and 13.

18. Calvin, ad I Tim. 2:2; English translation from D.W. Torrance and T.F. Torrance, eds., *Calvin's Commentaries: The Second Epistle of Paul the Apostle to the Corinthians and the Epistles to Timothy, Titus and Philemon* (Grand Rapids: Eerdmans, 1964) 206-207.

19. Tertullian, *Apology*, 32 (Migne: *Patrologia Latina* 1:508-509).

20. Apology 39 (Migne: *Patrologia Latina* 1:532); see also Tertullian *Ad Scapulam*, 2 (Migne: *Patrologia Latina* 1:778); but contrast *De Oratione*, 5 (Migne: *Patrologia Latina* 1:1261) where Tertullian opposes those who "pray for some protraction of the age, when the kingdom of God, which we pray may arrive, tends unto the consummation of the age. Our wish is that our reign be hastened, not our servitude protracted."

21. L.G. Patterson in his *God and History in Early Christian Thought* (New York: Seabury, 1967) p. 60 comments that "Christians had always shared with Rome itself, albeit on somewhat different grounds, the view that Rome [was] the last of the world empires." *"Quando cadet Roma, cadet et*

mundus" (Caractarus). Christians looked on Rome as the fourth and final kingdom of the prophecy in Daniel 2. In *De Resurrectione Carnis*, 24 (Migne: *Patrologia Latina* 2:874-877) Tertullian takes the Roman state to be the obstacle that, according to 2 Thessalonians 2, is for the moment holding back the appearance of the Antichrist before "the day of the Lord."

22. O. Cullmann, *Christ and Time*, rev. ed. (Philadelphia: Westminster, 1964) 164-166; or, in more detail for the second century, "Wann kommt das Reich Gottes?", reprinted in *Oscar Cullmann: Vorträge und Aufsätze 1925-1962* (Tübingen: Mohr, 1966) 535-547.

23. Origen, *Contra Celsum* II. 30; Eusebius, *Demonstration of the Gospel* III. 7, 30-35; see E. Peterson, "Der Monotheismus als politisches Problem," reprinted in his *Theologische Traktate* (Munich: Kösel, 1951) 45-147, in particular 83-93. Like Schlier, Peterson converted to Roman Catholicism. This essay dates from 1935.

24. See, for example, H. Schmid, *Zwinglis Lehre von der göttlichen und menschlichen Gerechtigkeit* (Zurich: Zwingli Verlag, 1959).

25. In 1 Timothy 2:8 "men"—by way of exception—means males. Here the author is being guided by Jewish practice in public prayer. There is no reason to think that the "good deeds" expected of pious women in verses 9-10 are restricted to females.

26. *Didachè* 14:3; Justin, *Dialogue with Trypho*, 41:2-3; etc.

27. Schlier, "Die Beurteilung" 8.

28. Ibid.

29. Ibid. 7.

30. "Even those who are such as we were [cf. v. 3]" (John Wesley, *Explanatory Notes upon the New Testament*, ad loc.).

31. Hanson, *The Pastoral Epistles* 183-193; cf. *Studies in the Pastoral Epistles* 78-96.

32. Hanson, *The Pastoral Epistles* 187-188.

33. Unfortunately John Wesley, following Bengel and the earlier Protestant tradition, identifies the beast with the Hildebrandine papacy. These days it is probably only liberal Roman Catholics who identify the pope with Antichrist.

34. "Vom Antichrist. Zum 13. Kapitel der Offenbarung Johannis," in Schlier, *Die Zeit der Kirche* 16-29.

35. See also H. Schlier, "Zum Verständnis der Geschichte nach der Offenbarung Johannis," written twenty years after the former article and first published in *Die Zeit der Kirche* (1956) 265-274. Imperial Rome is precisely the "*Weltstadt*": "*Im Rom der Cäsaren ist eine grausame und trunkene Welt-Polis aller Zeiten abbildebar und erkennbar*" (p. 267).

36. Schlier, "Vom Antichrist" 25.

37. Schlier, "Die Beurteilung" 14-15.

38. Schlier, "Vom Antichrist" 24.

39. Ibid.

40. The worship of the beast is "a usurpation of the worship due to God alone in a terrible hellish imitation of the *proskynesis* before God and the Lamb." J. Horst, *Proskynein* (Gütersloh: Bertelsmann, 1932) 263-264.

41. An inscription from an imperial statue reads: *Autokratori theōi Domitianōi Kaisari Sebastōi.*

42. Luther, Large Catechism, on the first commandment.

43. See G. von Rad, *Das erste Buch Mose* (Das Alte Testament deutsch), ad Gen. 1:26-28.

44. Schlier, "Vom Antichrist" 25.

38. Tertullian, *Apology* 21 (Migne: *Patrologia Latina* 1:461). The grounds Tertullian advances in *De Idolatria*, 18 for the impossibility of a Christian Caesar are more radical and render potentially malign the eschatological role of the Roman Empire: Christ's rejection of an earthly kingdom showed that "all secular powers and dignities are not merely alien from, but hostile to, God" (Migne: *Patrologia Latina* 1:766-767).

46. "It is not true that Constantine gave up all idea of an imperial cult in favour of Christianity. Rather, a transformed Christianity became the imperial cult by any other name . . . Constantine thus not only defeated the Church which his predecessors had failed to do, but enlisted the aid of the Church in unifying the Empire. And to add insult to injury, when Constantine reconstructed the imperial cult by which the wisdom of the world and the ambition of one man were given the absolute status of divine law, the Church actually pronounced this cult to be Christianity! . . . Did the Empire become a Christian state? No: Christianity sold its birthright for a pension and became the state religion" (A. Kee, *Constantine versus Christ* [London: SCM Press, 1982] 158-159).

47. H. Richard Niebuhr, *Christ and Culture* (New York: Harper & Row, 1951).

48. Questions of Christianity and politics received some treatment in my *Doxology*, especially chapters XI (Culture) and XII (Ethics), and in *The Ecumenical Moment* (Grand Rapids: Eerdmans, 1983), especially chapter IX (Revolution and Quietism).

49. *Institutes* IV, 20, 31-32. Calvin did allow that other agents might *unwittingly* do God's work in overthrowing wicked rulers (IV. 20, 30).

50. Where the state is at least open to the church and to the Christian faith, the best account of the proper relation of the Christian community to the civil community is to be found along the lines of Karl Barth's "analogy" whereby the Christian witness seeks to promote in society the values of God's kingdom, although this will be in an "exterior" and "provisional" form, whereas faith knows in an "interior" and "definitive" way those same realities of freedom, justice, peace, humanity, and the like; see his *Christengemeinde und Bürgergemeinde* (Munich: Kaiser, 1946; English trans-

lation in *Against the Stream* (New York: Philosophical Library, 1954). When a society or a government is not open to the Christian faith, the question of whence it draws even minimal standards of right and wrong raises the difficult theological theme for which "natural law" and "general revelation" stand as pointers. Further, whether it be a matter of minimal notions of right and wrong or of the more profiled values of God's kingdom, the complexities of human affairs are such that is seems there must always be room on our side for considerable variety of judgment in practical implementation and casuistical application.

14

Trinitarian Worship

In his conversation with the Samaritan woman, Jesus declared, "The hour is coming and now is, when the true worshipers will worship the Father in Spirit and in Truth, for such the Father seeks to worship him" (Jn 4:23). The hour is coming and now is. Some today would say that that hour has been and gone. Scarcely anyone has a good word for the Father. The Truth as it is in Jesus seems to many to be far too particularistic a basis on which to deal with modern science or other religions. When the Spirit is invoked, it is often to bless opinions and activities that have little to do with the virtues the Paraclete encouraged and enabled in the New Testament. It appears to me that liberal, and perhaps even moderate, Protestantism in North America in particular is in greater danger than ever of losing hold of the doctrine of the Trinity, which has been a touchstone of historic Christianity. To say nothing of particular relations with the Roman Catholic and the Orthodox Churches, the entire modern ecumenical movement has been built on trinitarian foundations: the basis for membership in the World Council of Churches characteristically declares that the churches "seek to fulfill together their common calling to the glory of the one God, Father, Son and Holy Spirit."

To see what is at stake, it will be useful to return to the origins and deep structures of trinitarian doctrine. We shall discover that its roots are sunk in worship, and that it finds its most significant continuing expression in the liturgy.

St. Basil the Great

A good place to begin will be the treatise of St. Basil the Great entitled *On the Holy Spirit*.[1] Written around the year 373, Basil's work expounds and defends trinitarian worship and doctrine in the face of Arian and Arianizing interpretations and attacks. It is the first fully systematic treatise to set forth the two complementary patterns of trinitarian devotion and understanding that have marked the Christian liturgy ever since. The argument centers on two pairs of Greek prepositions used in the formulation of praise to God: "Glory to the Father through [*dia*] the Son in [*en*] the Holy Spirit" and "Glory to the Father with [*meta*] the Son together with [*syn*] the Holy Spirit."

The first formulation appears to be the more ancient, and it was the more widely used in Basil's day. The Arians appealed to it, however, in an attempt to condemn the Nicenes out of their own mouths. This phrasing, it was alleged, implies a subordination of the Spirit and the Son to the Father, which is precisely what the Arians taught, to the point indeed of making the Son and the Spirit creatures of the Father. Basil of Caesarea undertook to defend the Orthodox meaning and use of the doxology with "through" and "in." He argued that all God's activity in creation, redemption, and sanctification takes place "through the Son" and "in the Spirit." It was, therefore, appropriate that our grateful response should occur "in the Spirit" and reach the Father "through the Son." Thus our thanksgiving corresponds to God's dealings with the world, the divine "economy."

This "mediatorial" pattern of God's relation with us and our relations with God does not, however, imply that the Son and the Spirit are creatures or are in any way less than God. To the contrary. Following a procedure already advanced by St. Athanasius in his *Letters to Serapion*,[2] Basil appeals to the faith confessed at baptism. Baptism takes place "in the name of the Father and of the Son and of the Holy Spirit." Not only are the three there ranked together, but our salvation is a work of God, and its agents cannot be less than God. Only God can give participation in God. When, therefore, we think of God in very being, a "coordinated" form of doxology is appropriate. It corresponds to the three mutually indwelling persons. While Basil is not always persuasive in the patristic precedents he cites for his use of the "with" form of the doxology, he has made a fair systematic case for its matching the immanent life of the God whom we know in the economy. Within a decade, the Ecumenical Council of Constantinople would not only reaffirm the Nicene faith in Jesus Christ as "Lord," "the only Son of the Father, eternally begotten of the Father, begotten, not made, consubstantial with the Father"; it would also confess the Holy Spirit as "Lord" and "Life-Giver," "who with the Father and the Son together is worshiped and glorified."

The New Testament

Having had St. Basil lay bare for us the deep structures of trinitarian faith and worship, we can now examine its New Testament origins. Its ground plan can be found there, as well as most of the building blocks with which the church would construct its developed and refined formulations in liturgy and doctrine. Here we can draw help from the important seventh chapter in the work of the Italian Benedictine Cipriano Vagaggini, *Il senso teologico della liturgia*.[3]

In the New Testament, Vagaggini finds a "way of communion between God and humankind" that can be described in the following circulatory fashion:

> Every good gift comes to us from the Father, through the medium of Jesus Christ his incarnate Son, in the presence of the Holy Spirit; and likewise, it is in the presence of the Holy Spirit, through the medium of Jesus Christ the incarnate Son, that everything must return to the Father and be reunited to its end, the most blessed Trinity. This is the Christological-Trinitarian activity of the sacred history of salvation, the plan of God in the world. The whole structure of the liturgy presupposes this activity, without which the liturgy would be incomprehensible.[4]

Christian worship, like the salvation it celebrates and advances, is summed up in the movement "from the Father, through Christ, in the Holy Spirit, to the Father [*a Patre, per Christum, in Spiritu Sancto, ad Patrem*]." Although the full cycle can rarely be found in single New Testament passages, there is an abundance of fragmentary arcs that allow us to divine the whole.

The Epistle to the Ephesians is particularly rich in this regard. There is, for example, the opening benediction (1:3-14):

> Blessed be the God and Father of our Lord Jesus Christ, who has blessed us in Christ with every spiritual blessing . . . In [Christ] you too have heard the word of truth, the gospel of your salvation, and have believed, and you have been sealed with the promised Holy Spirit, who is the guarantee of our inheritance until we acquire possession of it, to the praise of [God's] glory.

Or the cultically flavored passage, 2:18-22:

> Through [Christ] we both [Jews and Gentiles] have access in one Spirit to the Father. So then you are no longer strangers and sojourners, but you are fellow citizens with the saints and members of the household of God, built upon the foundation of the apostles and prophets, Christ Jesus himself being the cornerstone, in whom the whole structure is joined together and grows into a holy temple in the Lord; in whom you also are built into it for a dwelling place of God in the Spirit.

Or again, the doxology of 3:20-21:

> Now to [God] who by the power at work within us [i.e., the Spirit; cf. verse 16] is able to do far more abundantly than all that we ask or think . . . be glory in the church and in Christ Jesus to all generations for ever and ever.

Or there is the very concise passage in Galatians 4:4-6:

> When the time had fully come, God sent forth his Son, born of a woman, born under the law, to redeem those who were under the law; so that we might receive adoption . . . And because you are God's adopted children, God has sent the Spirit of his Son into our hearts, crying, "Abba! Father!"

It is also apparent that the Christians of New Testament times had begun to draw conclusions from the work of Jesus Christ and apply them to his person. By the fifties, the apostle Paul was able to draw on an even earlier hymn for the prospect that at the name of Jesus every knee would bow, and every tongue confess that "Jesus Christ is Lord, to the glory of God the Father." Philippians 2:5-11 there makes an astonishing echo of Isaiah 45, one of the most "monotheistic" passages in the Old Testament, and uses of Christ the name *Kyrios*, by which the Greek version of the Old Testament designates Yahweh. The one whom Thomas acclaims as "My Lord and my God" (Jn 20:28) is the risen Jesus, "the Word made flesh" (1:14); he "was in the beginning with God" and "was God," and "through him were made all things" (1:1-2). By 2 Timothy 4:18 and 2 Peter 3:18 Christ is receiving doxology as Lord and Savior. And in the book of Revelation every creature addresses "to the one who sits upon the throne and to the Lamb . . . blessing and honor and glory and might for ever and ever" (5:13). In his Letter to Adelphius, Athanasius fully embraces, and indeed actively exploits, the implications that the worship of Christ would be idolatry, were Christ not truly God.[5]

With the dubious exceptions of 1 Corinthians 6:19-20 and Philippians 3:3,[6] there is no case in the New Testament where the Holy Spirit is an object of worship as distinct from an enabling medium. Yet we have seen the systematic logic of a move from agency to being. And there are notable examples in liturgical history for praise and prayer addressed specifically to the Holy Spirit. Hymns in particular range from the Byzantine Pentecostarion *"Basileu ouranie"* and the Golden Sequence *"Veni, Sancte Spiritus,"* through a large batch of Wesleyan texts so addressed, to the most recent Pentecostalist choruses. There is a scriptural basis for this in the Fourth Gospel when Christ speaks of "another Comforter," who comes from the Father at his request and accomplishes divine functions. Usually it is "with the Father and the Son together" that the Holy Spirit "is worshiped and glorified."

To sum up thus far: we have seen how, in its origins and structure, trinitarian worship and doctrine is closely bound up with the nature of salvation: its source, its giving and reception, its celebration and enjoyment, its end. All of this implies, according to the Christian faith, the one God who works tripersonally and is in very being tripersonal: Father, Son, and Holy Spirit.[7] This deep structure has been transmitted in the official liturgies of the church. It has always needed interpretation and has often been under threat.

Present Difficulties

What, now, are the difficulties in our particular context? At the outset I hinted at difficulties with the sufficiency and finality, and therefore the reality, of the Incarnation. Some Christians may be tempted to weaken here for the sake, at least in part, of external apologetic in the face of other and shifting worldviews.[8] But the most acutely felt internal difficulty in our time and place seems to concern the designation of the second and first persons of the

Trinity as Son and Father, the latter being the sharpest problem of all. In efforts to avoid it, some are being led, perhaps involuntarily, away from the Trinity altogether. I shall suggest that here, too, it is the reality of the Incarnation that is at stake when the designations "Father" and "Son" are questioned. But let us for a moment isolate the problem of "Father."

Objections to calling God "Father" are of three kinds. The first has a background in Freudian psychology. "God the Father" or "the Father God" would then be the projection, onto a cosmic or even transcendent screen, of early experiences or unresolved neuroses. On Freud's own terms, we should be in the presence of an illusion. The second kind of objection is related to the social and cultural situation. With the breakup of the patriarchal family, or perhaps even of the family as such, it is difficult to find at the human end a reference point for the analogical attribution of Fatherhood to God. The third kind of criticism is the most biting of those expressed from within the church. It alleges that "Father" as a divine name is a reflection and buttress of sexist male dominance among humankind and even in the church. What can be replied on each of these three counts?

If taken strictly, the projectionist interpretation will, after the manner already of Feuerbach, reduce all theology to anthropology; the position cannot be refuted on terms acceptable to such of its proponents, but such proponents have in fact stepped outside historic Christianity. When the position is advanced in a more benign form, it is compatible with the view that the God who loves humankind accommodates to our psychological processes. Yet there is always the danger that we shall idolatrously exchange the Creator for the creature (cf. Rom 1:18-25). Our "images" of God must be permanently open to correction by God's own self-revelation. But that will bring us back precisely to the Incarnation, which I shall treat again presently.

With regard to our social and cultural situation today, there is (I think) an interesting piece of counter-evidence in the fact that several popular television series find it possible and desirable to present families, and even fathers, in a positive—indeed, affectionate—light; and that a leading comedian, Bill Cosby, can write a sympathetic bestseller under the title *Fatherhood*.[9] Theologically, it is in any case important to know which end of an analogy is determinative. According to Ephesians 3:14-15, it is the divine Father from whom every earthly fatherhood is named. The God revealed by Jesus is the corrective norm for every human father. The Incarnation again![10]

In the matter of sexism, I have no wish to support the oppression of any group of Christians, or indeed any human being at all, by any other. On the contrary. The injunction for those who would be followers of Christ is to mutual deference and service (e.g., Mk 10:42-45). But sympathy for some aspects of a cause, as with the position of women in society and in the church, is no reason for acquiescence in other tendencies of a movement that are dangerous, or even erroneous, but are not necessarily intrinsic to the cause. Proposals for linguistic change that threaten trinitarian worship and doctrine are to be resisted.

Arguments for Retaining the Trinitarian Name of Father, Son, and Holy Spirit

Feminist theologians who seek change in the divine name often stress the figurative or (as they say) metaphorical character of human speech in reference to God.[11] Now metaphor is not a simple category any more than the literal is.[12] It might be better to see "metaphorical" and "literal" as rough designations for ranges on a linguistic continuum. To this matter I shall return. But even supposing that all human God-talk were somehow metaphorical, it would not necessarily follow that all metaphors were equally appropriate or authorized or that they all functioned in the same way. We might have reason for holding that some metaphors were not exchangeable but rather indispensable and performed special functions.[13]

Among the wide range of figurative language used with divine reference in the Scriptures are the following similes:

> Thus says the Lord:
> "Behold, I will extend prosperity to
> [Jerusalem] like a river,
> and the wealth of the nations like an
> overflowing stream;
> and you shall suck, you shall be carried
> upon her hip,
> and dandled upon her knees.
> *As one whom his mother comforts,*

> *so I will comfort you;*
> you shall be comforted in Jerusalem."
> (Isaiah 66:12-13; my italics)

> Jesus said:
> "O Jerusalem, Jerusalem . . .
> *How often would I have gathered your children*
> *together as a hen gathers her brood under*
> *her wings,* and you would not!"
> (Matthew 23:37; my italics)

It is in accord with these texts that Julian of Norwich, when speaking of the maternal characteristics of God manifested in Christ, should have in mind the attitudes and acts of the Godhead as such *toward us—"our* Mother." Julian does not use "Mother" to designate the relations of the trinitarian persons *among themselves.* They remain Father, Son, and Holy Spirit.

Psalm 103:13 employs the following simile:

> As a father pities his children,
> so the Lord pities those who fear him.

Some of the language of Jesus in the Sermon on the Mount may remain in the same range of metaphor, as when he refers to the divine care for the birds of the air and the lilies of the field and argues *a fortiori* for the tender loving care of "your heavenly Father" toward his listeners. The fact that the hymn *"Veni, Sancte Spiritus"* can call the Holy Spirit also "father of the poor" suggests that parental care is an attitude of the whole Godhead as such toward us.

In these last cases we have seen comparisons drawn from positive human experience—whether of motherhood or fatherhood—to illustrate God's attitudes toward the world and people. But we have not yet reached the question of the trinitarian name. Here we need to look at the Epistles and, above all, the Gospels for the Father-Son relationship. It quickly becomes obvious that, if we are dealing with a metaphor, it is a highly privileged one. If a distinction between the metaphorical and the literal is to be maintained, I would hold that we have now moved toward the literal end of the scale.[14] Better still, in this case of Father and Son we have to do with *primary* language. Let us examine the key evidence.

Joachim Jeremias has highlighted the significance of Jesus' address to God as "Abba."[15] Although the uniqueness of this use may be hard to prove, it is a striking characteristic of Jesus that he should address his prayers by this intimate term which expresses both affection and respect when used by a child to address its father. The Aramaic word is transliterated at Mark 14:36, and we may suppose it to lie behind the Greek *"Pater"* when this occurs in accounts of Jesus praying in every strand of the gospel tradition. Jesus appears to have chosen this as the most appropriate way of expressing his relationship to the one who sent him and with whom he stays in constant touch (cf. Jn 11:41-42). The implications of that for Jesus' own identity are brought out in, for instance, Matthew 11:25-27:

> At that time Jesus declared, "I thank thee, Father, Lord of heaven and earth, that thou hast hidden these things from the wise and understanding and revealed them to babes; yea, Father, for such was thy gracious will. All things have been delivered to me by my Father; and no one knows the Son except the Father, and no one knows the Father except the Son and any one to whom the Son chooses to reveal him."

The Word incarnate can *define* language. In this context, "Father" and "Son" *mean* who the first two persons of the Trinity *are* and what the relation between them *is*. It is the divine ontology that sets the meaning of the terms, not an already established meaning of the terms that dictates the divine being.[16] The content of the Father-Son relationship, when expressed and lived out in the terms of the Incarnation, is to be discerned from the significant words and deeds of Jesus and the events of his life, death, and resurrection.

We cannot know "from the inside" the relationships among the trinitarian persons. The best hints provided in Scripture are those of a mutual indwelling that does not exclude the first person being what the Cappadocians would call "the fount of deity." In any case, the relationships are such that, when they are turned *"ad extra,"* the Son can reveal the Father:

> Philip said to [Jesus], "Lord, show us the Father, and we shall be satisfied." Jesus said to him, "Have I been with you so long, and yet you do not know me, Philip? Whoever has seen me has seen the Father; how can you say, 'Show us the Father'? Do you not believe that I am in the Father and the Father in me?" (John 14:8-10)

> No one has ever seen God; the only Son, who is in the bosom of the Father, he has made him known. (John 1:18)

The self-revelation of God in Christ becomes determinative, Christians believe, for all our understanding of God and of God's relation to the world and to us, and consequently of our proper response to God and of proper intra-human relationships.

In sum, it seems to me that the trinitarian name of God is *given* to us with Jesus' address to "Abba, Father," his self-understanding and career as "the Son," and his promise of the Holy Spirit. Christian reflection upon the divine self-revelation and the experience of salvation it brought led to the conclusion of an eternal divine Triunity. Classical Christian worship has therefore constantly followed the structure expressed in the two complementary formulations—mediatorial and coordinated—expounded and defended by Basil. And it has normatively employed the given name of the one God—Father, Son, and Holy Spirit—whenever the Trinity has been solemnly invoked. Thus the historic identity of the Christian faith is at stake if that structure is obscured or the best name we have is abandoned. It is vital that the structure and the name be maintained at such nodal points as the following:

* the baptismal questions ("Do you believe in . . .?") and declaration ("I baptize you in . . .");[17]
* the ecumenical creeds (Apostolic and Nicene);
* the eucharistic prayer;
* ordination to the ministry;
* the solemn benediction ("The blessing of God almighty, Father, Son, and Holy Spirit . . .").

The same pattern is found in familiar texts that have commended themselves down through the centuries: the Greater Gloria ("Glory be to God on high . . ."), the Lesser Gloria ("Gloria Patri . . ."), the Te Deum, and so on. The best hymn writers observe it, as does Charles Wesley in this hymn:

Father of everlasting grace,
Thy goodness and thy truth we praise,
Thy goodness and thy truth we prove;
Thou hast, in honor of thy Son,
The gift unspeakable sent down,
The Spirit of life, and power, and love.

Send us the Spirit of thy Son
To make the depths of Godhead known,
To make us share the life divine . . .

So fundamental is the pattern that it is natural for it to pervade all Christian worship. It is important that it continue to mark new compositions and extemporaneous prayer. Otherwise the old examples would risk being treated as fossils.

The trinitarian name and doctrine is precisely *not* an abstract formula.[18] It belongs to a living context. It must be kept firmly attached to the historical revelation through the telling and retelling of the story recounted in Scripture. It can thus carry with it all the associations of the God who has said and done such wonderful things and has received the praises of the people in such a rich abundance of language. The name and the doctrine need exposition in preaching and teaching. Further reflection may be needed to clarify their use, as took place, for instance, already at the Council of Nicea: "*eternally* begotten of the Father," "begotten, *not made*," "being *of one substance* with the Father."

This may be the place, however, to point out some tracks that would be false even if they were pursued with a view to explicating trinitarian doctrine, let alone replacing the triune name altogether (as some are suggesting). For example, "Creator, Redeemer, Sustainer" is either the listing of the three activities toward the world on the part of an otherwise undifferentiated Godhead (a kind of Sabellianism) or else runs the risk of dividing the Godhead in a Marcionite way. It is true that the tradition knows the careful and limited use of a principle of "appropriation," as in the Catechism of the Book of Common Prayer:

> First I learn to believe in God the Father, who hath made me, and all the world.
>
> Secondly, in God the Son, who hath redeemed me, and all mankind.
>
> Thirdly, in God the Holy Ghost, who sanctifieth me, and all the elect people of God.

But that is possible only in the context of a strong doctrine of the distinction, relations, and mutual coinherence of the three persons in the one God.[19] And such a doctrine is based precisely on the given name of Father, Son, and Holy Spirit. Or again, some are now speaking of "the Creator, the Christ, and the Spirit." This makes it sound as if Christ and the Holy Spirit were creatures; and Arianism, as Athanasius and Basil argued, forfeits our salvation, since only God can save.

So much is at stake in the matter of trinitarian worship that I have felt it necessary to give a fairly firm account of the traditional doctrine, and even at times to make a polemical point or two. But I would like to end on a more directly devotional note. I invite you to contemplate one of the most famous icons in Eastern Orthodoxy. Andrei Rublev depicts the persons of the Trinity in the guise of the three visitors to Abraham and Sara by the oaks of Mamre (Gn 18). The rhythm of the picture "folds" the three figures into one another in such a way as to suggest the mutual indwelling of the three divine persons in the one Godhead. Various details indicate that the figure we see on the left is the Father, the central figure is the Son, and the figure on the right is the Holy Spirit. Through a characteristic use of inverse perspective, the icon "reaches out" toward the beholder, who can thus be "included" in the scene. Salvation is to be drawn, in a way appropriate to creatures, into the very life of God, to be given by the graciousness of God a share in the communion of the divine persons.[20] The sacramental sign of the beginning of that process is baptism in the name of the Father, the Son, and the Holy Spirit. In the eucharist the Holy Spirit touches us and the bread and wine so that we may receive the body and blood of Christ and so be included in the Son's self-gift to the Father. To the one God we cry, "Holy, holy, holy . . ."

Notes

1. See Migne: *Patrologia Graeca* 32:67-218. Scholarly edition by Benoît Pruche in *Saint Basile de Césarée, sur le Saint Esprit*, rev. ed., Sources chrétiennes, no. 17 (Paris: Editions du Cerf, 1968). A modern English translation by David Anderson in *St. Basil the Great: On the Holy Spirit* (Crestwood, NY: St. Vladimir's Seminary Press, 1980).

2. See Migne: *Patrologia Graeca* 26:529-676. Modern English translation by C.R.B. Shapland, The *Letters of St. Athanasius Concerning the Holy Spirit* (London: Epworth Press, 1951).

3. See the English translation by L.G. Doyle and W.A. Jurgens, *Theological Dimensions of the Liturgy* (Collegeville: The Liturgical Press, 1976), in particular pp. 191-246.

4. Ibid. 191-192.

5. Athanasius, *Ad Adelphium* 3-4 (Migne: *Patrologia Graeca* 26:1073-1077).

6. For Augustine's exegesis of these two texts, see my book entitled *Doxology: The Praise of God in Worship, Doctrine and Life* (New York: Oxford University Press, 1980) 91-93.

7. See William J. Hill, *The Three-Personed God: The Trinity as a Mystery of Salvation* (Washington, D.C.: Catholic University of America Press, 1982).

8. See my essay entitled "The Doctrine of the Trinity: Where the Church Stands or Falls," *Interpretation* 45 (April 1991) 117-132.

9. Bill Cosby, *Fatherhood* (New York: Doubleday, 1986).

10. For a "secular" recognition (i.e., one that prescinds from substantial theological questions of normativity) of this kind of movement in connection with religious language, note the following passage from Kenneth Burke: "Whether or not there is a realm of the 'supernatural,' there are *words* for it. And in this state of linguistic affairs there is a paradox. For whereas the words for the 'supernatural' realm are necessarily borrowed from the realm of our everyday experience, out of which our familiarity with language arises, once a terminology has been developed for special theological purposes the order can become reversed. We can borrow back the terms from the borrowers, again secularizing to varying degrees the originally secular terms that had been given 'supernatural' connotations" (*The Rhetoric of Religion* [Berkeley: University of California Press, 1970] 7).

11. See, for example, Sallie McFague, *Metaphorical Theology* (Philadelphia: Fortress Press, 1982).

12. For theologically interesting discussions of metaphor, see Janet Martin Soskice, *Metaphor and Religious Language* (Oxford: Clarendon Press, 1985); and Roland M. Frye, "Language for God and Feminist Language: Problems and Principles" (Princeton: Center for Theological Inquiry, 1988).

13. In his collection of essays entitled *Divine Nature and Human Language* (Ithaca: Cornell University Press, 1989), William P. Alston argues against "irreducible metaphors" in theology, denying that what is said in metaphors could not, in principle, be said, at least in part, in other terms. But he does not argue *to* the interchangeability of metaphors in talk of God. To the contrary, he argues *from* the perception that some talk of God, at least, is literal.

14. This is an *ad hominem* way of stating a point that would really require a full exposition of my understanding of the principle of analogy and its ontological assumptions and consequences in religious and theological use.

15. See especially Joachim Jeremias, *The Prayers of Jesus* (London: SCM Press, 1967).

16. Georges Florovsky spoke of the *transfiguration* of human speech in this connection: "Man is created in the image and likeness of God—this 'analogical' link makes communication possible. And since God deigned to speak to man, the human word itself acquires new depth and strength and becomes transfigured" ("Revelation and Interpretation," in *The Collected Works of Georges Florovsky*, vol. 1, *Bible, Church, Tradition: An Eastern Orthodox View* [Belmont, MA: Nordland, 1972], in particular p. 27).

17. The maintenance of the trinitarian name at baptism is advocated, in a partial though by no means complete overlap of argumentation with the present study, by Catherine Mowry LaCugna in "The Baptismal Formula, Feminist Objections, and Trinitarian Theology," *Journal of Ecumenical Studies* 26 (1989) 235-250.

18. Cf. ibid. 242: "'God the Father' in the sense of 'Father of Jesus Christ' is a specific and personal way to name God, not an indefinite name for the divine essence."

19. Cf. ibid. 244: "Distinguishing persons by their function with respect to us does not sufficiently highlight the personal and relational character of God *as* God. The strong and bold claim of trinitarian theology is that not only is God related to us, but it is the very *essence* or *substance* of God to be relational." Or, as John Wesley put it in a letter of 3 August 1771 to Jane Catherine March: "The quaint device of styling them three offices rather than persons gives up the whole doctrine" (*The Letters of John Wesley*, ed. John Telford, vol. 5 [London: Epworth Press, 1931] 270).

20. For an exposition of the Orthodox view of worship as participation in God, see, for example, George S. Bebis, "Worship in the Orthodox Church," *Greek Orthodox Theological Review* 22 (1977) 429-443: Christian worship is "a continuous and an increasing experience, which is nothing less than a real communion with our God, the Father Almighty, the Creator of all things visible and invisible; a participation in the life of Jesus Christ, whose life is extended and thrives in the Church; and the unending reception of the Holy Spirit, who strengthens our life and prepares us to become members of the divine and heavenly household of God" (p. 429).

15

Canons, Cultures, and the Ecumenically Correct

"THOU HAST CONQUERED, O PALE GALILEAN," WROTE THE PROTO-NEOPAGAN poet Algernon Charles Swinburne, echoing the dying words of Julian the Apostate, *"Vicisti, Galilaee"*:[1]

> Thou hast conquered, O pale Galilean;
> the world has grown grey from thy breath.[2]

Swinburne's lament might be true, if the Enlightenment were an unalloyed product of Christianity, and if the Enlightenment's reductionistic generalizations, whether naïve or critical, about *homo sapiens* had been fulfilled. My thesis, however, will be that the Enlightenment's admirable thrust towards a universal humanism is better catered for, in terms of Christian theology, by a catholicity whose respect for particularity does not fall into the fragmentary irrationalisms of the post-modern. A canon set by the Revelation entrusted to the apostolic witnesses—the witness of "dead brown Judaeans"[3]—rejects religious relativism while providing a standard of holiness that allows for a variety of cultural expression without adulteration of the faith.

But let me backtrack, as far as the program committee's designation of the theme of this meeting: "Religious pluralism and/or the inculturation of theology." I was not privy to the committee's deliberations, but the studied ambiguity, as it seems to me, of that formulation gives rise to two sets of thoughts at least. First, the variant with "and" clearly supposes a certain linkage between religion and culture. Religion has a cultural dimension, and culture no doubt (à la Tillich) a religious dimension.[4] Religions have shaped and been shaped by cultures, and of course vice versa. With these two observations or contentions, taken phenomenologically, I would not disagree. The theological task, in our connection, would then be to consider how a religion (and, reflexively, its theology) might deliberately (for I take it that "inculturation" implies intention) come to express itself, for whatever purposes, in a culture in which it had hitherto not been at home and which had indeed been marked by another religion. Since the word "pluralism" usually carries positive resonances for those who introduce it, the expectation would be that such an inculturation would bring mutual enrichment to the two religions and their cultural carriers; so that, if appropriate circumstances arose, the adherents of the "second" religion might in turn seek to inculturate their religion in the home territory of the first. The underlying assumption is that of, at the least, a compatibility between the two religions, and perhaps even of their "ultimate" unity (whether already in some mystical or transcendent realm, or in a future history of humankind, or finally in some kind of eschatological realization).

Secondly, however, the version of the theme with "or" allows for a much more disjunctive approach. Maybe we have to do with two rather different issues, "religious pluralism" and "the inculturation of theology." Or, at least, two issues—perhaps the former an observed fact and the latter a desired process—whose relationship is quite problematical. It should be safe to assume that the program committee did not want us to make a total disjunction and hold two quite separate meetings, the one on religious pluralism and the other on the inculturation of theology. But I will understand the hiccup in their formulation of the theme as a milder disjunction in order to explore the problematic character, from a viewpoint within Christian theology (and I am not in a position to undertake any other kind of theology), of the inculturation—perhaps desirable, indeed in some sense unavoidable, and therefore finally possible— of the faith in human contexts hitherto untouched by the Gospel and in all likelihood occupied by some other religion(s). The modern history of the west shows that it would be unwise to look upon the inculturation of the faith as a permanent acquisition rather than a continuing task; and much of what I will say could be applied, *mutatis mutandis*, to the possibility of, and need for, *re*-inculturation of the faith in an apostate civilization; but for simplicity's sake, I will speak only of a first process of inculturation.

I was asked that my presentation should take the form, at least in part, of a report on current ecumenical thinking in respect to the named issue(s).[5] I shall now therefore give my paper its (third, if not fourth) start with the kerfuffle at Canberra, namely the controversy surrounding the lecture given by Chung Hyun-Kyung, of South Korea, at the Seventh Assembly of the World Council of Churches in 1991. The ecumenical discussion will then be made a bit more precise through attention to two perennial activities of the church that have both contributed to and benefited from the Christian ecumenical movement in the twentieth century, namely evangelization and liturgy; for both these enterprises involve questions of religion and culture of the kind sketched earlier. My own theological judgments will already have affected, implicitly or explicitly, this ecumenical reportage; so I shall then come clean with my own systematic discussion around the problematic relationship between our two assigned themes of "religious pluralism" and "theological inculturation," employing for the purpose my chosen binome of "canons" and "cultures." In conclusion, I shall advocate a return to an authentic ecumenism in place of the fashionably, or at least ironically so designated, "correct."

I. THE KERFUFFLE AT CANBERRA

On 8 February 1991 Professor Chung Hyun-Kyung provided for the entire seventh assembly of the World Council of Churches at Canberra its "introduction to the theological theme" under which it was gathered: "Come Holy Spirit, Renew The Whole Creation." Dancing barefoot on the "Holy Ground" of the "indigenous people of Australia," she recited a litany that invoked, among other spirits, "the spirit of indigenous people of the earth, victims of genocide during the time of colonialism and the period of great Christian mission to the pagan world," "the spirit of Earth, Air and Water, raped, tortured and exploited by human greed for money," "the spirit of the Liberator, our brother Jesus, tortured and killed on the cross."[6] Professor Chung then described her place of origin and the place of the assembly in this way:

> I came from Korea, the land of spirits full of *Han. Han* is anger. *Han* is resentment. *Han* is bitterness. *Han* is grief. *Han* is broken-

heartedness and the raw energy for struggle for liberation. In my tradition people who were killed or died unjustly became wandering spirits, the *Han*-ridden spirits. They are all over the place seeking the chance to make the wrong right. Therefore the living people's responsibility is to listen to the voices of the *Han*-ridden spirits and to participate in the spirits' work of making the right wrong.[7] These *Han*-ridden spirits in our people's history have been agents through whom the Holy spirit has spoken her compassion and wisdom for life. Without hearing the cries of these spirits we cannot hear the voice of the Holy spirit. I hope the presence of all our ancestors spirits here with us shall not make you uncomfortable. For us they are the icons of the Holy Spirit who became tangible and visible to us. Because of them we can feel, touch and taste the concrete bodily historical presence of the Holy Spirit in our midst. From my people's land of *Han*-filled spirits I came to join with you in another land of spirits full of *Han*, full of the spirits of the indigenous people, victims of genocide. Here, in Australia, we are gathered together from every part of our mother earth to pray for the coming of the Holy Spirit to renew the whole creation.

The following paragraph occurred at a later point in Professor Chung's speech:

For me the image of the Holy Spirit comes from the image of *Kwan In*. She is venerated as Goddess of compassion and wisdom by East Asian women's popular religiosity. She is a *bodhisattva*, enlightened being. She can go into Nirvana any time she wants to, but refuses to go into Nirvana by herself. Her compassion for all suffering living beings makes her stay in this world enabling other living beings to achieve enlightenment. Her compassionate wisdom heals all forms of life and empowers them to swim to the shore of Nirvana. She waits and waits until the whole universe, people, trees, birds, mountains, air, water, become enlightened. They can then go to Nirvana together where they can live collectively in eternal wisdom and compassion. Perhaps this might also be a feminine image of the Christ who is the first born among us, one who goes before and brings others with her?

The speech provoked great excitement, even uproar. An extra session for clarification and debate revealed that Professor Chung had not been relying on poetic license but intended to be taken with theological seriousness. The whole episode undoubtedly colored the critical responses of the Evangelicals and the Orthodox to the Assembly. The World Council of Churches had begun to woo the Evangelicals, who for their part have been coming to a stronger sense of the need for the visible unity of the church; but in their subsequent "Letter to Churches and Christians worldwide," participants at Canberra who confessed themselves to "share evangelical perspectives" felt bound to declare, in all courtesy:[8]

> As the Assembly discussed the process of listening to the Spirit at work in every culture, we cautioned, with others, that discernment is required to identify the Spirit as the Spirit of Jesus Christ and thus to develop criteria for and limits to theological diversity. We argued for a high Christology to serve as the only authentic Christian base for dialogue with persons of other living faiths . . . The ecumenical movement needs a theology rooted in the Christian revelation as well as relevant to contemporary problems. At present, there is insufficient clarity regarding the relationship between the confession of the Lord Jesus Christ as God and Saviour according to Scripture, the person and work of the Holy Spirit, and legitimate concerns which are part of the WCC agenda. We share many of these concerns, such as those related to justice, peace and the integrity of creation, to the contextualization (or inculturation) of the Gospel, and to religious pluralism. This theological deficit not only conspires against the work of the WCC as a Christian witness but also increases the tensions among its member churches.

The Eastern Orthodox and Oriental Orthodox Churches have, in fact, come to a sharper crisis than ever concerning their continuing membership in the World Council of Churches. The following extracts from the "Reflections of Orthodox Participants" subsequent to Canberra give the flavor of ecumenically minded Orthodox theologians on our theme ("ecumenically minded," be it well noted; *not* the views, say, of the monks on Mount Athos):[9]

> The Orthodox note that there has been an *increasing departure from the Basis* of the WCC. The latter has provided the framework for Orthodox participation in the World Council of Churches. Its text is: "The World Council of Churches is a fellowship of churches which confess the Lord Jesus Christ as God and Saviour according to the scriptures and therefore seek to fulfil together their common calling to the glory of the one

God, Father, Son and Holy Spirit." Should the WCC not direct its future work along these lines, it would be in danger of ceasing to be an instrument aiming at the restoration of Christian unity and in that case it would tend to become a forum for an exchange of opinions without any specific Christian theological basis. In such a forum, common prayer will be increasingly difficult, and eventually will become impossible, since even a basic common theological vision will be lacking.

The tendency to marginalize the *Basis* in WCC work has created some dangerous trends in the WCC. We miss from many WCC documents the affirmation that Jesus Christ is the world's Saviour. We perceive a growing *departure from biblically-based Christian understandings* of

a) the trinitarian God,
b) salvation,
c) the "Good News" of the gospel itself,
d) human beings as created in the image and likeness of God, and
e) the Church . . .

The Orthodox follow with interest, but also with a certain disquiet, the developments of the WCC towards the broadening of its aims in the direction of *relations with other religions*. The Orthodox support dialogue initiatives, particularly those aiming at the promotion of relations of openness, mutual respect and human cooperation with neighbours of other faiths. When dialogue takes place, Christians are called to bear witness to the integrity of their faith. A genuine dialogue involves greater theological efforts to express the Christian message in ways that speak to the various cultures of our world. All this, however, must occur on the basis of theological criteria which will define the limits of diversity. The biblical faith in God must not be changed. The definition of these criteria is a matter of theological study, and must constitute the first priority of the WCC in view of its desired broadening of aims.

Thus, it is with alarm that the Orthodox have heard some presentations on the theme of this Assembly. With reference to the theme of the Assembly, the Orthodox still await the final texts. However, they observe that some people tend to affirm with very great ease the presence of the Holy Spirit in many movements and developments without discernment. The Orthodox wish to stress the factor of sin and error, which exists in

> every human action, and separates the Holy Spirit from there.
> We must guard against a tendency *to substitute a "private" spi, it,
> the spirit of the world or other spirits for the Holy Spirit* wno
> proceeds from the Father and rests in the Son. Our tradition is
> rich in respect for local and national cultures, but we find it
> impossible to invoke the spirits of "earth, air, water and sea
> creature." Pneumatology is inseparable from Christology or
> from the doctrine of the Holy Trinity confessed by the Church
> on the basis of Divine Revelation.

It is only fair to Professor Chung to mention that her speech was favorably received not only by the bureaucratically entrenched Liberal Left but also by such a thoughtful veteran of the ecumenical movement as the Italian Waldensian theologian Paolo Ricca who found in it, less a "decline into pantheism," than a link between the voices of the victims of creation and history and the voice of the Holy Spirit (cf. Rom 8:18-23), and an indication that "the God of all peoples and cultures may be intending to use encounter and dialogue with other worlds of the spirit, religious and secular, present among humanity in order to reveal to us some still unknown aspects of that 'fulness' of his revelation in Jesus Christ which we are far from having completely explored."[10]

Nevertheless, the controversy provoked by Professor Chung's address serves to signal two concerns that are inevitably raised for Christian theology by our themes of "religious pluralism" and "inculturation." The twin concerns may be labelled as *relativism* and *syncretism*. The relativistic threat to the unique and universal status accorded Jesus Christ in the traditional Christian confession may be illustrated anecdotally from a walk I took through the foyer of the WCC headquarters in Geneva two or three years ago with someone who had previously held high office in the organization. As we passed by the banners commemorating Assemblies of the WCC (Evanston 1954: "Jesus Christ the Hope of the World"; New Delhi 1961: "Jesus Christ the Light of the World"; Nairobi 1975: "Jesus Christ Frees and Unites"), we finally came to "Vancouver 1983: "Jesus Christ the Life of the World," and my companion said with confidence in her voice, "That's the last time we'll see *his* name on a banner." And whereas syncretism has usually in the past been repudiated as a denial of the purity and sufficiency of the Christian Gospel,[11] we can now find the ecumenically influential Indian theologian M.M. Thomas speaking rather more positively of a "Christ-centred syncretism."[12] Quoting Raimundo Panikkar's characterization of western Christianity as "ancient paganism, or to be more precise, the complex of Hebrew-Hellenic-Greek-Latin-Celtic-modern religions converted to Christ more or less successfully," Thomas writes that "all Christians are pagan in parts. Synthesis is a long way away, it is almost 'eschatological'. Syncretism with a sense of Christian direction is all that we can now realize."[13]

The issues of relativism and syncretism arise in connection with the practices of evangelization and liturgy to be treated, in no more than an indicative way, in the next section (II), and they will come up again in the ensuing, and slightly more developed, systematic reflections on canons and cultures (III).

The lengthy quotations so far given provide us with ample material for theological debate; but in case any readers are tiring of the reportage style and are looking for something more directly systematic on the author's own part, they should now skip directly to section III. Thereafter they may return, if they wish, to section II for a little more technicolored approach.

II. EVANGELIZATION AND LITURGY
IN ECUMENICAL PERSPECTIVE

Here I can do no more than indicate some current trends and tensions in two areas of ecclesial practice—evangelization and liturgy—that are not only perennial works of the church but have also, and indeed consequent upon their belonging to the permanent charge of the church, figured prominently in the twentieth-century ecumenical movement. It is, of course, still the themes of religious pluralism and/or the inculturation of Christianity which occupy us.

Evangelization and/or Dialogue

Here I introduce my own hiccup into the title, in order to signal a problematic relationship.

"The evangelization of the world in this generation" was the banner under which the ecumenical pioneer John R. Mott marched at the turn of the nineteenth century into the twentieth. The event from which the modern ecumenical movement is conventionally dated was precisely the World Missionary Conference at Edinburgh in 1910, at which the testimony from the "overseas" mission fields concerning the "scandal" of Christian disunity as an obstacle to evangelization started to put pressure on the "home" churches to set their own house in order. The International Missionary Council (IMC) was founded in 1921 and, despite the variety to be found among evaluations of "other religions" in Christian eyes, the major drive of its concerns and work was towards evangelization or the explicit preaching of the Gospel. When the IMC became integrated into the World Council of Churches in 1961, misgivings were expressed by some about a possible blunting of the evangelistic thrust through the diffusion of interests in the larger body. Although "world mission and evangelism" remains a part of the WCC structure and programs, an increasing prominence has been achieved by a new sub-unit, established in the early 1970s, on "Dialogue with People of Living Faiths and Ideologies."[14]

But instead of taking once more an example from the World Council of Churches, let us look instead at the tense question of "evangelization and/or dialogue" as it appears from a Roman Catholic angle, the Roman Catholic Church having become a full partner in the ecumenical movement as a result of the Second Vatican Council in the 1960s. It may even suffice to quote a few extracts from the writings and speeches of Cardinal Francis Arinze, the Nigerian President of the Pontifical Council for Interreligious Dialogue.[15]

First, from "Prospects of Evangelization, with reference to the areas of the non-Christian religions, twenty years after Vatican II" (1985):[16]

> Jesus Christ, the Son of God made man, is our Saviour . . . [He] carefully prepared his apostles to bring his salvation to all men, of all times, in all places . . . [He] founded his Church as the sacrament of salvation and sent his apostles into the whole world, just as he himself had been sent by his Father (cf. Jn 20:21; Mt 28:18; Mk 16:15). He gave his Church a mission, an assignment, a task, an apostolate: to evangelize, to bring the good news of salvation to all men, to be witnesses of his love and service, to share with all men the superabundant riches of the salvation which he so lovingly worked for us . . .

> This assignment includes . . . "the dialogue in which Christians meet the followers of other religious traditions in order to walk together towards truth and to work together in projects of common concern." Such interreligious dialogue is not aimed at conversion, although it is not opposed to it. True interreligious

> dialogue is concerned to promote for both parties progress in movement towards God, more sincere search for the truth, greater obedience to God, and therefore greater openness to divine action, and so to salvation . . .

> Interreligious dialogue would be unnecessary if all men believed in Jesus Christ and practised only the religion which he established . . .

> By dialogue the Church puts herself as an instrument into the hands of Divine Providence and in God's working out of his own mystery of salvation for mankind. In interreligious dialogue the Church discovers the working of God in the other religions, elements of truth and grace, seeds of the Word, seeds of contemplation, elements which are true and good, precious things both religious and human and ways of the truth which illumine all mankind.

Difficulties are recognized. First, on the Christian side:

> The tension between the missionary thrust of Christianity and the call to respect the religious views of others can lead some Christians into untenable positions. Some can come dangerously near to holding that all religions are essentially the same, that everybody is an anonymous Christian, that every religion is equally a way to salvation and that the era of missionary work and conversion should now give way to a new emphasis: that of respectful dialogue and fraternal coexistence of all religions. Others are tempted to the other extreme: not to see much good in non-Christian religions and to regard interreligious dialogue as a marginal exercise which busy bishops and priests cannot afford.

And on the other side:

> Some non-Christians are not sure of the Christian motives of dialogue. They fear that it is conversion. They are afraid that dialogue is a trojan horse which Christians want to bring into the fortified cities of the non-Christians. They need assurance that dialogue, although not opposed to conversion, does not aim at conversion but at mutual exchange and enrichment, deepening of one's faith and greater fidelity to God and openness to his action.

Or again, from "Interreligious Dialogue: Problems, Prospects and Possibilities" (1987):[17]

> Religious pluralism in the world of today is a fact which is being noticed more and more because of the growing ease of communication . . . These religions are the way of life of a greater part of humanity. They are the living expressions of the souls of vast groups of people. They carry with them the echo of thousands of years of searching for God. They possess an impressive patrimony of deeply religious texts. They have taught generations of people how to live, how to pray and how to die. The Catholic Church cannot afford to ignore them.

And yet (or is it "Precisely so"?):

> [The] divine plan has its centre in Jesus Christ, God and Man. It is in Christ that people find the fulness of their religious life. It is in him that God has reconciled all things to himself (cf. 2 Cor 5:18-19). God wants all men and women to be saved and to come to the knowledge of the truth. Jesus Christ is the one and only mediator between God and man (cf. 1 Tim. 2:4-6). He is the only Saviour of all mankind (cf. Jn 4:42) . . .

> Therefore all human beings are included in the great and unique design of God in Jesus Christ, even when they are not aware of it. Through the Holy Spirit the mystery of Christ can be operatively present even in the lives of those who are not Christians, who have other religions and who are not conscious of this link with Christ. All human beings are related to Christ not only as individuals but also with the best of their cultural and religious values.

That last mention brings us nicely to the question of inculturation, for which liturgy often provides a test case.

Liturgy and the Treasures of the Nations

By virtue of its own symbolic character, the ritual of worship often serves as a focus for matters that occur more widely in doctrine or life.[18] The modern liturgical movement has been ecumenical in scope, although the leadership has often come, in both theology and practice, from the Roman Catholic side. From its start early in the twentieth century, it has aimed at intelligent, active participation by all the assembled people of God, beginning in a western world that was already showing, in varying degrees and forms, evidence of secularization. But, in order to avoid the admitted problem of the need for *re*inculturation in a waning Christendom, let us look at the more classic case of liturgical indigenization amid cultures marked by other religions. Two somewhat contrasting examples, again from Roman Catholicism, will have to suffice.[19]

In 1974 the National Biblical Catechetical and Liturgical Centre in Bangalore produced some experimental *New Orders of the Mass for India*. A reading from Indian scriptures was included in the liturgy of the word, with this justification:

> This inclusion does not imply that problems concerning revelation in non-Christian religions and the inspiration of the non-Christian scriptures have been solved to everyone's satisfaction . . . These problems stand a better chance of a just solution if they are examined, not in the abstract, but in the light of experience—experience of those who have used these texts for reflection and prayer in the context of the Bible. Besides, even if we recognize only the "seeds of the Word" in these scriptures, the final manifestation of the Word of God in Jesus Christ does not render the "seeds" pointless and irrelevant. Jesus has come to fulfil, not to destroy . . . The non-Christian scriptures, even if they represent only a cosmic revelation, still form part of the dynamism of the Word and are better understood when placed in this context. In the liturgy, the non-Christian scriptures are never read alone, but always in the context of the Bible.

Again, the eucharistic prayer praised God for his self-revelation in the religions of India. The "cosmic covenant with all men" is applied to the Indian context through successive mentions of the animistic religions (with their worship of God as Power present in nature), of the Hindu religion (with its three paths to salvation: *karma, jnana, bhakti*), of Buddhism and Jainism together, and finally of Islam:

> God of the nations,
> You are the desire and hope
> of all who search for you with a sincere heart.
> You are the power almighty
> adored as Presence hidden in nature.
> You reveal yourself
> to the seers in their quest for knowledge,
> to devout who seek you through sacrifice and
>   detachment,
> to every man approaching you by the path of love.
> You enlighten the hearts that long for release

> by conquest of desire and universal kindness.
> You show mercy to those who submit
> to your inscrutable decrees.

The Roman authorities prohibited the use of this rite.

On the other hand, in 1988 Rome approved a new *Missal for the Dioceses of Zaïre*.[20] The opening invocation of the saints includes "our ancestors, who have served God with a good conscience." During the singing of the *Gloria in excelsis* there is a dance around the altar. Drums are used. The eucharistic prayer reads, in part:

> Lord our God, we thank you, we praise you,
> you, our God and our Father,
> you, "sun too bright for our gaze,"
> you the all-powerful,
> you the all-seer,
> you, the Master of men,
> the Master of life,
> the Master of all things,
> it is you we praise,
> it is to you that we give thanks,
> through your Son Jesus Christ,
> the one who is our mediator with you.

> Holy Father,
> we praise you through your Son Jesus, our mediator.
> He is your Word, the Word that gives life.
> Through him you created heaven and earth;
> through him you created our river, the Zaïre.
> Through him you created our forests, our rivers,
>   our lakes.
> Through him you created the animals who live in
>   our forests,
> and the fish who live in our rivers.
> Through him you created the things we see,
> and also the things we do not see.

> You have made him Lord of all things;
> you have sent him among us to be our Redeemer and
>   Saviour.
> He is our God made man.
> By the Holy Spirit, he took flesh of the Virgin Mary.
> You sent him, with the task of gathering all people
>   together,

> of making all mankind one family: your family.
> He obeyed you: he died on the cross.
> He conquered death, he rose from the dead.
> Death has no longer any power over him.

In African terms, this is a splendidly Nicene affirmation concerning the divine Person of Christ and his mediating role in creation and redemption, mediating God to humankind and humankind to God.

III. CANONS AND CULTURES

Under canons and cultures I want to address, respectively though also somewhat mutually, the perceived threats of relativism and syncretism. The normative notion of canon is intended by its users as a safeguard against relativism, although the fact that phenomenologically a plural is needed indicates that claims to absolute truth do not go uncontested (hence "religious pluralism"). There is no problem for Christian theology in recognizing a multiplicity of human cultures, at least insofar as they are receptive of the Gospel and subject to the sovereignty of Christ; "inculturation" of the faith is problematic only to the extent that religious features incompatible with the Christian canon may thereby get imported in a syncretistic process into Christianity. I shall argue that Christian theology requires a *religious canon* (specifically the apostolic faith, which defines historic Christianity and includes a confession of the unique and universal significance of Christ) and allows a *cultural pluralism* (as part of an ecclesial catholicity in time and space that allows grace to transform rather than destroy culture). The concept and reality that join these two together is that of an *assimilative tradition*.

The Canonicity of the Apostolic Faith

Within early Christianity, the notion of canonicity comes formally to the fore in the late second century with Tertullian and Irenaeus and their *regula fidei* or *kanôn tês alêtheias*.[21] The heart of Christian belief found expression in slightly variable summary statements which, in their trinitarian structure and their rehearsal of the *Heilsgeschichte*, closely resemble the baptismal creeds of the time; minor variations in the formulation are verbal rather than substantial. Irenaeus and Tertullian used this "rule of faith" as a "canon of truth" to dismiss Gnostic accounts of reality and offers of salvation that somehow claimed Christ but in fact conflicted with the revelation and redemption given by God in Jesus as this had been transmitted in the testimony and practice of the dominically authorized apostles and their appointed successors in the catholic church.

Roughly simultaneously, the catholic communities were settling on lists of writings appropriate for reading in church (*"legi in ecclesia"* is the phrase of the so-called Muratorian fragment whose dating and location is currently controversial among historians). According to Justin Martyr, in Rome around the middle of the second century, the Sunday liturgy included readings from "the writings of the prophets" and "the memoirs of the apostles."[22] While the historical importance of the case of Marcion as a stimulus to the fixation of a scriptural canon is disputed,[23] it is impossible to under-estimate the theological significance of the retention by catholic Christianity of the Scriptures of Israel (whatever the fluctuation in the precise limits and form as recognized and used by Christians), for the God of Israel was thereby being confessed as the one and only God, the universal creator and consummator. The Christian "retention" of the Scriptures of Israel implied also, it has to be said, a theological claim to them. The Scriptures of Israel constituted the literary, historical, and religious context into which Jesus came, and they provided the terms in which his person and work were first interpreted. The particularity of Israel was here sharpened, accord-ing to Christian confession, to a single figure, to whom was attrib-uted a unique and universal significance—"Jesus Christ is Lord," "the Savior of the world"—that would eventually require a trinitarian theology of Father, Son, and Holy Spirit. The status recognized to Jesus by Christians as the Son who mediates a new and universal covenant meant that the Scriptures of Israel were now to be read "in Christ," witnessing to the character, operation, and purposes of a God who had now taken his revealing and redeeming presence and action to the point of incarnation, atoning death, life-giving resurrection, and the start of a fresh pouring out of the Spirit on all flesh in anticipation of a final and everlasting kingdom.

Now there cannot be any doubt that the early Christians were making truth claims of public, indeed cosmic significance for their faith—claims which brought them into substantive conflict with those Jews who had not (yet) accepted Jesus, and with pagans who proposed other views of reality and ways to salvation. Positively put, the Christians offered a Gospel of salvation to both Jew and Gentile (Rom 16:25-27; Eph 2:11-3:21). They did not do it tentatively, relativistically, but forthrightly, absolutely: "There is salvation in no one else [than in Jesus Christ of Nazareth], for there is no other name under heaven given among men by which we must be saved" (Acts 4:12; cf. Rom 10:5-17; Phil 2:9-11).

The soteriological importance of the *regula fidei* is illustrated by the trouble which the church has time and time again taken to preserve it substantially intact in face of deviating tendencies within or on the fringes of Christianity. The single most decisive case was the prolonged struggle over Arianism. However reluctantly, the Council of Nicea was prepared to introduce the nonbiblical term *homoousios* into the confession of faith in order to safeguard the deity of the Savior who, as Athanasius and the Cappadocians would never tire of arguing against all variants of Arianism, had been confessed and named at baptism and who, if less than divine, would be less than a (biblical) Savior. (Whether the Nicene Creed means that "God must remain Greek" is a question to which I shall return under the discussion of "an assimilative tradition.") It is linguistically interesting that conciliar statements excluding heretical positions continue to be called canons.

That the notion of the *regula fidei* is still alive in the contemporary ecumenical movement, at least in Faith and Order work, is shown, for instance, in the questions put to the churches for their response in connection with the Lima text of 1982 on *Baptism, Eucharist and Ministry*:[24] How far can your church "recognize in this text the faith of the Church through the ages"? And what consequences can your church draw for its relations with other churches, "particularly with those churches which also recognize the text as an expression of the apostolic faith"? BEM evoked an unprecedented amount of attention and number of responses from the churches.[25] Dogmatically more significant was the decision to make the Nicene-Constantinopolitan Creed the "theological basis and methodological tool" for the Faith and Order study "Towards the Common Expression of the Apostolic Faith Today." This study is still in process.[26] It is highly significant that the doctrinal component in the search for the restoration of ecclesial unity is here set within the context of witness—evangelistic, apologetic—towards a world marked by many religions and ideologies, a world which is also culturally various.

Clearly, the Christian Churches continue to make a general offer of the Gospel and the faith with which they believe they have been entrusted. From the viewpoint of systematic theology, the intriguing question continues to concern the relation between the particular and the universal, or (more sharply put) the "scandal of particularity" involved in the offer and claim of Jesus as the universal Savior and Lord.[27] This incarnation of God was always a philosophical problem for a certain Greek mentality that kept an unbridgeable ontological gulf between the divine and the material, and the difficulty lived on in Lessing's dictum that "accidental truths of history can never become the proof of necessary truths of reason." In a sense, this is less of a problem for apologetics today, since western epistemologists now usually suppose that whatever can be known is known somehow "historically," in space and time (this is certainly the supposition of, say, Foucault's "genealogical" approach to knowledge). The greater problem lies with the post-modern contestation of an ontological coherence in the world and an intellectual and moral rationality in the human knower. Christian apologists have a stake in maintaining some kind of a Logos doctrine (as illustrated in many recent writings of T.F. Torrance[28]), which itself was early given Christian use—in a way which broke the bounds of its Greek origins (for John 1:14 declares that "the Word *became flesh*")—in order to state, as in Justin, the universal reference of Christ and the possibility of salvation for those who had lived before the time of Jesus.[29] The virtue of a Logos doctrine is to allow an account to be given of a coherent creation and a potentially universal salvation, the whole focused on Jesus Christ who can function criteriologically as Lord (a judge who embodies the divine law that both accuses and guides) and redemptively as Savior (who forgives and sanctifies), however difficult it may be for *us*, across cultural differences, to perceive where he is transformatively at work to bring people into God's kingdom (we must look in our own and others' lives for hints of a "Christ pattern" as this is described in the canonical witness to Jesus[30]).[31]

The kind of issues that arise in connection with Christocentrism in the key area of evangelization have been illustrated in section II of this chapter.

It is the particularity of Jesus Christ which, in Christian eyes, requires there to be a religious canon. It is the claimed universality of his significance which allows the question of cultural pluralism to expect, when set in the right framework, a positive answer. To that we now turn.

Cultural Pluralism in a Universal Frame

There is a distinct thinness, even a mere formality, to what many in the age of the Enlightenment were willing to affirm, philosophically, about humankind. It was, theoretically, a very gray world: "Reason" edged out emotion and the corporeal; mathematics was advocated as a universal method; causality was reduced to the efficient mode; transcendence gave way to self-sufficiency; what observation and speculation predicated as common to all people amounted to very little.[32] It is no wonder that the postmoderns, by reaction, seek "thick description," delight in the difference, suspect the grand theory . . . Yet the Enlightenment project of a universal history retained something valuable from the Christian *Heilsgeschichte* that is lost in the nihilistic fragmentation characteristic of postmodernism; and the Enlightenment's exaltation of Reason, though the quality of its human exercise seems to have been viewed with exaggerated optimism, bears tribute to some such coherence of reality as is confessed in the Christian doctrine of creation but denied by many postmoderns.

My contention would be that the Christian story and vision provide a universal frame within which diversity, both in its positive and its negative aspects, can be made sense of. That frame is set by the "one God, the Father, the Almighty, maker of heaven and earth, and of all things visible and invisible"; by the "one Lord, the only Son of God," who, when we had fallen from the communion with God to which we who were made in his image were called, "for us men and for our salvation came down from heaven, and was incarnate by the Holy Spirit from the virgin Mary," "was crucified" and "rose again" and "ascended into heaven" and "shall come again with glory"; and by "the Holy Spirit," who binds believers into "one holy, catholic and apostolic church" in anticipation of "the resurrection of the dead and the life of the world to come."

The positive diversities among humankind can be viewed as the work of a richly resourceful Creator and providential Lord of history, into whose final kingdom all the treasures of the nations will be brought. But some differences in human culture can be attributed, theologically, to a greater or lesser present conformity among a fallen and not yet fully redeemed humankind to the will of God and the destiny to which God calls us. Rather than taking H.

Richard Niebuhr's five "typical" attitudes as fixed and divergent stances of the Christian faith towards all human culture, it is more appropriate to see them as indicating the possibility of, and need for, a discriminating attention on the part of Christians toward every human culture at all times and in all places.[33] Whereas a particular cultural configuration may appear as predominantly positive or negative in relation to the saving purposes of God, it is likely that most cultures will contain some elements to be affirmed, some to be negated, resisted, and even fought, some to be purified and elevated, some to be held provisionally in tension, and some to be transformed.

The *regula fidei* is self-referential in confessing a church that is "holy, catholic, and apostolic." A church that abides by the apostolic norm will display its catholicity by including in its life those features from the variety of human cultures that prove marked or markable by the holiness revealed in the person and work of Jesus Christ and released in abundance by the pentecostal outpouring of the Holy Spirit. It is the observance of the apostolic norm that prevents syncretism in the sense of adulteration.

The kind of issues that arise in connection with catholicity in the key area of liturgy have been illustrated in section II of this chapter.

In the final part of section III, I want to argue that the notion and reality of a regulative religious canon and the possibility and actuality of a positive cultural pluralism are combined in the church understood as an assimilative tradition.

The Church as Assimilative Tradition

The earthly church is to be understood as an ongoing body in time and space, functioning as a transmissive vehicle and hermeneutical continuum for the original Gospel amid the historically and geographically changing cultures of humankind. In order to be able, without adulteration of the faith ("syncretism" in the frankly negative sense), to integrate into itself people and features from hitherto unevangelized cultures, the tradition needs to abide by its own substantive norm, the apostolic canon. In turn, the translatability of the canon is an indicator of the points of contact in the other culture and the transformative power of the Gospel.

According to John Henry Newman's *Essay on the Development of*

Christian Doctrine, one of the notes of a vital tradition is its "power of assimilation." In contrast with (say) "mathematics and other abstract creations,"

> doctrines and views which relate to man are not placed in a void, but in the crowded world, and make way for themselves by interpenetration, and develop by absorption. Facts and opinions, which have hitherto been regarded in other relations and grouped round other centres, henceforth are gradually attracted to a new influence and subjected to a new sovereign. They are modified, laid down afresh, thrust aside, as the case may be. A new element of order and composition has come among them; and its life is proved by this capacity of expansion, without disarrangement or dissolution. An eclectic, conservative, healing, moulding process, a unitive power, is of the essence, and a test, of a faithful development.[34]

Newman's argument led him, within Christianity, to the Roman Catholic Church. More generally, his perception of the "power of assimilation" provides a theologically valuable perspective for a Christian understanding of the place of the gospel tradition amid the religions and cultures.

It is within this optic that some recent Christian theologians risk a yet more positive use of the word syncretism than we have so far discovered.[35] The Orthodox Demetrius Constantelos writes approvingly that "it was a syncretic approach that won Christianity its followers in the first five centuries." With more precision, the Lutheran Wolfhart Pannenberg writes: "Christianity affords the greatest example of syncretic assimilative power; this religion not only linked itself to Greek philosophy but also inherited the entire religious tradition of the Mediterranean world." According to the Reformed Jürgen Moltmann, this process had been presaged in the Old Testament: "Israel achieved a syncretism between the religion of the nomad and of the Canaanite peasant through historicizing the latter in struggle." Enough is known about these theologians for us to be sure that they judge the "syncretism" to have occurred under the norm of a particular revelation.

Now it is the canonical Scriptures which tell the "full story" of which the *regula fidei* of an Irenaeus or a Tertullian or the Nicene-Constantinopolitan Creed is both a distillation and (consequently) an hermeneutical key. What happens with the translation of the

Scriptures illustrates both the degree of receptivity in the culture to which the Gospel is being brought and also the power of the Gospel to overcome obstacles and effect transformation. The Gambian theologian Lamin Sanneh, himself a convert to the Christian faith from Islam, has recently demonstrated in his book *Translating the Message* the renewing impact of Bible translations upon many vernacular cultures.[36] When a people has accepted Christianity, it in turn becomes part of the Christian tradition, which it enriches, thus making available an even greater variety in the form in which the faith can be further transmitted.

This is the perspective in which I should like to answer the question provocatively put by Robert Hood in his book *Must God Remain Greek?*[37] One could soften the question to "may," but I myself would be prepared, in a second step, to return an affirmative answer even to the "must" question. If God "became" Greek by the efforts of the early Greek-speaking Christian theologians, then God *may* remain Greek insofar as those early theologians were faithful to the apostolic witness. In an (unpublished) address to the American Theological Society in 1986 on "The New Testament and Nicea," Leander E. Keck argued that Athanasius was a legitimate interpreter of the apostle Paul:

> A thread that runs through Paul's diverse ways of regarding the situation of the unredeemed, unrectified self, is the self's inability to save itself . . . Athanasius too held a radical view of human nature and its salvation. And it was precisely this radical need that he sought to satisfy by insisting that the savior was nothing less than *homoousios* with the Father. No one less would do, could do, what needed to be done. Does the same logic lie latent in Paul's understanding? . . . In deepening the inherited theology of rectification to redemption, Paul—in his own way—seems to have sensed this.

And if the *homoousios* is in that way a necessary clarification of the Gospel, then God *must* remain "Greek." An anecdote will help to explain the sense in which I mean that. When the WCC Faith and Order Commission was debating whether to make the Nicene-Constantinopolitan Creed the "theological basis and methodological tool" of its study "Towards the Common Expression of the Apostolic Faith Today," it is instructive that a Jamaican Baptist, who by his cultural and confessional origin was at first understandably

suspicious about a text that contained "Greek metaphysics" and
had, to boot, been "imposed by imperial authority," came to see that
Commission members who advocated the use of the creed were on
his side in affirming the deity of the Savior, whereas it was, in part
at least, the questionably orthodox among the western liberals who
opposed the use of the creed. Somewhat similarly, at the 1990
meeting of the American Theological Society Kosuke Koyama affirmed that Japanese Christians understood very well what was at
stake in the *homoousion*, even if they would have great difficulty in
translating the term. In my judgment, the "Greek" tradition must be
maintained because it was there that a crucial dogmatic clarification
was made and a conciliar decision taken in order to sustain the
apostolic *regula fidei* for the permanent guidance of a Christian
tradition that would certainly become wider than the Greek even
while having already been enriched by it. Nor must the transformative effect of the Christian faith upon the Greek philosophical and
cultural tradition be forgotten. A radical change was made in the
Greek conception of deity when it was affirmed that "One of the
Trinity suffered," so that the "impassibility" of God became a way
of talking, not about God's distance from the world, but rather
about a compassionate and condescending God's victory over human sin for our salvation. Thus Athanasius:

> [The incarnate Word/Savior] remains as he is, impassible in his
> own nature, not merely unharmed by the passions, but destroy-
> ing them completely; while men, their passions transferred to
> the impassible and thereby destroyed, actually become impas-
> sible, freed from their passions from now on and for ever. This
> was the teaching of John: "You know that he appeared in order
> to take away our sins; and sin is not in him" [1 John 3:5] . . . The
> flesh can answer the contentious heretic: "I am indeed made of
> the earth, and am naturally mortal. But subsequently I have
> become the flesh of the Word. He has borne my passions,
> although he is impassible; I have become free of them, and
> because of the Lord who has freed me, I am no longer aban-
> doned to their service."[38]

****

Midnight approaches, and tomorrow I have a plane to catch for
Jerusalem and Rome. In Jerusalem there will take place the first
conversations in a "bilateral dialogue" between the World Method-

ist Council and the Anglican Consultative Council. In Rome I shall visit Cardinal Cassidy at the Pontifical Council for Christian Unity, and Cardinal Ratzinger at the Congregation for the Doctrine of the Faith, in connection with the work of the Joint Commission between the Roman Catholic Church and the World Methodist Council, a commission that has now been in existence for twenty-five years. For all my adult theological life I have been engaged in the cause for Christian unity. The classic ecumenism—for which the Orthodox and the Evangelicals appealed after Canberra and to which the Roman magisterium is clearly committed—rests upon a determination for conformity to the apostolic canon of faith and (consequently) for proclamation of the Gospel of Jesus Christ to people in every culture. It rests upon the prayer of Jesus that his disciples may be one in order to bear witness to his divine mission of reconciliation (Jn 17:20-23), and upon the insight of the apostle Paul that only by living together in harmony may Christians suitably praise with one heart and one voice the God and Father of the Lord Jesus Christ (Rom 15:5-6). To the realization of that vision I devote my theological energies.

Notes

1. Theodoret, *Hist. Eccles.* III.20.
2. A.C. Swinburne, "Hymn to Proserpine."
3. I am afraid I have no more distinguished source for this phrase than the spoof "ancient letter discovered" that is reported in "The Seminary Crisis at Nicopolis" in *The Christian Century*, 5-12 February 1992, 116f.
4. "The religious dimension is never absent in cultural creations even if they show no relation to religion in the narrower sense of the word." Paul Tillich, *Theology of Culture* (New York: Oxford University Press, 1959) v. This would mean that even a "secular ideology" could, *mutatis mutandis*, function as a "religion"—which may, of course, according to Tillich be "demonic."
5. Besides having been engaged for nearly thirty years in the work of the World Council of Churches, particularly on the Faith and Order side, I have recently served as an editor of a hefty *Dictionary of the Ecumenical Movement* (Geneva: World Council of Churches; Grand Rapids: Eerdmans, 1991).
6. My quotations are taken from the mimeographed typewritten document of the Assembly, PL 3.3; punctuation is original.
7. Surely the reverse is intended: making the wrong right.

8. "Evangelical Perspectives from Canberra," in *Signs of the Spirit: February 1991*, ed. Michael Kinnamon (Geneva: World Council of Churches, 1991) 282-286.

9. Ibid. 279-282.

10. Paolo Ricca, "Echi di Canberra," *Protestantesimo* 46 (1991) 136-141; "Gli Ortodossi, il Consiglo Ecumenico e noi," ibid. 192-200.

11. As in Hendrik Kraemer, *The Christian Message in a Non-Christian World* (London: Edinburgh House, 1938); W.A. Visser 't Hooft, *No Other Name: The Choice between Syncretism and Christian Universalism* (London: SCM Press, 1964).

12. M.M. Thomas, "The Absoluteness of Jesus Christ and Christ-Centered Syncretism," *The Ecumenical Review* 37 (1985) 387-397.

13. M.M. Thomas, "Syncretism," in N. Lossky and others, eds., *Dictionary of the Ecumenical Movement* (Geneva: World Council of Churches; Grand Rapids: Eerdmans, 1991) 964-966.

14. Note the *Guidelines on Dialogues with People of Living Faiths and Ideologies* (Geneva: World Council of Churches, 1979; revised 1990) which includes a list of "consultations" and a bibliography of WCC publications on the theme.

15. Francis Arinze, *Church in Dialogue: Walking with Other Believers* (San Francisco: Ignatius Press, 1990).

16. Ibid. 9-49. The following quotations come from pages 9, 10, 15, 37-38, 38-39 respectively.

17. Ibid. 160-183. The following quotations come from pages 166 and 170 respectively.

18. See Geoffrey Wainwright, *Doxology: The Praise of God in Worship, Doctrine and Life* (New York: Oxford University Press, 1980).

19. Interesting writing, both historically and theologically, comes from the Filipino Benedictine Anscar J. Chupungco, notably *Cultural Adaptation of the Liturgy* (New York/Ramsey, NJ: Paulist Press, 1982) and *Liturgies of the Future: The Process and Methods of Inculturation* (New York/Mahwah, NJ: Paulist Press, 1989).

20. See Jean Evenou, "Le Missel romain pour les diocèses de Zaïre," *Notitiae* no. 264 (1988).

21. See, for instance, H.E.W. Turner, *The Pattern of Christian Truth: A Study in the Relations between Orthodoxy and Heresy in the Early Church* (London: Mowbray, 1954).

22. Justin Martyr, *Apology* I. 67.

23. A crucial role was assigned to Marcion's case by Harnack.

24. *Baptism, Eucharist and Ministry*, Faith and Order Paper no. 111 (Geneva: World Council of Churches, 1982).

25. See the six volumes of *Churches Respond to BEM*, ed. Max Thurian (Geneva: World Council of Churches, 1986-1988).

26. *Confessing One Faith*, Faith and Order Paper no. 140 (Geneva: World Council of Churches, 1987); *One God, One Lord, One Spirit*, Faith and Order Paper no. 139 (Geneva: World Council of Churches, 1988); *Confessing the One Faith*, Faith and Order Paper no. 153 (Geneva: World Council of Churches, 1991).

27. I have discussed the issue in terms of universality and particularity in my *Doxology* (as in note 18) pp. 357-362, although the whole of Chapter 11 (pp. 357-398) bears on our current themes.

28. T.F. Torrance, *Theological Science* (London: Oxford University Press, 1969); *God and Rationality* (London: Oxford University Press, 1971); *Christian Theology and Scientific Culture* (Belfast: Christian Journals, 1980); *The Ground and Grammar of Theology* (Belfast: Christian Journals, 1980); *Reality and Scientific Theology* (Edinburgh: Scottish Academic Press, 1985).

29. Justin, *Apology* I. 46. The case of those who lived historically "before" Christ can by analogy be extended to cover those who live existentially "outside" the hearing of the Gospel.

30. For what I mean by a (concrete) "Christ pattern," which is not an (abstract) "Christ principle," see my *Doxology* (as in note 18) 68-69, 106, 144-146, 359-360.

31. I suppose that no religious Jew has difficulty, in principle, with the notion of a revelational and redemptive particularity that has an ultimately universal scope. The "scandal" of the Christian confession (1 Cor 1:23) is not that there should be a Messiah, but that the Messiah has come in the crucified Jesus. Without that first confession of Jesus as the Christ, it is of course obvious that Christians would not even have begun to develop their doctrine of God in a trinitarian direction; see my article "The Doctrine of the Trinity: Where the Church Stands or Falls," *Interpretation* 45 (1991) 117-132.

32. A recent study of the Enlightenment from a Christian viewpoint is Michael J. Buckley's *At the Origins of Modern Atheism* (New Haven: Yale University Press, 1987).

33. H. Richard Niebuhr, *Christ and Culture* (New York: Harper and Row, 1951).

34. J.H. Newman, *Essay on the Development of Christian Doctrine*, Part II, Chapter V, Section 3, quoted from the 1878 edition as printed in paperback (London: Sheed & Ward, 1960) 135.

35. These examples are borrowed from M.M. Thomas, "Syncretism." I have traced the Pannenburg quotation to "Toward a Theology of the History of Religions," in his *Basic Questions in Theology*, vol. 2 (London: SCM Press, 1971) pp. 65-118 ("syncretism" is treated on pp. 85-87).

36. Lamin Sanneh, *Translating the Message: The Missionary Impact on Culture* (Maryknoll, NY: Orbis, 1989). Issues touching on the inculturation of Christianity in Islamic contexts are interestingly treated in J. Dudley

Woodberry, "Contextualization among Muslims: Reusing Common Pillars," in *The Word Among Us: Contextualizing Theology for Mission Today*, ed. Dean S. Gilliland (Dallas: Word Publishing, 1989) 282-312.

37. Robert E. Hood, *Must God Remain Greek? Afro Cultures and God Talk* (Minneapolis: Fortress, 1990).

38. Athanasius, *Against the Arians* III.34, quoted from *Documents in Early Christian Thought*, ed. M. Wiles and M. Santer (Cambridge: Cambridge University Press, 1975) 57.